N

RUGGLES' REGIMENT

UNIVERSITY PRESS OF
NEW ENGLAND

Hanover and London, 1982

RUGGLES' REGIMENT

The 122nd New York Volunteers in the American Civil War

DAVID B. SWINFEN

UNIVERSITY PRESS OF NEW ENGLAND

Brandeis University
Brown University
Clark University
Dartmouth College
University of New Hampshire
University of Rhode Island
Tufts University
University of Vermont

Publication of this volume has been aided by a grant from the
NATIONAL ENDOWMENT FOR THE HUMANITIES.

Library of Congress Catalog Card Number 81–69940
International Standard Book Number 0–87451–230–1

Printed in the United States of America

Library of Congress Cataloging in Publication Data will be found on the last printed page of this book.

To Marilyn and Jean-Pierre
for their many kindnesses

CONTENTS

LIST OF PLATES

ACKNOWLEDGMENTS

In writing this book I have benefited greatly from the help of many people. I should like to thank in particular the librarians and their staffs of Dundee University Library (especially the archivist, Joan Auld), St. Andrews University Library, and the National Library of Scotland; on the American side, the Keeper of the National Archives, Washington, D.C., and the Chief Librarian of the Public Library in Syracuse, New York. I would like to single out five people without whose aid and advice the book would never have been written. The first is Richard Wright of the Onondaga Historical Association in Syracuse, New York, whose knowledge of the region's history is awesome, and whose generosity is without limit. I also owe a special debt to my friend and colleague Peter Parish, whose own expertise on the Civil War was inspiring and reassuring, and who was the first person (it is to be hoped not the last), to read the whole text through. My thanks to Jean Humphries and Margaret Greatorex who between them deciphered my handwriting and turned it into a typescript. I should like to thank my wife, Ann, for her understanding.

I also acknowledge with gratitude the permission of the Dundee University Library to publish the Ruggles drawings, and the Onondaga Historical Association to publish extracts from the letters of Herbert Wells. Thanks are also due to the Geography Department of Dundee University for preparing the map.

D. B. S.

INTRODUCTION

In the late summer of 1862 a young carpenter from Syracuse, New York, called William Eugene Ruggles added a couple of years to his age and enlisted as a private soldier in the Union army. There was nothing very unusual in this—he was only one amongst thousands of young men of the city who responded with remarkable enthusiasm to President Lincoln's call for extra men to help defeat the South. Nor was Ruggles' military career unique, though it had moments of high drama, adventure, and shame. As a member of the 122nd Regiment New York Volunteers, William Ruggles fought in most of the major battles of the Virginia theater, was captured by the Confederates, and tried several times though without success, to desert. Indeed, he finally mustered out of the army under sentence of court-martial.

It is what Ruggles did after the war, rather than during it, that makes the 122nd New York Volunteers *Ruggles'* regiment. Like many of his surviving comrades, once the war was over he clung to his wartime associations, attended regimental reunions, and joined the local branch of the veterans' organization called the Grand Army of the Republic, taking full part in its parades and ceremonies. Moreover, though the exact circumstances remain obscure, he collaborated with a Syracuse engraver, Philip M. Ostrander, in the creation of a remarkable series of drawings of his regiment in action. These drawings lack any real artistic merit, but have considerable historical interest. So far as is known, they are the only series from the American Civil War that depicts the military experiences of a single regiment in all its most important engagements. The drawings are reproduced herein; the story of the Ruggles–Ostrander collaboration is told in the final chapter.

Curiosity about the many questions and conundrums posed by the Ruggles–Ostrander pictures, and a desire to see them more widely known and appreciated were among my reasons for writing this history of Ruggles' Regiment. A number of regimental histories of the period have, of course, appeared over the last hundred years, but not one, as it happens, concerns the 122nd. A history of its sister regiment, the 149th, of which Ostrander was a member, was published toward the end of last century. Like many of its kind, it was written by a former member of the regiment—but no one did a like service for the 122nd. And yet the regiment deserves to have its story told—few others can have had a more active, glorious, and bloody existence. Narrowly missing involvement in Antietam, the 122nd served for most of the war in Sedgwick's famous

Sixth Corps, and hardly missed a battle, major or minor, during the rest of the Virginia campaign. It fought at Fredericksburg and churned its way through the morass of Burnside's "Mud March." It returned to Fredericksburg for the storming of Marye's Heights and was involved in an important side action at the time of Chancellorsville. Side by side with the 149th, it beat back the fierce Confederate attack on Culp's Hill during the crucial battle of Gettysburg. It was present at Rappahannock Station (where William's brother Philo was killed by a shell) and at Mine Run. The terrible slaughter of the Wilderness brought it well over a hundred casualties, including over twenty killed and mortally wounded, and it went on to fight under Grant's leadership at Spotsylvania Court House and Cold Harbor. Even during the long drawn-out seige of Petersburg, when other regiments remained static, if bored, behind in the Union breastworks, the 122nd was pulled out to defend Washington, D.C. against Jubal Early's daring surprise attack, then thrown into the Shenandoah Valley campaign, where, under Sheridan, it stormed the Confederate stronghold at Fisher's Hill and held the line during the near disaster of Cedar Creek. Finally, it took part in Lee's ultimate defeat, and was at or near Appomattox Courthouse at the time of the great Confederate leader's surrender. The regiment fought hard, often, and over a long period of time, and suffered a commensurate loss in killed, missing, and wounded.

An account of the campaigns and battles in which the regiment fought forms the major part of this study: it follows the life of the 122nd from its mustering in, to its ultimate discharge and homecoming in the summer of 1865. This account details the extremes of misery and discomfort, the occasional heroism, the long boredom of waiting, which is the lot of all soldiers in all armies, and the numbing fear of battle when every bullet seems to have one's name on it. In these early chapters the story of the regiment is set against the background of the war itself, because what the regiment and its members actually did formed, of course, only part of a larger strategy and a larger struggle.

Later chapters focus attention not on battles but on the day-to-day concerns of army life—conditions in camp, the arms and equipment carried by the men, their entertainments, and private worries. In particular, these chapters examine the cause for which this regiment was fighting by exploring the minds and motives of those who fought. Did they see the struggle as a defense of the Union, an antislavery crusade, or something more mundane or more personal? Did they hate the rebels, or only fight them? What was their attitude toward national politics, and whose side did they take in the crucial wartime election of 1864?

The 122nd Regiment may have had no published history, yet it has not been without its historians and in a real sense, the present account is very much the work of veterans of the regiment. The contribution of William Ruggles has already been mentioned, but others have also played a significant part. Published extracts of the diary of Maj. Theodore L. Poole and the reminiscences of Capt. (later Col.) James M. Gere illuminate their unit's role in the Wilderness and at Spotsylvania Court House. One of the most informative sources has been a series of private letters to his family, written by Lt. (later Captain) Herbert Wells, a former millwright who fought with great distinction throughout the regiment's existence. Yet the author of the fullest contemporary account remains, apart from a single initial, unidentified and unknown. As with many locally raised units, the 122nd retained a strong connection with its hometown through the medium of the local press— in this case, the Syracuse *Journal*. The *Journal* had as its regular correspondent a member of the regiment known only as D. D's reports were full of detail, clearly expressed, and well balanced, but also remarkably impersonal. Only occasionally are we allowed a glimpse of him—visiting a hospital, following up the regiment after Fisher's Hill, sitting in a group laughing at the antics of the great war illustrator, Alfred R. Waud. D's letters were published regularly, until the fall of 1864, when they suddenly terminated. In the search for D amongst the rolls of dead or wounded in the exhausting Shenandoah campaign, no obvious candidate emerges. But if Ruggles prompted the execution of this history, D provided much of the material which made it possible.

The American Civil War was not only the most devastating war which the American people had so far experienced, it was also a war concerned with great political, economic, and moral issues. Though the war did not resolve those issues in full, it did decide that the Union was not to be dissolved, slavery was not to be preserved. In this outcome the 122nd Regiment played a notable part, and its bravery, suffering, and loss should not go unchronicled.

I · THE ROAD TO WAR

On August 25, 1862, a great celebration took place in the village of Lafayetteville, in Onondaga County. Crowds poured in from the country, the village people turned out en masse, and "Beard's Hall was thronged at an early hour in the afternoon with the beauty, fashion and grace characteristic of the fair portion of our population." This was indeed a special day for the ladies of Lafayetteville. At a ceremony which had its parallels across the North, the ladies were to present an "elegant and costly banner" to the newly raised Third Onondaga Regiment—a banner "gorgeous in material" fringed with bullion, with tassels and cords of gilt. It had been worked by the patriotic ladies themselves at a cost of $107.[1] Unfortunately, the flag did not survive the war and after being shot almost to ribbons in various engagements, it was eventually replaced.

Such a ceremony called for speeches. The commander of the regiment, Col. Silas Titus, received the flag on behalf of his men with a few suitable words. The principal speech, and a fine one at that, was delivered for the ladies by Mrs. M. E. Gage. The purpose of her speech was to explain why men should fight on the Union side—not to acquire territory, nor to subjugate a people, but to uphold the principles of liberty and popular government. She saw the war as a struggle between opposing principles, and she contrasted the Northern cause of liberty, union, and the poor man's rights, with the Southern stand on slavery and the rule of the few.[2]

We cannot know to what extent the men of Onondaga County shared Mrs. Gage's view of the principles at stake in the Civil War. We do know that very many of them shared her enthusiasm for the Northern cause, and enlisted by the hundreds in the 122nd (Third Onondaga) Regiment, New York Volunteers, and in her two sister regiments. The Union, after more than a year of war, faced a crisis, and to this crisis they responded.

All wars it seems, once begun, are expected to be over by Christmas. At the start of the Civil War, both sides had been confident of a quick victory, and in the North, Lincoln's initial call for troops, or rather, militiamen, had specified enlistment for only three months. A proclamation issued by the president in May, 1861, not only increased the size of the regular army but also brought into being a new army of volunteers which was to bear the brunt of the war effort for the next few years. The initial call was for forty-two thousand men in forty regiments—a figure that was almost immediately greatly exceeded. When Congress convened in July, it authorized a call for another 500,000 troops and, after Bull Run, a similar number. On July 1, 1862, the president called for an additional three hundred thousand men, and on the next day the governor of New York state issued a proclamation appealing for volunteers. To make provision for the organization of the forces to be raised, a circular was duly issued from the adjutant general's office, directing the division of the state into regimental districts, corresponding to existing senatorial districts, with a rendezvous camp appointed for each. At the same time, the circular appointed a War Committee for each such district that was charged with raising and organizing troops within the area under its jurisdiction.[3]

The need for quick action was evident to all, and the next two months were to be critical. In Virginia, the Union forces were now organized into two armies. The Army of the Potomac, under McClellan, lay safe but motionless on the James Peninsula. In the Shenandoah Valley, Pope had been brought across from the west to command the Army of Virginia. Military logic might have suggested the mounting of a giant pincer movement whereby the two armies would converge on Lee and settle the issue outright. Such logic would have ignored McClellan's constitutional inability to attack without an impossible preponderance of numbers, and the personal animosity which had quickly sprung up between the two Northern commanders. General Halleck, appointed general in chief on July 11, 1862, advised the strategic withdrawal of the Army of the Potomac from the James peninsula back to

the area south of Washington, but the movement, ordered on August 3, was not begun until midway through the month. This was Lee's chance. Before McClellan's evacuation had even begun, Lee was sending more and more of his troops north to threaten Pope. Jackson had a sharp brush with Pope's vanguard at Cedar Mountain on August 9, and then was sent with half the Confederate army around Pope's position to Manassas Junction. After sacking the important Union supply depot there, Jackson, who was soon to be joined by the remainder of Lee's army, fought off Pope's attack at Second Bull Run (August 29–30) and forced the latter to scurry home to the shelter of Washington.

It was against this background of Northern discomfiture that the new regiments from Syracuse were raised and formed. In Onondaga County, the twenty-second district, events moved remarkably fast. Within days of the adjutant general's circular, a committee of ten leading citizens had formed and held its first meeting on July 15, at which it passed three resolutions. The first requested that the inhabitants of various townships in the county appoint a committee of three to act in concert with them. At the same time the governor of the state was called upon to summon the state legislature into special session to discuss the question of bounties to be offered to volunteers, and thus ensure uniformity of action on this matter. Finally the committee decided to hold daily meetings from then on at seven thirty in the evening at the mayor's office.[4]

William Ruggles' regiment, the 122nd Regiment New York Volunteers, was one of the first fruits of the committee's work. Enlistment rolls opened on July 20, only five days after the first meeting of the committee, and they closed exactly one month later, on August 20, with the regiment possessing a full complement of officers and men totaling 1,078.[5]

The 122nd, as we shall see in a later chapter, was almost entirely composed of civilian volunteers, and only a small handful of the more senior officers had had any previous military experience. Many of the officers were lawyers from Syracuse; the bulk of the enlisted men were farmers and farm workers from Onondaga County. Despite the regiment's lack of experienced personnel, little time could be found for military training, and in the few days available between enlistment and the departure for Washington, the only training the men received was in musket drill.[6] On August 25, the flag presentation ceremony was held, and on the twenty-eighth the regiment was mustered into the United States service. By noon the next day, Saturday, the last bounty had been paid, and Colonel Titus telegraphed the governor with the news that his men were ready to move and awaited orders. The reply was prompt. Preparations were to begin at once, and they were to set out as early as possible on the Sunday morning. The suddenness of the move took the local citizenry by surprise. "It was," commented the *Journal* "like many of the recent movement of our armies, a complete surprise—to its friends." Despite attempts to keep the order secret, it was in fact widely known, but not so widely believed. The immense crowds that had thronged the presentation ceremony were not to be seen as the regiment marched quietly out from Camp Andrews and made its way without parade to Central Station. As they entered the city, however, the news began to spread, and by the time the station was reached, the number of onlookers, relatives, and friends had swelled to several thousand. Numerous leave-takings delayed the departure, but by ten o'clock all had embarked, and the train with its twenty-one cars and more than a thousand men finally left for the war.[7]

The regiment's primary destination, Washington, was a four-day journey that lasted from Sunday morning to the afternoon of Wednesday, September 3. From Syracuse they traveled to Albany, arriving in time for an excellent supper at Delevan House, then across the Hudson by ferry and to New York by train. There the men were issued weapons and other equipment—Enfield rifles and five rounds of ammunition per man—before embarking on the steamboat for Perth Amboy late on Monday afternoon. It began to rain, and the storm kept up all night. By the time the men reached Perth Amboy, spirits were beginning to droop, and they were not raised by the inferior accommodation provided on the train from there to Philadelphia. The men reacted to this shoddy treatment with soldierly dispatch, staving in the car windows with the butts of their new rifles and throwing the seats out the windows. Philadelphia was an improvement. After a substantial breakfast provided by the Volunteer Relief Association, the regiment left by train for Baltimore.[8]

Something less than a welcome was expected from this Maryland city, but in any event there was no trouble. One of the men in Captain Brower's company wrote home:

We reached the Monumental City at five o'clock, Tuesday afternoon. We marched through the city, passed the place where the Massachusetts Sixth were stoned. There was not a single sneer cast upon us on our way through Baltimore, but the stars and stripes were waving everywhere, and the ladies and children waved their hankerchiefs and gave us cheers. Our reception at all the places along our route from home was very hearty and gratifying.

At nine the next morning the regiment entrained for the final leg of the journey, arriving in Washington at 4:00 P.M. on September 3.[9]

At this time, the strategies of both Lee and McClellan centered upon Harper's Ferry, the key to the Potomac River. For the time being this strong point was held by Union forces under Col. D. S. Miles, but his position was threatened by Lee's forces on the south side of the river, while the rest of the Confederate army, in scattered formations, rampaged around Maryland on the north side. Lee's intention was to force Miles to surrender, while his units in Maryland kept McClellan at bay, then move the rest of his army across the river and attack the Army of the Potomac in strength. For his part, McClellan planned to mop up Confederate units in Maryland, before hurrying to the relief of Miles. He was too slow, and the result was the fall of Harper's Ferry and the battle of Antietam.

Those parts of Lee's army which were already in Maryland had, by early September, occupied South Mountain, in a range of hills running southeast across the state to the Potomac, east of Harper's Ferry. McClellan learned of Lee's plans through the discovery of a general order at Frederick, and pushed on in pursuit, meeting up with the rebels at Turner's and Crampton's Gaps on September 14. At Turner's Gap, Meade and Hooker, commanding the right wing of McClellan's army, inflicted heavy losses on the enemy: those killed and wounded

numbered two thousand; fifteen hundred were taken prisoner. Franklin at Crampton's took four hundred prisoners and seven hundred small arms. The Confederates had lost the battles and the men, but they had won time—with Franklin's troops no more than six miles distant, Miles' garrison at Harper's Ferry surrendered at eight o'clock on the following morning.[10]

The 122nd had earlier joined McClellan's forces but was to take no active part in these two engagements, nor in the major battle of Antietam which followed. The news, when the regiment arrived in Washington at the beginning of the month, had not been encouraging. General Pope, they learned, had been defeated at Chantilly, and Lee was rumored to be crossing into Maryland. The original plan had been for the regiment to march to Fort Pennsylvania for training and drill instruction. They got as far as Long Bridge, where there was a delay before they could cross the river into Virginia. Before their turn could come, orders were changed: they found themselves marching back through Georgetown to encamp at Chain Bridge, some ten miles from the capital, only to be told to be ready to move again to the relief of Harper's Ferry. Three days' rations and forty rounds of ammunition were issued to each man. All heavy equipment—tents, blankets and even knapsacks—was to be left behind. A member of the regiment described the march:

Part of the march was performed in the evening. All were ordered to be silent. Rifles were loaded and bayonets fixd. The march was an exacting one. At one time Col. Titus ordered "Halt! Front! Charge bayonets!" It was a moment of excitement, and many of the boys no doubt were frightened.

We have changed position almost every day since. On the 10th we passed Poolesville, and saw the effects of the battle of the Monday before. On Thursday, the 11th, we went to Noland's Ferry, at the mouth of the Monocacy at the point where the rebels destroyed the Chesapeake and Ohio Canal, took a position so as to guard the ford, and remained there till Saturday, all the time under arms, ready to "fall in" any moment. There were 10,000 or 12,000 of the enemy beyond the hills, ready to cross here. Our two brass guns were so planted as to command the ford. . . .

While at Noland's Ferry, we heard the firing of the battle which commenced at Frederick. On Saturday we started in the direction of the firing which then continued, and at night camped on a camp left by the rebels in the morning. The boys found many things that were curious to them. Much old clothing was found, and it is supposed that they received large contributions of clothing in this State, as they have strewn all their camps with old garments. We think this camp was about three miles from Point of Rocks. On Sunday, 14th, we moved on, and passed through much of the finest and best cultivated country that we have seen in this State. We advanced about fourteen miles, probably. From a ridge of the Blue Ridge we enjoyed a beautiful sight of the valley through which we had passed, and passing on a short distance, beheld one of the finest views that I ever saw, including Harper's Ferry Gap, etc. We have found more patriotism amongst the inhabitants than since we left Baltimore. At night we stopped near Burkittsville. On Monday, the 15th, we started early and found the Church at Burkittsville filled with wounded, mostly ours. By the side of the Church, as he fell, lay a dead rebel, the first that we had seen. There were many prisoners. Within half a mile of this place was the battle field of South Mountain Pass—Gen. Slocum's field. . . A description of the scenes of this battlefield would be only a repetition of what has been attempted so many times, and like all others, a failure. Its horrors cannot be known except they are seen.

We passed many troops moving in the same direction we were. After we passed this field, Gen. Slocum, the hero of yesterday, rode through our lines in the road, and the whole division sent up long and loud shouts that reverberated far away along the mountainside. We moved on, and took a position where it was suppose[d] that the enemy would pass on his way to Harper's Ferry. The whole division were under arms all the time. Prisoners came in frequently; many gave themselves up and said they were glad to do so.

Tuesday evening it was said that our pickets were driven in. We were drawn up in line of battle and ordered to rest. We remained so till four o'clock when we were aroused and started at half past five for Harper's Ferry. We arrived at Harper's Ferry about noon. The Chasseurs and the right wing of our regiment were sent up the mountain that commands the Ferry. When nearly to the top, a horseman rode up in haste and ordered the whole division back to this place to re-inforce Gen. McClellan, and back we went, and arrived near the battlefield in the evening. The firing was terrific just at night. Many troops were moving in the same direction, and you can form no correct idea of the immense baggage trains that we passed for miles. Not really baggage trains, for there are no baggage trains. Many regiments carried nothing but blankets, haversacks and canteens; amongst those is the 122nd. They are ammunition and provision trains.

Yesterday, early, we moved into position on the field where we are now supporting a battery of four pieces of artillery. The field is thickly strewn with the dead; hundreds may be seen by walking a few rods from this place. They were killed day before yesterday. The wounded have all been cared for. In one place, near a small burying ground, the ground looks as though nearly a whole regiment had fallen. Canister and a charge of the Irish Brigade did the terrible work. Nothing was done yesterday, except by sharpshooters and skirmishers. An arrangement was entered into under a flag of truce to exchange wounded and bury some of the dead. At five o'clock the time was up, and two of our men were carrying one of their wounded on a stretcher, when, without any notice, they were fired at, and one of them was wounded. I saw him ten minutes after he was shot, and the man who was with him told me they opened a full volley, and I assure you there was a scattering. The picket lines were not more than twenty rods apart.

The rebels have moved over the river, and we are to go after them. There is heavy firing at the front. I am writing amid the whizzing of balls. A six pounder is firing over our heads, and the balls strike a short distance beyond. Just now we are ordered into line. There is a general advance of the lines of this great army.[11]

The 122nd then had avoided direct involvement in the battle of Antietam, having been sent off toward Harper's Ferry to thwart an expected enemy flanking movement which never actually materialized. They were fortunate. In desperate attempts to take and retake the cornfield which bore the worst of the action, another New York regiment, the thirty-fourth, was cut to pieces. The Fifteenth Massachusetts, which went into battle six hundred strong, emerged with only 134.[12] Passing across the battlefield on the nineteenth and twentieth, a regimental observer was sickened by the

many traces of the terrible conflict that had taken place. The course of the charges of the Irish Brigade could be traced by the heaps of dead and their arms and equipment. In one line between a small burying ground and the woods, it seemed as though nearly a regiment of the rebels had fallen in line. Many of the dead had

turned black, and the stench was almost unendurable. The ground in the woods in which the rebels were stationed was covered with branches torn from the trees by the storm of shot and shell. I counted thirty cannon ball holes in a house that stood near the woods. Some lengths of fence were torn entirely away, and the marks of bullets could be seen on everything.[13]

Having spent the eighteenth and nineteenth on the battlefield, the 122nd, together with the rest of Couch's division, marched to Williamsport.[14] Here the regiment came upon a band of rebels, and formed into line of battle behind a small rise. Although Colonel Dwight narrowly escaped being shot by sharpshooters during a reconnaissance, Private Hunn, the first casualty in the regiment, was hit in the leg, and a neighboring Long Island regiment had four men killed or wounded; the whole line was ordered to withdraw before they could retaliate. The reasons for this order remained mysterious and cause for some cynical comment.

It is said that the "Rebs" had a masked battery planted on our left that would have raked our flank had we not fallen back; also that the Rebels were making an attempt to turn our left flank, to counteract which we were compelled to fall back. It was also said that the discovery was made that the enemy greatly outnumbered us, and that it would be unsafe for us to attack them; and again some say that we had greatly the advantage of the enemy, and it was feared that in case a battle ensued we should gain a Union victory at the expense of the Rebels.

Whatever the reason, the withdrawal was accomplished in good order—"all our retreats are masterly"—and without loss. On the way to the rear some of the men paused to club apples

off the trees, "which was regarded as a thrilling instance of bravery, patriotism, and love of apples."[15]

General McClellan's irritating disinclination to move in to the kill, which had lowered his reputation with Lincoln and the politicians, was obviously causing some frustration for the soldiery also. Men who had recently joined the army in the hope of glorious action and a quick, decisive end to the war now saw these hopes receding. McClellan had already caused some eyebrow raising by his willingness after Antietam to arrange a truce for the Confederates to collect their wounded and bury their dead. This respite the rebels used to advantage to make themselves scarce. "Were it not for fear for hurting Gen. McClellan's feelings," commented the regular correspondent of the *Standard,*

I would hazard the opinion that he was either "tremenjusly sucked in" by the "Rebs," or else he thought it better for the country that they should live to work the cotton plantations, to be vacated by the colored population by virtue of the President's Proclamation, than to run the risk of killing or disabling a few thousand of them by making them fight when they wanted to be let alone. . . "Mac" is young but there is great room for improvement.[16]

At Williamsport also, the readiness of the higher command to find reasons for a withdrawal did not increase the men's confidence.

If the regiment was spoiling for a fight, its hopes were to be continually disappointed over the next few weeks. After staying on at Williamsport for the next couple of days, they moved on to camp at Downesville, where they underwent training and drill at the hands of that expert drill master, Maj. (later Major General) Joseph Hamlin. This period of relative inactivity was enlivened by an occasional inspection, or by intermittent false alarms, orders and countermanded orders. On the twenty-fifth, a Mr. Seager of Syracuse visited the camp and received a warm welcome. On October 2, Major General Slocum was called in to make a few appropriate remarks, and another local man, Edward Thurber, brought welcome news from home and from the 122nd's sister regiment, the 149th. October 3 was an even more special occasion: the regiment marched to Bakersville to be received by the president himself. It seems that Lincoln did not make the same good impression on everyone. "The first time I saw Abraham," commented one witness, "he looked much better than I expected. This time he looked much worse." On the eighth, the regiment was again inspected, and the day was further enlivened by Lieutenant Webb, who accidentally shot himself in the leg while cleaning his revolver.[17]

After a few days of this, the men were ready for a change. On the tenth, orders to prepare for a march were issued, but almost immediately rescinded. On the twelfth, the orders were renewed, and the regiment moved off at two in the morning, but covered less than a mile before being sent back to camp. Two days later they were up and ready at 5:00 A.M., but made no move at all. The next day they were again drawn up and ready to move, and did so—back to their tents. At last, on the eighteenth, they did actually set off—through Downesville, Williamsport, and Clear Spring, marching at a good pace until 2:00 A.M. That night they camped in a field where "stone is more prevalent than grass," and without tents.[18] These conditions did not deprive everyone of sleep—the adjutant slept so soundly that someone stole the loaf of bread he was using for a pillow, and obliged him to forage for his breakfast.[19] On the nineteenth they set off again toward Hancock, passing along a route which "abounds in pleasant scenery," covering a further fifteen miles and arriving in late afternoon. Pausing here for only two days, they set off again on the march, back along the road to Clear Spring for about ten miles, and finished up at Indian Springs, where they camped for the next two weeks. The march, though relatively short, had been a hard one. "We started about dusk," reported a soldier.

It soon began to rain and continued to do so until just before we camped, or rather bivouacked for we had no tents, and as there was no moon it was so dark you could not see your hand before your face. Beside all this, the road was of the genus "up hill" almost the entire distance. We were fortunate enough to be halted in the immediate vicinity of a large straw stack, which added materially to our comfort, as the weather was extremely cold before morning.

Winter was fast approaching and cold, even in a proper encampment, was soon to be a serious problem. The expectation was that the whole division would soon be moved to winter quarters, "unless a short active campaign is decided upon."[20]

Whether or not the regiment would find itself involved in a "short active campaign" was soon to be decided, but in the meantime, for the rest of October, it was moved restlessly and, so it seemed, purposelessly, from point to point. On the twenty-second, while the unit lay in camp at Cherry Run near Indian Springs, Colonel Titus received word to move at daylight. He waited until dawn broke before giving the order, and sure enough the men spent the whole day standing in readiness, until five o'clock when they were stood down and told to pitch camp again.[21] On Saturday, the twenty-fifth, an order was published to prepare for a thorough inspection the following day, but fortunately this was rained out. In the evening the order to march at daylight came again, the regiment arose at four thirty and stood around in the rain until nine. Major Hamlin did his best to keep up morale

by riding up and down the line, and commanding, *sotto voce,* "I want you to be ready at sharp seven. You will be ready to move at precisely seven. Any man not ready will be immediately shot with a pack-saddle." Or, "Colonel, you will immediately report yourself under arrest for not having your regiment ready," etc. etc. all with an air of profound gravity and mock severity that much amused the boys, made them smile out loud some considerable, and put all in a good humor.

Eventually the waiting came to an end, and the regiment set off to march the thirteen miles to Williamsport—pitching camp on the very spot where they had had their skirmish with the rebels less than a month before. Here, in a very short space of time, they laid out their camp—tents in parallel rows gave the appearance of a small and tidy village.[22] All to no avail—the men had scarcely settled in when they were off again in the direction of Downesville. This time the 122nd was given a particular job—to act as guard for the divisional wagon train. Obliged to keep in close contact with the slow moving line of mule drawn wagons, they were late getting into Downesville and had no time to pitch camp that night. This they did the next day, Thursday, and although the task was carried out with customary care, it was evident that their stay at Downesville would be short. Company commissaries were up most of the night, taking in and dividing up rations and stores; company cooks were kept busy preparing breakfast. Sure enough, at two o'clock, the order came to be ready to move out at three thirty, at which time the main body of troops took the direct road to Rohrersville, while the 122nd and the train followed a more roundabout route through Boonsboro. After a short stop to collect their pay, they caught up with the rest of the division a short distance beyond Rohrersville. There an impressive sight awaited them—a huge gathering of men and equipment, composing, so it was said, the whole of the Sixth Army Corps. "Judging from appearances by moonlight and camp fires, the troops were massed over the whole field about as closely as they could lie, and the camps extended for miles." Reveille came at two in the morning, and within half an hour the whole division was on the move, passing over South Mountain and the battlefield of Crampton's Gap before dawn[23] (Plate 1). Perhaps now, at last, there would be some real action.

The men are all pleased with the onward movement, and hope that something is to be done, and that instead of running up and down along the river, there is to be no falling back. It is said here that 40,000(?) troops crossed here yesterday, among which was the 149th N.Y.S.V. The crossing commenced last Sunday and has been going on ever since. I do not know whether the rest of the corps moved this morning. Newton's division is still arriving here and arranging on the field on this side of the river. The division train includes about 270 wagons, each drawn by four or six mules or horses, and about thirty five ambulances, and, probably, is some four miles in length.[24]

For the time being the 122nd found its destiny closely connected with that of the train; regardless of the train's speed, the regiment was obliged to keep pace with it. Wagon guard duties also involved them in an embarrassing and potentially dangerous incident. At the rear end of the train came the ambulance corps. It so happened that a number of ambulances belonging to other divisions had attached themselves to the end of the train without the knowledge of the officer commanding the rear guard:

The order to this officer (our Lieutenant-Colonel) was "follow the train," and when the train reached this place [Berlin] all but these ambulances turned off and parked in a by place, not seen from the road. The officer saw the long line of ambulances on the bridge and turned after them and crossed the pontoon bridge on an independent expedition into Dixie. The ambulances pushed off at a run, and the guard pushed on after the train. Meeting General Burnside a short distance from the river, he asked what troops those were and was told it was the rear guard of Newton's wagon train, to which he replied "all right." Assured by this, the officer pushed on, and went some three miles into the heart of Old Virginia, when he began to smell a large-sized "mice," because no train was visible, and because he could get no trace of it.—Halting his command he rode ahead and made enquiries at Burnside's headquarters at Lovettsville, and learned that no such train had passed. He rode back, and said a few naughty words—got his command ready to take the back track, when an orderly dashed up with a peremptory order for the Lieut. Col. commanding to return to camp with his command, and report himself at once at

FROM MEMORY.
W.E RUGGLES.
122ᵈ REGT. N.Y.

·:(((THE 6ᵀᴴ CORPS,   ON THE MARCH TO SOUTH, MOUNTAIN.)))):·
PASSING SUGAR LOAF MOUNTAIN, MD. POOLVILLE IN THE DISTANCE.

1. The 6th Corps on the March to South Mountain

brigade headquarters. They trudged back, the boys in high glee at their trip in advance of the rest, and calling it "Dwight's grand raid into Dixie," while that officer went up and made his explanation, which was cheerfully accepted.[25]

The regiment soon tired of wagon guard duties, and longed for a place in the advance. Their involuntary excursion in Virginia was soon followed by a general movement of the army in the same direction. The crossing was made at Berlin on November second, and two days later camp was pitched at Union, in Virginia, the state which was to be their home and battlefield almost without interruption for more than two years.[26] The military situation at this point was explained in a letter home by Capt. James M. Gere, of Company H:

Affairs look very promising to us just now. Some nine weeks ago, or when we first came out, our forces were making a great *defensive* effort to preserve Washington itself and Baltimore, and Philadelphia even, and to expel the enemy from Maryland. Now we are making the most formidable demonstration, not upon Richmond only, but upon the whole State of Virginia, that ever was made, and with a good prospect of success.

Our forces about here hold all the important gaps in the mountains, and seem to be cutting the rebel forces in two, compelling them to fight separate or to fall back far in order to unite. I think now that our chance is good to reach Richmond before the main body of the enemy's forces, and if we do not, that our relative situation and forces will enable us to overwhelm them, and then reach Richmond. Things look now as if Christmas would find us in possession of the rebel Capital, if not a much shorter time.

When we started from Washington, and affairs looked so threatening, my faith was just as strong that we should expel them, and in our final triumph; but I must confess that my faith today is a much more comfortable one than that of two months ago.

Monday of last week we crossed the Potomac at Berlin into Virginia, marched more or less of the time for three days, reaching this place the night before last, just at dark. We are lying in the woods, on a hill, just by the side of the Valley, and within a quarter of a mile of the Railroad. Yesterday we had a snow storm, the first that we have seen. About two inches of snow fell. The roads were dry and good—the weather has been fine. The snow I think will disappear today, and the roads will probably be not much worse, and I am in hopes of general good weather for a while yet.

We have made ourselves very comfortable through the storm, with our shelter-tents and all the wood we are willing to cut, and fires all about among the tents, which stand thickly around. I am quite well and feeling well, going ahead with my duties—and feeling especially well when each step that I take is one more towards Richmond. When tired and weary on the march, that thought is the best encouragement that I can have.[27]

Gere's optimism was, of course, misplaced. The capture of Richmond and the end of the war would not be achieved by this Christmas, nor the next, nor the next. Nothing indeed had been done in the weeks following Antietam to bring about a victory. The purposeless wanderings of the regiment and the rest of the army along or sometimes across the line of the Potomac served no purpose other than avoidance of military disaster—a wholly negative achievement. Changes were on the way, changes both of command and of strategy, which would at last bring the 122nd into direct contact with the enemy. It can hardly be said, however, either for the regiment or for the Union cause at large, that these changes were an improvement.

II · FROM FREDERICKSBURG TO GETTYSBURG

Richmond. To capture the Confederate capital, so tantalizingly near, seemed to many, including James M. Gere, the obvious strategy. To take Richmond would, or so it then appeared, trump all Lee's cards and bring the war to a quick and decisive end. To move against Richmond had been at the heart of McClellan's plans, however cautiously, even timidly, executed. This strategy was also central to the plans of his successor, General Burnside.

McClellan's procrastination had, by early November, finally exhausted Lincoln's patience. McClellan, as one historian notes, had most of the necessary military talents, except the ability to put them to the greatest use.[1] His failure to follow up Antietam, his lack of any new plan, his unwillingness to do with his army what Lee was so manifestly prepared to do with the Confederate Army, brought about his own downfall. It was unfortunate both for the Union cause and for the man himself that Ambrose E. Burnside was chosen as McClellan's replacement; Burnside was an able lieutenant but a disastrous commander.

Amongst McClellan's many military virtues, was his ability to attract the loyalty of his men. His dismissal caused widespread resentment amongst his supporters in the army who believed, not wholly without cause, that he had been made the victim of political persecution. In early November, the *Journal*'s regular correspondent reported that:

Of course the all engrossing topic is the removal of Gen. McClellan and the devolvement of the command upon Gen. Burnside. Why the change was not made before the army was put in motion, if it was to be made at all, seems to be the main question asked. While many of the officers and men regard it as political persecution, all admit that McClellan was opposed to the movement, and that was known months ago, and nearly all admit that a man opposed to the movement should not be obliged to manage it, but once having begun and having met with the most perfect success this far, the change will be interpreted by many to have a political significance, whether correctly or not.[2]

McClellan had indeed opposed the decision, made by Lincoln on Halleck's advice, to evacuate the Army of the Potomac from the James Peninsula and reposition it to the south of Washington. "Little Mac" had devised a number of plans for an offensive from his existing position but had made them all contingent upon being provided with reinforcements on a scale matching his grossly exaggerated estimate of Confederate strength. Although it was true that certain radicals in Congress were out for his blood, critics of his performance were not confined to his political opponents, and finally Lincoln could see no alternative but to replace him.

The general's farewell to the Army of the Potomac was a typically stage-managed and emotional affair.

He took leave of this part of the army yesterday morning, riding along the road on the sides of which the troops were drawn up without arms. As he appeared at the head of his suite, the men made the welkin ring with their cheers and were most enthusiastic in their reception. He rode at a trot, cap in hand, while by his side rode the "coming man," Gen. A. E. Burnside, looking with his broad, full, pleasant face and thoughtful massive brow, like the man equal to the task. After them came their suites and a troop of cavalry, and then Gen. Schurz and staff, Gen. Sigel and staff, and various other officers.

While Gen. McClellan looked well, he evidently was sad at heart, and had a cast of countenance as if trying to suppress tears.—The acclamations of the soldiers seemed not to raise his spirits, but to make him more heavy-hearted still; and one thing is most certain, he carried with him the sympathy of all beholders.

Gen. Burnside bore his new honours meekly, and seemed to be noticing anything but the show or ceremony going on as he passed.—His appearance was in the highest degree favourable, and impresses the observer with the conviction that he is a thinking clear-headed man.[3]

First impressions are notoriously unreliable, and the "clear-headed" Burnside was soon to involve the 122nd and the rest of the Army of the Potomac in the expensive fiasco of Fredericksburg. But in the meantime he was not a man to be envied. The soldiers cheered his respected predecessor, reminding him, if he needed to be reminded, that his job was to do what his former chief had failed to do—to take some decisive action against Lee's forces.

Burnside's plan, accepted only reluctantly by Lincoln and Commander in Chief Halleck, was to move the army eastward to the area round Fredericksburg on the Rappahannock, and from there march against Richmond. It was a plan, as Lincoln rightly understood, which could only work if carried through quickly, before Lee could get himself into position to defend Fredericksburg. But speed was lacking—owing, as far as one can gather, to Halleck's tardiness in providing the pontoons needed to cross the Rappahannock. Not until a month after his appointment on November 8, was Burnside able to transfer the army from one side of the river to the other, and the delay proved fatal.

The 122nd, now in the Left Grand Division (Franklin's) of the Army of the Potomac, joined the march toward Fredericksburg on November tenth. After camping for a few days, as James Gere had described, at the west end of Thoroughfare Gap, they moved on to Stafford Court House. Here they halted, prevented from moving on by bad weather and lack of food. "The intermediate state of the weather," reported a letter from the regiment, "along between rain, snow and fair weather, which gives us a sort of raw, cold, damp time, and mud from two inches to two feet deep, and the almost entire absence of rations, have kept us here." "All this," the letter went on optimistically, "may have been a part of the programme."[4] At last things began to move, and supplies began to come up from the mouth of Acquia Creek—only four hours' running time from Washington.

The delay had given Lee his chance to reinforce Fredericksburg, but the regiment remained confident that when the expected battle came, they would triumph. "We have been and are still expecting a fight in this vicinity every day," wrote D. G. S. from Stafford Court House at the end of November,

for as near as I can learn the Rebs are in heavy force at Fredericksburg, and from all accounts mean to make a stand there, but if you were here and travel for miles around and see the vast army we have and the amount of artillery at our command, you would say at once that it was just as easy for the leaders of this rebellion to enter the Kingdom of Heaven, as for them to resist the pressure of our forces.[5]

On December 4, still dogged by bad weather, the regiment moved from Stafford Court House to a new camp near Belle Plaine. They arrived "in a pelting rain, which turned to snow soon after we had dived into a thick pine forest, filled with undergrowth, for a camp, and the comforts of our position were not those of an exalted character."[6]

These conditions had to be endured for the next week. But on the tenth, Herbert Wells wrote home in expectation of an imminent battle. The usual preparations had been made. Every man "had 40 rounds of cartridges and last night were ordered to furnish ourselves with 3 days cooked rations and the men supplied with cartridges enough to make 60 rounds and be in readiness to move any moment. But we are here today and expect orders to move at any moment. When they do come we shall probably cross the river and then the fun will commence or the rebs will skedaddle."

That same day, camp was struck, and the regiment moved to join the general transfer of the army across the river, marching approximately nine miles to a crossing point some two miles below Fredericksburg. Pontoons had at last been brought up and laid across the river by the engineers on the night of December tenth. Early the next morning it was the 122nd's turn to cross. A tremendous artillery duel that had begun at about 5:45 A.M. was kept up all day, but at the crossing point, heavy covering fire from the Union side enabled the troops to get over safely. By the next morning the bulk of the army had crossed the river and taken up their positions. That morning "the ball opened and the battle of Fredericksburg had begun."[7]

Burnside's attempt to storm the heights of Fredericksburg on December 13, in the words of one Northern historian, "must ever remain as the darkest, bloodiest and most fruitless sacrifice of our brave soldiers during the whole war."[8] Lee had used the Union delays to good advantage, and by the time Burnside was ready for the attack, some seventy-five thousand Confederate troops had been positioned behind breastworks along the bluffs. The rebel guns, possibly as many as three hundred, had been so placed as to command every foot of ground across which an attack might come, and Marye's Hill to the rear of the city and in front of the Union army was defended by a four foot stone wall. In attempting to take these heights, Burnside was condemning many of those involved to certain death. The Irish Brigade, commanded by General Meagher, suffered the greatest loss and, according to Meagher himself, of the twelve hundred he had led into action, only 280 appeared on parade the next morning.[9] The correspondent of the London *Times* commented "that any mortal man could have carried the position before which they were wantonly sacrificed, defended as it was, it seems to me idle for a moment to believe."[10]

Fortunately for the 122nd, it was not involved in the storming of the heights. Indeed, its members seem to have survived the battle almost unscathed. As part of the Left Grand Division, the regiment was on the Union left, three miles or so south of Fredericksburg, in reserve for the Union attacks on Prospect Hill. On the afternoon of the thirteenth, the division moved up and took position behind a line of three batteries. There they were exposed to enemy fire for three hours—"a perfect hail storm of shot and shell." Only four casualties in the regiment, however, were reported, and one of those had shot off his own finger by mistake. "Our men," commented a soldier, "behaved splendidly—not one flinched, but they laid mighty flat, with shell and shot whizzing just over their heads. The Colonel got a big strap and cracked everyone over the head that didn't lie low in obedience to General John's orders."[11]

Herbert Wells described his experience of the battle in a letter to his parents written on Christmas Day:

I went into the fight with Co.G as First Lieut. having been promoted just about an hour before we crossed the Rappahannock on Friday morning December 12th. We were under fire soon after we got over, but no one in our regt. was hurt that day.

Sat. the 13th we were ordered to the front to support a battery. Late in the afternoon the rebs commenced shelling us while the batteries in front and on the left of our regt. answered back. We were lying down at that time and the shell flew over and burst around us quite lively. We had everything that would encumber us thrown off for we expected a lively charge from the rebs on our battery or that we would advance on them, but after dark the firing (heavy firing) ceased and late at night we were relieved or withdrew, having only 2 or 3 men in the regt. wounded.

We were very lucky, had we fell back or even stood up at the time of the shelling we would have lost a good many men.

Sunday Dec. 14th (I have been told since) our Division was to drive the rebs from the hills and works in front. The order was given and partly written but countermanded for some reason or other. Monday we supported another Battery but did not draw much fire and in the night our army was withdrawn from the south side of the river. The rebs were very strongly fortified and were in a very advantageous position. It would cost many thousands of lives to storm the hills and I understand that there were 50 or 60 guns bearing on our immediate position which they had not yet opened on us.

Our troops on the right (those engaged in the main attack on Marye's Heights) suffered terribly, charging Batteries. Of course you know we were in the Left Grand Division of the army and were about 2 or 2½ miles below F—. I visited Capt. Petitts Battery at Falmouth day before yesterday 23rd December, they are yet in position the north side of the river and above F—. They are on a hill, just back of Falmouth and threw shell across at the time of the fight. I could see the rebel earthworks on the other side, redoubt after redoubt on every hill and there were 3 ranges of hills, each rising above the other as they went back. It is no boys play to go over those hills extending for miles from right to left and would cost probably 40 or 50 thousand lives.[12]

The regiment, as Wells described, had been withdrawn on Sunday, but on Monday (the fifteenth) the men were back at the extreme front, fully expecting to come under heavy fire; however, all was quiet. About nine in the evening the army began what was discreetly described as a "change of base" back across the Rappahannock. By 3:00 A.M. all were across but the pickets who retired on a signal, closely followed by those of the rebels. Little seems to have been done to hinder the Union retreat. Some Confederate guns began shelling, but Northern artillery put a stop to that. Then rebel sharpshooters opened fire on the engineers who were removing the pontoons—though with no serious effect. A correspondent to the *Journal* described one incident where the Confederate intentions were foiled—a description couched in that mixture of jocularity and callousness typical of such accounts:

One group of rebel officers and men had gathered near a house we had used as a hospital, and were getting a gun into position, when one of our gunners planted a 5-inch shell right in their midst, which exploded as it struck. The meeting suddenly adjourned, with numerous riderless horses and horseless riders. A sneaking butternut was working down the steep bank to get a shot at our engineers. A chief of piece planted a shell right under his feet. It burst. Secesh took a rise of a few feet, and then pursued his course to the river, "heels over head."[13]

The regiment then fell back somewhat, paused for a couple of days, and finally withdrew to camp near Falmouth.

Regimental comments on the battle were remarkably unconcerned, perhaps because the regiment had been only marginally involved in the battle and, as noted, had suffered negligible casualties. Thus the defeat does not seem to have been recognized as the serious setback to Northern hopes which it undoubtedly was. "Our army," claimed one such report, "fought with splendid courage and drove the enemy on the left somewhat, and at one time held his front battery and line, but we were forced to retire upon failure of ammunition."

It was conceded that the North lost heavily in trying to storm Marye's Heights, and that the army had been beaten back "from an almost impregnable position by the overwhelming number of the enemy." But, the report concluded, "Our gallant boys displayed the most determined bravery, and though beaten, won fresh laurels. The repulse has not had the effect to dishearten the troops in the least, and the rebels freely admit the heroism of our soldiers."[14]

So ended the first major battle in which the regiment had taken an active part.

The whole army sat back for a time and licked its wounds, while General Burnside tried to pick up the pieces of his ruined strategy. The 122nd, like the rest, went into camp near Falmouth and was not to move out again for more than a month. The move, when it came, proved almost as disastrous as the attack on Fredericksburg, although in a different way.

The Fredericksburg debacle had had repercussions both within and beyond the army itself. Despite the *Journal* correspondent's claims that the defeat had not served to dishearten the troops in any way, in fact, army morale plummeted, and thousands deserted. Generals Newton and Cochrane made a trip to Washington to confront Lincoln directly with the news of demoralization within the ranks and amongst the officers. Although Lincoln assured the troops that "although you were not successful, the attempt was not an error nor the failure other than an accident,"[15] he knew where the fault lay and so peremptorily ordered Burnside not to make any movement of the army without letting him know first. Burnside's response, not unnaturally, was to offer his resignation; he did so twice, but Lincoln was not at this stage in a position to find a replacement. Burnside, for the moment, was stuck with the job.

Perhaps as an attempt to retrieve the shreds of his military reputation, the reluctant commander of the Army of the Potomac offered a new plan. This involved a projected recrossing of the river in force at Banks's and United States' Fords, up river from Fredericksburg, with an attempt, made simultaneously, to deceive the enemy into believing that the crossing was to be made at Seddon House, some six or seven miles downstream. Whatever the merits of this plan may have been, they disregarded a crucial factor—the weather. On January 20, the army began the movement soon to be notorious as Burnside's "Mud March" (Plate 2). The sad history of this march was told by a *Journal* correspondent on January 27:

On the 20th all worked well. We marched to Berea Church, and encamped at dark, in a piece of woods, all ready to cross the river (about two miles in front) at daylight. Wagons, guns, pontoons, etc., coming up by another route to the crossing, and the enemy not yet alarmed. But at eight in the evening, the clouds that had been slowly banking up from the east all day gave the first premonitory sprinkle, and it began to rain, and soon settled into a steady heavy storm.

It rained all night, and when we got "under-weigh" at daylight of the 21st, it rained in steady torrents, with a furious gale of wind from the east.

We marched within half a mile of the river, and then halted, and several thousand men stacked arms and were sent to help the guns, wagons etc. along. The rain still poured, and at twelve o'clock of the 21st the roads were simply utterly impassable. Any-

where off the roads a wagon would sink to the hubs instantly. Wagons were overturned, broken down guns stuck in the mud; caissons broken down and abandoned; pontoons smashed and capsized, while the supply and ammunition trains were miles in the rear jammed fast, and unable to advance or retreat. In some cases eighteen horses were put upon a single gun, and then it could not be moved a mile per hour. In some batteries the hind wheels and chest were left and an effort made by doubling teams to draw the forward half and one limber chest up to the front, but this was given up as impracticable. The mud was in many places more than up to a horse's body, and men could only get along by skirting the road single file.[16]

The original intention had been to carry out the maneuver under cover of darkness, but such was the difficulty of moving at all through the morass that daylight revealed the entire army floundering about in full view of the enemy and immediately vulnerable to attack. Fortunately, the Confederates were sensible enough not to embroil themselves in a mud bath and remained satisfied with guarding the fords over which Burnside had hoped to cross. Curiously, the unhappy general escaped censure in the columns of the *Journal*. "Although the boys have nicknamed Burnside as "Old Stick-in-the-Mud," commented one correspondent, "there is general confidence felt in him," while another claimed, as far as one can tell without irony, that "General Burnside certainly won golden opinions for the determined manner in which he encountered obstacles, and for the manner in which he gracefully yielded when he saw that further effort would only wear out his men. I think that it is universally regretted that he is relieved from the command of the army in Virginia."[17]

2. Gen. Burnside Under Difficulty, Va.—January 24th, 1863

But even the *Journal* could not overlook the effect of this ordeal on morale. More men were lost by desertion after the "Mud March," it was estimated, than were lost by death and wounds at Fredericksburg. No longer was there any possibility of a winter campaign in Virginia. "Mud is king, and will continue to reign."[18]

One casualty of the Virginia mud was Burnside's position as commander of the Army of the Potomac. On January 25, 1863, he was replaced by "Fighting Joe" Hooker, a general whose qualities of courage and leadership were matched by a capacity for intrigue. Although Lincoln believed him to be partly responsible for the unsettled state of the army and its lack of confidence in Burnside, he gave Hooker complete responsibility for reorganizing the army and infusing it with a new spirit—a task Hooker performed with a great deal of success. In two months he had made welcome improvements in the organization of supplies, in military discipline, and in the arrangements for pay and furlough. By early April he had built up an army larger than any seen before in the United States, with one hundred and thirty thousand men, thirteen thousand cavalry, and at least five hundred guns.

Hooker's campaign plan, which was to lead ultimately to the Confederate victory at Chancellorsville, was initially well conceived. Avoiding the crude frontal assault employed so unsuccessfully by his predecessor, Hooker settled on a long flanking movement up stream hoping to turn Lee's left. The Confederate army would then be forced either to emerge from its strong defensive position and fight in the open or be pushed back in the direction of Richmond. A major part of this plan called for Sedgwick's Sixth Corps (including the 122nd) to be sent across the river two miles south of Fredericksburg to create a diversion.

A mile or two downstream from Fredericksburg, the 122nd and the rest of Sedgwick's corps prepared to cross the river on pontoons. "April 28th," Wells wrote home,

we broke camp and started for the river. We halted when near the river and waited for darkness. We were detailed to carry the pontoons down to the river for waggons and horses would make too much noise. Each Company took a boat. We got them all down there just before daylight and Pratt's Light Division jumped in the boats and went across to take the bank and hold it—so that they could build the bridge in the morning for the rest of our Corps to pass over. Everything was still when they started and as our regiment with others had been at work hard all night we lay on this side listening for the first sound of battle. Suddenly crack went a volley and whizz flew the minies. The rebs had heard the boats and fired but the gallant fellows soon landed and so Reb had to fall back. So we got the bank and held it. This was about a mile and a half below the City of F— and just where we crossed at the time of our first fight. Our brigade did not cross over until Saturday night May 2. Our fellows still held the bank at this point, but had not as yet farther advanced. We went over first at dark and rested till towards midnight and then started for the city of F—.

We took the river road. The 1st U.S. or rather the 65 N.Y. led off and our regiment came next. Thus we felt our way along a strange road and near the enemy expecting every moment we should catch a fire from an unseen foe. We had flankers thrown out on each side of the column from each company. When we reached the edge of F— the head of the column was fired on and quite a number wounded. We pushed on, however, went into the city and came out at the foot of the heights on which were the rebel batteries and rifle pits and that *stone wall* you heard or read so much about in our first fight. We moved part way up the hill and joined line of battle. Col. Shaler, who commands our brigade gave orders to get ready to charge that battery, meaning the one on the hill right in front of us and so near were we to the rebs that their commands could be heard by us. Everything was thrown off for the charge. Our regiment was in the front line and all expected time, but it was dark and as we were going in on our uncertainty our General concluded to wait for daylight. So we fell back just to the edge of the city.

Morning came, we had not slept any and in the forenoon of Sunday May 3rd the charge was made after the usual amount of commanding had been done. Our regiment was not in the front line of the charging party but followed up as soon as the charge was made to support them and hold the hills. Just before we started forward and while we yet were on the edge of the city my Captain (who was standing right beside me, and we were talking about the same time) was struck by a minie and badly wounded. We were watching the effect of the charge. As soon as he was wounded I took him away from the place where he had been hurt but the grape and canister seemed to come thicker where we went so we went back for I thought that would be as safe a place for him as anywhere. The next moment we were ordered forward and I had to take command of the company. The rebs were falling back. After getting up the heights part of our regiment (my company included) were deployed as skirmishers, we soon came upon the rebel skirmishers and the fuss commenced. All the firing our regiment done was while skirmishing. It was a continual crack of rifles and whistling of balls from both sides. I had one man slightly wounded while skirmishing. At the time of the charge Sunday forenoon it was estimated that our Corps lost about 900 men in about 11 minutes, killed wounded and missing.

Well after our skirmish we took a road from F— and started towards where Hooker was but after getting about 2½ miles from F— we came upon the rebels in force and Sunday about 4 P.M. a terrible infantry fight ensued and for about 2 hours it seemed as if everything was let loose. We were ordered to relieve a regiment in the front and done so, but the firing had ceased mostly for that night and we were again lucky. The dead and wounded of both sides lay thick around and a good many of the wounded rebs that could walk came into our lines. They seemed to think they could get better care at our hands than they could get in their own lines. Well after dark I deployed my company as skirmishers in front of the regiment and near a piece of woods where the rebs were supposed to be but we were not fired upon that night and at 4 in the morning we were relieved by another regiment of our Brigade.

Monday we found that Hooker was falling back and had to act in the defensive, consequently the rebs sent a heavy force to oppose us. They got around between us and F— and as Hooker was falling back and we could not form a junction with him we had to fall back and we crossed over on this side of the river early Tuesday morning at Banks's Ford, some miles above F—. I think if the 11th Corps had done well Hooker would have continued to advance and our Corps could then have joined him. You see Hooker was fighting at or near Chancellorsville some 8 or 10 miles from us but he had to fall back and consequently our Corps could not join him.[19]

Wells' letter provided a remarkably complete account of his own part in battle, but it has to be fitted into context. On May 2, Sedgwick had been ordered to move his corps across the river in order to join up with Hooker at Chancellorsville. The crossing was carried out without difficulty, and after skirmishing around Fredericksburg, the Sixth Corps found itself in front of Marye's Heights on Sunday morning, near the fatal stone wall mentioned by Wells before which so many Union men had perished in December. Meeting with strong enemy fire, the men moved back to the edge of the city. There they were joined by Gibbons' division, bringing the number under Sedgwick's command to nearly thirty thousand. The rebels continued to hold Marye's Hill where they had a number of guns in position, and the difficulty of mounting a successful assault against them was increased by a canal located on the enemy's left. One attempt to clear the rebel rifle pits at the foot of the hill was beaten back, but another, successful assault was made at eleven in the morning by three columns of General Howe's Second Division. Two hundred prisoners were taken, but the capture of the hill proved expensive—in the course of only eleven minutes about nine hundred Union soldiers were killed or wounded.[20]

The 122nd had not been in the van of this attack but in a supporting column which passed over the hill, wheeled to the right, and within a short distance came up against a fortified hill occupied by a rebel unit with two guns. This the regiment was ordered to carry and did so promptly, with the loss of nine men[21] (Plate 3).

This was only a curtain raiser. Having successfully taken Marye's Heights, Sedgwick was now able to move on in the direction of Chancellorsville, about nine or ten miles to the west, but he could get no further than Salem Church, which was only four miles along the road. A strong Confederate force defended the position grimly, and after a bitter battle lasting two hours, no headway had been made. Sedgwick's position became critical. More and more rebel forces, flushed with victory at Chancellorsville, arrived to reinforce the strong point, threatening Sixth Corps' left flank. On Monday, the fourth, the attack began. The Union forces were pushed back to the river and, ultimately, back over it at Banks's Ford. A bridge was laid across the Rappahannock at nightfall and held by the 122nd until three in the morning; they were the last regiment to cross. The maneuver cost the Sixth Corps approximately five thousand casualties. By the eighth, the regiment was back in camp, only a small distance from where it had started out.[22]

In the two major engagements in which it had so far been actively involved—Fredericksburg and the Chancellorsville campaign—the regiment had performed well and lost comparatively few men in action. It was impossible to ignore the fact, however, that both battles had been Northern defeats, and it is surprising, if it was true, that morale seems to have suffered so little. No one could have known then that a Northern victory was in fact only a few weeks away—a victory in which the regiment would take not only an active but even a decisive part. But the road to Gettysburg was long and hard, and the regiment spent most of the intervening period in restless movement along that road.

Early in June, Lee began his preparations for a new invasion of Maryland and Pennsylvania. He started by moving part of his army up along the south bank of the Rappahannock. These

FROM MEMORY,
W. E. RUGGLES, 122D N.Y.
(((((MARYS' HEIGHTS, FREDERICRSBURGH, VA.))))))
MAY 3D 1863.
THE 122D REGT, N.Y. WITH SHALER'S BRIGADE, STORMING THE HEIGHTS.

3. Marye's Heights, Fredericksburg, Va.—May 3rd, 1863

movements were carefully screened from the Northern forces, but Hooker grew suspicious, and on the sixth of June sent Howe's division of the Sixth Corps, including the 122nd, back across the river to Fredericksburg on a reconnaissance. Rightly or wrongly, Howe concluded that there had been no reduction of rebel strength in the area and withdrew to the north bank on the thirteenth. On the ninth, the *Journal's* regular correspondent in the regiment sent this report from on the field near Fredericksburg:

We broke up camp on Friday last, and moved to the river at what is now called Franklin's crossing—our old place. The bridges had been laid with a sharp resistance in which Capt. Cross of the Engineers, a Captain of a New Jersey regiment and several men were killed, and eighteen wounded, in all a loss of about twenty five. We then crossed and took position on the south bank and threw out our pickets. My own impression is that the move was made under the idea that the heights were abandoned, as the rebels had been moving, in large numbers, up to the right; but our demonstration soon showed that they were here, for in the afternoon of the 6th, the long heavy columns of grey backs, with nothing shining but their muskets, moved over the hills and into their works, and a heavy picket line on our front showed them on the *qui vive*. Johnny Butternut is not very good natured this time either. We hold a front of almost half a mile, while our picket line is fully a mile and a half long, the farthest part about three-fourths of a mile from the river. On the front and left everything is lovely: but on the right they are as waspish as a nest of bumble-bees after we have mowed over their nest in the old meadow at home. A fine old house and some out-buildings, just in range of our line there, and between it and Fredericksburg, furnish a den for their sharpshooters, and they have been pop, pop, popping at our pickets ever since we have been here, but our fellows understand the game and none of them had been hurt. Until this morning the orders have been not to return the fire, but just now ten of the Berdan Sharpshooters have been deployed, with long telescopic rifles, and the rebs have pretty much closed up the business. Yesterday and day before a battery opened on the houses, and made splendid shots, rattling the rebs out in fine style, but they would skulk back as soon as the fire was stopped. . . .

We hold a strong position on the south bank and have the city right under the fire of our guns. It is hardly possible that the rebels will attack us, and if they do it is almost a dead certainty that they will get terribly defeated. The army is in good spirits, and the fighting Sixth Corps look on the frowning heights in the rear of the city as their peculiar property, and something they want to take once more to keep.[23]

They were not, of course, to be given the chance. On the thirteenth the entire Union force was ordered back to the north side of the Rappahannock. While they crossed in the pitch dark, a tremendous rainstorm hid their movements from the enemy. The next three days were spent in hard marching: on the fourteenth to Stafford Court House, the fifteenth to Dumfries, on the sixteenth to Fairfax Station where they were given a day's rest. The pace was killing—pronounced by the oldest soldiers to be the worst they had ever endured—and the heat and dust did not add to the comfort. Captain Brower and Captain Lester both collapsed from sunstroke, though they soon recovered. The eighteenth saw the regiment on the move again, this time to just beyond Fairfax Court House, where they rested up for six days.[24] Then on the move again: on Wednesday, June 24, from Fairfax to Centreville, where they

4. Gettysburg, Pa.

expected to stay on picket duty. On Thursday a change of plan—they were sent out at night to picket on the old field of Blackburn's Ford, then next morning off again to Dranesville in the pouring rain where they camped for the night. But there was no rest yet.

On Saturday morning, the 27th, we moved at four o'clock, for Edwards' Ferry and Poolesville, and that afternoon camped again on the banks of the Potomac at the Ferry, waiting for the trains to get across, when we shall take up our "winding way" in Maryland, "My Maryland." We move twelve miles on Friday and fifteen miles on Saturday. These marches weary our men very much—the sun beats down hot and scalding, and the dust is very oppressive—but all are full of grit.

Rumors reach us that the rebels have heavy forces at Williamsport, South Mountain, Hagerstown and opposite Harper's Ferry,— thus holding the old classic ground of Maryland, where we are to try over the issues that were fought here a year ago. This regiment (the 122nd) encamped at Poolesville Saturday night, and will move on to meet the invaders of Pennsylvania tomorrow (Sunday).[25]

It took the 122nd three days to march to Gettysburg, at an average pace of more than twenty miles a day. Although exhausted when they arrived they had only an hour's rest before being sent to the front. Adj. Osgood V. Tracy described their experiences to his mother in a letter written on the battlefield:

We arrived at Manchester, Md., on the night of the first; laid still on the 2nd, until about 5 o'clock when we received orders to march. We marched all night and the next day until about four P.M. making in all about thirty miles. During the night I was so sleepy I had to get off my horse and walk to keep awake. After our arrival near Gettysburg we laid quiet for about an hour and then were ordered up to the front and there remained all night. The next morning (Friday) our brigade was detached and ordered to report to General Slocum. We were put behind a breast work of logs, with the rebels behind a stone wall about 200 yards in front. I happened to be with the left wing when the 1st Maryland who were in front of us got out of ammunition and came running in. As soon as we learned the state of the case the left six companies advanced and took position behind the front breastworks. I tell you the bullets whistled *some*. We kept our position and finally drove the rebels from theirs. Soon after we took possession of the works, a regiment came up and relieved the regiment on our left; and judge of our surprise and pleasure on finding it was the 149th. Was it not remarkable that the first time the two regiments from Onondaga met should be fighting behind the same breastworks?[26] (Plate 4)

Tracy's account of the regiment's involvement in Gettysburg is almost certainly mistaken as to dates, and there remain some discrepancies between surviving commentaries. It seems most likely that the 122nd actually arrived on the afternoon of Thursday, July 1. That night Green's brigade of the Twelfth Corps fell back from a line of rifle pits to the regiment's right, only to find on the Friday morning following that these had been occupied in the interval by the rebels. It was at this point, as Tracy describes, that Shaler's brigade (including the 122nd) was placed under the command of General Slocum and ordered to regain the pits. According to the *Herald* correspondent:

The 122nd New York took the lead, and troops never loaded or fired with greater rapidity or surer effect than the gallant soldiers of the regiment, cheered by their intrepid leaders. Their sixty rounds of ammunition was exhausted upon the rebels, when the Long Island regiment advanced to relieve them. As the muskets of the latter were raised the entire body of the rebels in the pits rose up with white flags and surrendered. There were between three and four hundred of them in the breastworks, and all preferred capture to a repetition of the regimental fire they had first received.[27]

The regiment's mission had been successfully accomplished, but the battle had still one day to run. Although the third day is chiefly remembered for the slaughter of Pickett's charge, fighting on the Union right was also fierce and the outcome vital. Here the rebel attack, led as on the previous day by General Ewell, would, if successful, have broken the Northern army's right flank and left the whole line vulnerable. That it was not successful was largely because of the stubborn defense put up by the regiments of Shaler's First Brigade, the 122nd among them, positioned on Culp's Hill. Here, from nine to eleven in the morning of the third, the 122nd took its place in the front line. This it held until relieved by the 82nd Pennsylvania. The cost had been high. The regiment's losses in the battle totaled forty-four killed, wounded, and missing, more than all those in the rest of the brigade put together. But few would now dispute that the outcome of Gettysburg was crucial to the outcome of the war at large. The "high water mark of the Confederacy" had been reached—and passed.

III · INTO THE WILDERNESS—AND OUT AGAIN

The Confederate Army's defeat at Gettysburg and the fall of Vicksburg have long been considered major turning points in the Civil War. After these losses, the fortunes of the South went into an irreversible, though intermittent, decline. Southern morale, however, was by no means destroyed. The South still had Lee, and Lee still had plenty of fight left in him. But, militarily, the South had lost the initiative and, worse still, had lost the war of supply. Following Gettysburg and Vicksburg, the war machine in the North gathered new momentum, and Northern troops, at least on paper, were from that time on to outnumber the enemy's. Only one factor could have won the war for the South—the loss of Northern determination to win.

This situation, so apparent to us years later, was by no means clear at the time. Southern leaders, especially Jefferson Davis, seriously viewed the outcome of Gettysburg as a draw. And in some respects this perspective was valid, as Meade's failure to follow up by crushing Lee as he lay almost helpless on the northern side of the Potomac at Williamsport, allowed Lee to escape and his army to keep the Confederate cause alight for almost two more years. The aftermath of Gettysburg in the eastern theater proved to be a kind of stalemate, at least until after the winter when the whole weary process had to be begun all over again.

This is not to say that the Army of the Potomac was totally inactive for the remaining months of the 1863 campaign. The 122nd, still with Sedgwick's Sixth Corps, found plenty to occupy itself with until just into the New Year. After wintering in Sandusky, Ohio (probably, though not certainly, as part of the guard at the prisoner of war camp on Johnson's Island), they began on a new and bitter campaign, in the course of which, in the Wilderness and at Cold Harbor, they were to sustain their highest casualties of the war.

Their immediate task after Gettysburg was to take part in the cautious pursuit of the rebel army in retreat. As Lee withdrew toward the river, the 122nd's brigade followed him to Middletown and from there, across the mountain to Funkstown, Maryland. Arriving on July 14, they found the rebels in a good defensive position behind breastworks and so sheltered by a grove of trees that the Northern artillery could not be brought to bear on them. A number of courageous volunteers undertook to chop down the intervening trees in full view of the rebel guns, but their exploit was in vain: in the morning, when the attack was to have been made, the enemy was found to have fled. The Union army pressed on to Williamsport, a distance of four miles, and captured the rebel rear guard, but instead of following up this success, they recrossed the Potomac and pitched camp at Warrenton, Virginia.[1]

The 122nd was to remain in camp about a mile and a half from Warrenton from July 24 to September 15. In Wells' view, no new attack on Lee's army was likely until the Union troops had been reinforced, unless of course Lee attacked first. The regiment, like its fellows in the brigade, was now seriously under strength, and Wells waited anxiously for the result of the latest draft in Onondaga County. Warrenton itself aroused mixed feelings among the soldiery—as a town it was acknowledged to be a pretty enough place, but as Wells commented, "the war has about used it up. All the stores are closed because they cannot get goods and I guess the inhabitants do not live much better than we soldiers do." The most uncomfortable aspect of Warrenton, apart from the heat, was the unfriendliness of the local inhabitants who were "mostly Secesh—ladies and all."[2] In addition, the area was a hotbed of guerrillas. Despised and feared by the Union soldiers, these guerrillas, "honest farmers," as they were contemptuously referred to, had the disconcerting habit of ambushing stray Northern soldiers and then, when a sortie was sent out against them, turning into innocent farmhands, fully equipped with government passes falsely acquired by perjured oaths of allegiance.[3] The activities of these guerrillas were among the factors which changed the attitudes of Northern soldiers toward the Confederates from a kind of comradeship in adversity to active hatred.

This extended stay at Warrenton, however, was no doubt a welcome respite from the months of almost uninterrupted campaigning. Wells was able to catch up with his paper work on the company muster rolls and build one of his elaborate, semipermanent "shanties." Time was also found for some full-scale brigade and division drills—possibly the regiment's first. By early September Wells was able to comment with some satisfaction that "we can get around in most any shape now."[4] But the regiment could not be allowed to remain inactive forever. On the fifteenth they were moved to White Sulphur Springs, where they camped at Stone House Mountain until October 1. From there they marched in heavy rain to Catlett's Station, arriving on the third and remaining on guard with the rest of the brigade for the next ten days.

In the small hours of October 13, the regiment was roused up and marched to Warrenton Junction, where they were positioned in line of battle about a mile east of the junction to protect the wagon trains and the flank of the main army as it moved north. That evening the brigade moved to Kettle Run, not far from Bristoe Station, and then on to Centreville on picket. This movement was in response to the rebels having edged their way around the army's right flank, thus threatening the lines of communication with Washington. The Confederates had closed on Centreville in the hope of being able to occupy its fortifications, only to find on their arrival that three Union corps had got there first and were already in possession. Assuming correctly that the Northern trains would be close behind this position, the rebel forces wheeled right and attacked the train, while at the same time coming into contact with the flank of the Second Corps. Undismayed, the men of the corps counterattacked fiercely and repelled the attack, inflicting heavy losses. This engagement was called Bristoe Station.[5]

The next few days were equally eventful. On the sixteenth the regiment marched to a position four miles north of Centreville and waited for the enemy to attack. There was hard fighting for two days before the rebels were pushed back toward Gainesville, then to New Baltimore, and finally back to Warrenton, where the Confederates withdrew across the river. Morale in the Army of the Potomac was now higher than it had been for some months. A dangerous Confederate move that came close to threatening Washington had been dealt with successfully. It was now time for the North to take the initiative. This General Meade proposed to do by attempting yet another attack in the Fredericksburg area, some twenty-five miles west of the town itself. On November 7, he sent Sedgwick with the Fifth and Sixth Corps from Warrenton to Rappahannock Station, to a location on the north bank of the river that the rebels had strongly fortified in order to protect their pontoon bridge.[6]

The battle of Rappahannock Station was one of the 122nd's most successful, but one in which it also incurred serious losses (Plate 5). Sedgwick's troops came up about noon, taking time to rest and carry out a thorough reconnaissance before making any moves. The decision was then made to carry the enemy's works by a direct assault. Union troops dashed forward, carried the position, and captured sixteen hundred prisoners, two thousand small arms, and four cannons. The regiment's *Journal* correspondent described the 122nd in action:

We engaged the enemy about 2.00 P.M. Cos. "A", Lieut. Clapp, "G", Lieut. Wooster, and "I", Capt. J. M. Dwight, being engaged as skirmishers, and the rest in close support.

Our skirmishers drove in the enemy's in the most gallant style, firing one volley at them and charging with the bayonet, and each of the above officers distinguished himself very highly. Our skirmishers took a position within close rifle shot of the rebel works and held it through the above fight, under a heavy fire, inflicting severe damage to the enemy. The rest of the regiment supported Ayre's Battery, and the whole regiment behaved with the most determined bravery.[7]

The result in terms of losses to the enemy was creditable, but it was paid for: the 122nd had thirteen killed and wounded.[8] Amongst the former was Sgt. Philo Ruggles, William Ruggles' elder brother, who was killed along with two companions by a percussion shell.[9] At considerable cost, Northern control of the ford was now complete, and Lee was obliged to fall back on Culpeper before withdrawing across the river on the following day.

One final task lay ahead of the regiment before the old year could give way to the new, and active campaigning put away on the shelf while the armies, Northern and Southern, recouped their strength in winter quarters. This was the Mine Run campaign of late November and early December, 1863 (Plate 6).

FROM MEMORY
W.E.RUGGLES
122ᴰ. N.Y.

(((((((THE BATTLE OF RAPPAHANICK, STATION, VA.)))))))
NOV. 7TH 1863.

THE 122ᴰ REGT. N.Y. IN THE 1ST, LINE OF BATTLE, SUPPORTING COWANS BATTERY.

5. The Battle of Rappahannock Station, Va.

After the success of Rappahannock Station, the regiment had moved back to Brandy Station on about November 10 and had spent a fortnight in camp. On Thanksgiving Day the men were ordered out on the march; they crossed the Rapidan at eight in the morning as part of the Third Corps.[10] Once over the river, their corps was soon engaged in a brisk fight in dense woods and undergrowth. Taking advantage of this cover, the corps commander placed eight guns together in a small field with orders to open fire slowly. The enemy fell into the trap. Believing that such ineffective fire could be coming from no more than a couple of guns, they charged, but when they got within close range "eight Napoleons opened up with canister, clearing up about five acres of brush and the same quantity of rebels. The enemy stuck to it with good pluck, and had the same bad luck, till they gave it up and left us the field, with all their killed and wounded."[11]

The 122nd had not been directly involved in this engagement. Instead, on the twenty-eighth, it had marched across to the left to join up with the Second Corps. Heavy rain fell throughout the day, and there were fears that if the rain persisted it would result in the loss of every gun, caisson, and wagon in the train. Fortunately, on the morning of the twenty-ninth the skies cleared, and after a brief interlude, the regiment moved to a position opposite the enemy's right flank. Here the enemy had taken a strong position, defended by swamps and gullies in front and flank, and had worked like beavers throwing up breastworks, and we laid in their front all day expecting to *go in*. Rumor says that Gen. Warren received an order to that effect, and replied that he could do so, but that no Second Corps would be left if he did, and asked Gen. Meade to look at the position of the enemy first; that Gen. Meade did so, and warmly complimented Gen. Warren on his discretion, and revoked the order.[12]

That night, having seen little action and suffered no casualties, the unit fell back to the river, recrossed it the following day and returned to their old camp at Brandy Station on the third. The campaigns of 1863 were over.

The Mine Run campaign had been a strenuous one in physical terms, though one which incurred no loss to the regiment, and the break in the weather came as a warning to the army command not to make the mistake that Burnside had made in attempting a winter offensive. The campaign had also been enlivened by an incident involving Alfred R. Waud, the famous Civil War artist, on a visit to General Shaler's camp. The *Journal*'s regular correspondent, D, happened to be present at the time:

About 2 p.m. as it was bitter cold, the men were seated and lying round their fires, and I was lying near the fire of Gen. Shaler, with a group of officers and Mr. Houston, of the Herald Staff, and Mr. A. R. Wand [*sic*], the artist of Harper, all laughing at the drolleries of Wand, who had no overcoat, and a blouse all torn and ragged, and kept vowing he wasn't cold, and keeping everybody else warm with his jokes and witticisms. He had just finished a side splitting imitation of a Chatham-street Jew clothes-dealer, and all were laughing, when whiz! bang!! and a shell burst over our heads and fiz! whiz!! rattle!!! came the framents amongst us.

If you ever saw a debating society dissolve when the gas was turned off, or a colony of chipmunks disappear at the crack of some urchin's gun, or a crowd of dogs scatter when a junk bottle made its appearance in their midst from a fourth storey window, you can form some idea of the adjournment of our convention.

6. Mine Run—November 29th, 1863

Houston rolled heels over head, and the artist's tattered garments streamed out as he struck out in the wind's eye for his horse; the staff sprang to their horses; the Colonel sprang to his feet and turned to his regiment, singing out the command "Lie down *close*, men!" Another stepped quickly to a spot near his command, and simply said "Down, there!" and then we all waited for the next. It soon came, but wide, and a ten pounder rifled Parrott of ours shut the fellow up in three shots. No one was hurt, but I observed the gentlemen of the press *diggin'* down the road to the rear, soon after, and small blame to them.[13]

This was one Civil War incident of which *Harper's Weekly* did *not* publish a Waud drawing.

To appreciate fully the part played by the 122nd regiment in the Northern offensive in the spring of 1864, it is first necessary to understand the national scene and take note of certain important changes in leadership, and consequently in strategy, within the army high command. The most important change, one from which all others followed, was the appointment of General Grant as commander of all the Union forces, with the rank of Lieutenant General. At long last the president had an army chief who thought along similar strategic lines as himself, and who was prepared to act decisively and ruthlessly. The man Grant replaced, General Halleck, was retained in the new post of chief of staff where he played a vital role as Grant's liaison with Lincoln by freeing the new commander from the necessity of staying in Washington, close to the President. Grant knew that his place was in the field, and he chose to establish his headquarters with the Army of the Potomac, leaving the able Meade in command of the Army itself.

This unified command structure made possible a coherent strategy based on two simple principles. The first principle, which neither McClellan nor Burnside nor Hooker had ever succeeded in grasping, was that the Union's primary objective must be not the capture of the Confederate capital but the destruction of the Confederate army. In fact, this meant the destruction of two armies—Lee's forces in Virginia, and Joe Johnston's in Georgia. The second principle of the new strategy was that this objective was to be achieved by massive and unrelenting pressure—making the best use of the North's greatest single advantage over the South, its preponderance of men and war materials. In Georgia, Grant had an able and like-minded lieutenant in General Sherman, a man who understood perhaps ever better than Grant that a civil war must inevitably be a war against the civil population. This policy Sherman carried out mercilessly but effectively, destroying not only the rebel forces, but also the fields, farms, and possessions of the Southern people and with these, their will to continue the fight.

For the men of the 122nd Regiment, the appointment of Grant had two major consequences. The first took immediate effect and resulted in a thoroughgoing reorganization of the Army of the Potomac: the former five corps were now reduced to three, under, respectively, General Hancock (Second), General Warren (Fifth) and General Sedgwick (Sixth). To this already formidable force was later added Burnside's Ninth Corps, bringing the total fighting strength of the Northern army in the east to well over one hundred thousand. Within the Sixth Corps, reorganization resulted in the 122nd becoming part of the Fourth Brigade in the First Division of the corps.[14] The second consequence of Grant's appointment

7. Battle of the Wilderness, Va.—Morning of May 6th, 1864

was that his policy of unremitting pressure was applied as much to the Union army as it was against the Confederates. From May 1864 to April 1865, the 122nd campaigned with scarcely a break. The cost in battle casualties alone was devastating—the regiment lost approximately 360 men in the last year of the war, compared to only around sixty-five in the previous year. Almost a third of these new losses were incurred in the terrible carnage of the Wilderness.[15]

Grant's Virginia campaign of 1864 opened in May with a move against Lee's army, south of the Rapidan. The choice lay between an attack against the enemy's left flank, passing through relatively easy open country, or one made against his right flank, across more difficult terrain. Grant chose the latter, partly because he preferred the advantages it offered in the way of a waterborne supply route, and partly because he hoped thereby to get between Lee and Richmond and grasp control of the rebels' supply lines. For the 122nd the choice was disastrous. Along with the rest of the army, they plunged into the dense, almost impenetrable, undergrowth of the Wilderness, where the advantage of numbers counted for little. The battle which ensued was less a conflict between armies than a series of desperate struggles between small groups isolated from their companions by the trees and scrub. The following extracts from the diary of Maj. Theodore L. Poole, provide a graphic picture of the confusion and devastation felt by the entire regiment:

May 4, 1864. Left camp near Brandy Station at daylight. Our brigade is rear-guard and is with the wagons of the corps. At about 11 p.m. marched eastward and went into camp at Gold Mine Ford. At the ford we found the entire wagon trains of the army, and they were then crossing the Rapidan. We spread our blankets on the ground and slept till daylight.

May 5. Did not cross the river until late in the afternoon, when we marched about two miles and encamped, still being the wagon-guard. A battle was in progress all day in front of us, continuing till late at night. It is impossible to learn anything definite.

May 6. We were awakened at midnight and leaving the wagons behind us, marched several miles to the right and took up line of battle. Crossed over a portion of the battle ground of yesterday and saw many of the dead. The battle commenced at daylight; but at this hour (6 a.m.) we have taken no part. Word has come that we shall soon make a bayonet charge. 2 o'clock p.m. Attempted the charge and failed. We advanced twenty rods and halted, took what cover we could and opened fire (Plate 7). Continued firing about twenty minutes, when both sides ceased; our skirmishers, however, kept up fire during the day. Our losses up to this time in the regiment are, one man killed and 41 officers and men wounded. Besides these 15 are missing, and we have reason to suppose some of them are killed or wounded. My company (I) lost Captain Dwight, wounded in the left leg below the knee, not supposed to be serious; privates Howard and Brooks, both wounded severely; Lieutenant Wilson, of Company A, wounded in the shoulder (proved fatal); Lieutenant C. B. Clark, wounded in the leg; (Captain Dwight, wounded early in the morning at 8 o'clock, and I have since been in command of the company). Corporal Isaac, of my company, is missing and I suppose him killed; Corporal F. Patterson, of Company D, belonging to my color-guard, is also wounded. . . .

At 6.30 p.m. the rebels made an attack upon our works, in front, right flank and rear, the attack being made by Gordon's division (Plate 8). Our regiment and the entire brigade were driven back in great confusion and with heavy loss, many of our

8. Battle of the Wilderness, Va.—Evening of May 6th, 1864

regiment being killed and wounded and others falling and being taken prisoners. The extreme right, consisting of our division, was driven back and completely broken to pieces, being left in fragments in the woods. We retreated nearly two miles, seeking to rally the men, but the panic was such we found it impossible. Captain Clapp and myself finally got half a dozen of our regiment together, and as we had our regimental flag it gave us a rallying point, and with our little band we started back to the front. Other small squads were found, and we soon had quite a force together. I had only three men in my company out of 30. Our force went back a quarter of a mile or so, gathering strength as we went. Here we were joined by Lieut-Col. Dwight, Capt. Walpole, Lieuts. Hoyt and Wells and five or six more of our men. Col. Upton, of the 121st New York, took command of our division (what was left of it) and soon formed a line of battle. We and the 1st Long Island regiment (67th N.Y.) consisting of about forty men, were made the second line. At 11 p.m. we were attacked in force, but we drove the enemy back easily. At about 1 o'clock p.m. (sic.) we moved to the right again, and lay down behind a battery and rifle pits. I have no idea what the loss of our regiment is, but it is very great. Capt. Platt, Lieut. Ostrander are both prisoners. I think our entire loss so far will be nearly or quite 2,000. Out of nine sergeants and corporals belonging to my color-guard, only one is with me.

May 7. Soon after daylight, the rebels attacked us once more, but we drove them back, our battery doing us great service. Adjutant Tracy is missing and is supposed to be wounded and a prisoner. Col. Dwight has detailed me as Adjutant, and Lieut. Wilkins has taken my company. Lieut. Hall and a squad of men have just come in. At 8 a.m. moved again to the right about two miles and occupied rifle-pits, where we lay quietly all day. At 9.30 p.m. fell in, moving towards the left and marching all night.[16]

Poole's account of the confusion and heavy losses suffered by the regiment in the Wilderness seems to have been in no way exaggerated. The picture he presents is corroborated by the later recollections of Capt. James M. Gere, who was himself amongst those taken prisoner in this engagement. Gere began the battle with the rest of the regiment on the extreme right flank of the army, but in the ensuing disorder he lost contact with his unit and was eventually captured. According to his account, the battle started with a charge by General Gordon's division against the Union right flank, driving in the skirmishers and falling upon the protective screen of cavalry. The rebel attack pressed on until it struck the 122nd, who were driven to the left about a quarter of a mile. At this point General Shaler appeared; gathering together about 500 men, he made a rally and charged Gordon's men. These held their ground until the attack was almost upon them and then broke. Shaler, the only man there on a horse, set off to the rear to bring reinforcements but had the bad luck to ride straight into the rebel line—and inevitable capture. The rest of the five hundred kept on with their charge and managed to drive the rebels back to where they had begun their attack. Attacked from the rear by another force of Confederates, Shaler's men turned and scattered them, then tried to find their regiments and re-form.

In half or three-quarters of an hour, the rebels were heard cheering up through the woods. There was with us one stand of colors belonging to a Maine regiment; this was planted in the road, and in a minute about 150 men rallied around it facing the enemy. Raising a yell, they charged the on-coming brigade of rebels with such fury that (probably thinking the little squad was only the advance of a heavy charging column) they broke and ran, and were pursued a mile, till they joined a larger body of the rebel army.[17]

At the end of two days of hard fighting, it was difficult to say which side had gained the advantage. The losses to both had been enormous; casualties on the Union side were far in excess of the two thousand estimated by Poole. The loss to the Sixth Corps alone was put by Colonel Titus of the 122nd at approximately seventy-five hundred, and total Northern casualties were probably not less than seventeen thousand.[18] Confederate casualties though fewer, could not be replaced. The real significance of the battle, however, lay less in a calculation of losses than in the events that happened next. Grant's strategy had suffered a major setback. If he had followed precedents set by Burnside at Fredericksburg or Hooker at Chancellorsville, he would have retired or held off, taking time to reorganize and recoup. Grant did none of these things—he moved on. Lee was now to feel the full weight of Northern pressure as the Union forces raced him for control of the vital crossroads at Spotsylvania Court House.

Spotsylvania Court House, an important road junction, lay some twelve miles to the southeast of the battlefield of the Wilderness. Control over it would obviously enable Grant to move round Lee's right flank and position his forces between Lee and Richmond. But if Grant could grasp this point, so could Lee, and the race to get there first was won—by the narrowest of margins—by the rebels. What Grant might have taken simply by moving with extra speed, he was now obliged to do battle for; the fighting was the hardest either side had yet encountered. The worst carnage took place on the salient or "bloody angle" before the Confederate defenses, when on May 12, Grant and Meade, in desperation, attempted a costly and fruitless frontal attack.

The 122nd Regiment was closely involved in much of this bitter struggle, which lasted from the eighth to the twenty-first. Major Poole's diary recorded the whole of the engagement as he experienced it:

May 8. Passed through Chancellorsville and took the road to Spotsylvania Court House. About noon our advance met the enemy and engaged them. During the afternoon we supported a battery and at 5 o'clock moved into some breast works, together with the 6th Maine and 119th Pennsylvania. Here lost one man. At 9 p.m. were attacked, but there had been no general engagement during the day. Our entire loss up to this time had been 130—less than 30 of them prisoners. Gen. A. Shaler and Gen. Seymour are among the latter. The Chasseurs (65th N.Y.) and 1st Long Island (67th N.Y.) have lost very heavily. Capt. Tracy (of the Chasseurs) and Capt. Cooper, of the Long Island, are both killed, and a number of officers are wounded in both regiments.

May 9. Moved at daylight to the line, and lay upon an open plain supporting a battery. Gen. John Sedgwick, commanding the 6th Corps, was killed this morning by sharpshooters. During the afternoon we were exposed to the enemy's shells and sharp shooters, but met with no loss. Up to this time officers and men have behaved splendidly; but all are worn down with fatigue, hard marches, continued fighting and loss of sleep. During Monday night we were attacked three different times by the enemy. I am almost sick, and many are worse off than I am. We have about 200 men left for duty and eight officers, besides the colonel and myself. Some of the best men of our regiment are gone, but I hardly have time to think about them.

May 10. Orders came at 2 o'clock this morning that we, in conjunction with our entire force in front, would advance upon the enemy at daylight. Daylight came, however, and we did not move. During the afternoon Col. Dwight was sent back to hospital sick and worn out, and Capt. Walpole took command of the regiment. The battle commenced early in the morning and up to this time (4 p.m.) has raged with terrible fury. Fortunately for us, we have not suffered much along our portion of the line, and our brigade has not been harmed.

Orders have come. The Chasseurs have taken knapsacks and haversacks, and started forward. The Long Island and our own regiment have moved into some rifle pits to the left. The charge took place at about 6 o'clock, and lasted some forty minutes. We could hear but not see what was going on. Directly in our front the charge was successful, but we were finally driven back with heavy loss. The charging column consisted of the 5th and 6th Maine, the 5th Wisconsin and the 14th and 56th New York regiments. They took 1,500 prisoners and a battery of four guns; the guns, however, they were forced to leave.

May 11. Our regiment went out on picket to the left. Sharp picket firing all day. Lost five men, wounded; also Capt. Walpole supposed to be taken prisoner. He had given me orders early in the morning to advance the left wing, which I had charge of, and at the same time directed the right wing to advance (Plate 9). We drew upon us a heavy fire, and Walpole has not been seen since. He was either shot or went through the lines and was taken prisoner. The right wing of our regiment was relieved at night, Captain Clapp now assumed command and sent for me to report to him, sending Lieut. Wells to take command of the left wing. We returned to the place we had started from in the morning and remained till daylight.

May 12. Our brigade fell in at daylight and marched off to the left. Early this morning, Gen. Hancock, with his [2nd] corps, made a grand charge on the enemy's lines and was successful, capturing 5000 prisoners, including three Major Generals and about 20 cannon. In going through a piece of woods, our regiment, which was in the rear, was cut off by another column. We were exposed to a heavy musketry fire, and also to rain which lasted all day. We could find nothing of our brigade, and as we were near the front, our little band of about 100 decided to go in, and accordingly attached ourselves to the 2nd corps, and went forward into some breastworks which had been taken by Hancock this morning. Here we remained till late in the afternoon, fighting hard all day.

Just behind us was a spot so exposed to the rebel fire from their breastworks in front of us, that no soldier could live there a moment. [The "bloody angle"]. One section of a battery, two guns and a caisson, came down on a run to occupy this spot, with a view of shelling out the rebels about thirty rods in front of us, when they were fired upon and every man and horse killed instantly. Not one escaped. The rebels made desperate attempts to drive us out of our works and partially succeeded. We lost but few men ourselves, but the carnage around us was fearful. About 4 o'clock we were relieved, and as night set in found the rest of our brigade.

May 13. Our brigade moved and occupied the same rifle pits we had occupied the day before. The rebels during the night had fallen back, leaving their dead and wounded in our hands. Our skirmishers were sent out immediately, and soon reached the skirmish line of the enemy. Col. Dwight rejoined us this morning from the hospital and Captain Cassitt from a sick-leave. Gen. Meade published an order this morning which I read to the regiment, announcing that so far we had been successful, capturing 18 cannon, 22 colors and 8,000 prisoners. We remained in these

9. Battle of Spotsylvania Court House, Va.

pits all day and until two o'clock at night, when we fell in again and marched to the left, to the support of Gen. Burnside.

May 14. Crossing the Po River and skirmishing. No battle. After crossing the stream, threw up breastworks, and our regiment, detailed for picket duty, immediately went out. Heavy rain for three days impeding the progress of the army.

May 16. Our regiment relieved from picket duty.

May 17. A false alarm brought us all to the rifle pits, but nothing came of it. Soon after dark we fell in quietly and took up our line of march to the extreme right of the army, where we arrived about daylight.

May 18. Found that our corps formed a line of battle, column-by-divisions, appearances indicating that a charge in that form was contemplated. Our brigade was sent to the extreme right and flank, as a guard against a flank movement by the rebels. So matters stand at 9 o'clock, a.m. The charge was attempted and failed, and in the afternoon we were marched back to our former position. Here we remained till daylight, May 19. Early in the morning moved to a new position still further to the left, where we were busy all day building breastworks. An attack was made near night upon our right flank and rear, the object being the capture of our wagon trains. Moved about 11 o'clock p.m. to the support of the 2nd corps, which was engaged with the enemy. The battle was over before we reached the ground, and we encamped for the remainder of the night.

May 20. Engaged in building breastworks. Portions of the army engaged with the enemy.

May 21. About 9 a.m. marched off to the extreme left. Found the entire army moving in the same direction [toward Lee's strong defensive position on the North Anna]. Halted near the position occupied on the 20th, and half our regiment sent back on picket to the rear. About dark, the rebels made an attack a little to the right of us, which was easily repulsed. Our position is strongly posted with 16 pieces of artillery. At 11 p.m., ordered to fall in, and marched again to the left, marching all night. Halted at Holladay's for breakfast, thence to Guinea's, a station of the Fredericksburg and Richmond Railroad, distant from the latter place about 45 miles. We can hear cannonading in the direction of Bowling Green, towards which our advance is making. Remained here in camp at the farm on which is the negro hut in which Stonewall Jackson is said to have died after his wound at Chancellorsville. At 6 p.m. moved again, marching about five miles, when we encamped, and remained till 9 o'clock a.m., Monday May 23.[19]

Poole's account of Spotsylvania is remarkable not only for its detail, but also for its relative detachment. It may very well be that these published extracts were later polished and edited. Herbert Wells, in two letters from the battlefield written on the thirteenth and twentieth, appears to have been more affected by the regiment's experience—"the greatest fighting that I ever witnessed or took part in." Writing of the bloody twelfth, he described that day as "a terrible day, and it may be that today the fighting will be just as hard. There is probably about 300 men of the three regiments of our Brigade left present for duty. Our folks have lost very heavily and the rebels have lost as many if not more than we. It has been raining and it is very muddy. The dead lay thick around this part of the line. . . . Such fighting I never saw before. . . . An army cannot last a great while at such a rate."[20]

The awful butchery of the bloody angle left a deep impression in the minds of all who survived it, and years later the Veterans' Column of the Syracuse *Weekly Recorder* described the salient as a "slaughter pen, where both sides fought like incarnate heroes offering themselves as a willing sacrifice to the God of war."[21]

What had been gained by this sacrifice? On the face of it, from the Northern point of view, very little. Union casualties stood at about seventeen thousand, greatly exceeding those of the Confederacy, which have been estimated at around eleven thousand. Not only had Grant failed to dislodge Lee from this key position, but other parts of his grand strategy in the Virginia theater had also gone awry. A planned diversion by Ben Butler to take a force of thirty thousand men up the James River to City Point, from where he could threaten Petersburg, or even Richmond itself, ended with Butler establishing himself in a defensive position at Bermuda Hundred. Although he may have been safe from attack, Butler was kept a virtual prisoner by Beauregard. Franz Sigel, in the Shenandoah Valley, was defeated by a smaller force led by Breckinridge and retreated.

But once again, Grant refused to be upset by the series of setbacks. With Lee established in a new and strong defensive position behind the North Anna River, Grant again began to feel his way cautiously toward the southeast in a new attempt to pass around Lee's right flank. As the Northern army crept closer to Richmond, Lee was forced to follow. The two armies converged on the next great battleground at Cold Harbor.

The 122nd, it will be remembered, had left the field of Spotsylvania Court House on the twenty-first and rested in camp for the next two days. On the twenty-third and twenty-fourth they marched; they spent the twenty-fifth helping to tear up about a mile of the Gordonville Railroad and on the twenty-sixth, marched through the night and into the next day, when they crossed the Pamunkey River at Hanover Town, less than twenty miles from Richmond.[22] Herbert Wells took the opportunity to write home with the latest military news:

Dear Folks at Home,

We have stayed in one place all night and have had one full night's rest for a wonder—We marched night before last all night and until the next day about noon and yesterday crossed the Pamunkey River. I hardly know what the crossing is called or what place we are near, but if you look at the map (a good one) and find the White House on the river and then trace the river up about 15 miles and you can see where we are. We are about 15 or 18 miles from Richmond. We moved down here from Noels Station which is between the North and South Anna Rivers and crossed the Pamunkey about 15 miles up the river from the White House. I believe there is only our Division and about 10,000 cavalry here at this point. Don't know whether the rest of the Corps and Army will come down here or not. I think we have got on Lee's flank and I guess he will have to fall back from Hanover Court House and the South Anna River, and if he sends much of a force down here to whip us it will weaken his front at the South Anna. Our cavalry that went on that raid were within 2½ or 3 miles of Richmond—could hear the bells ring the alarm in the city. I wish they could have been well supported by infantry and artillery so they could have taken the city and liberated our men that are prisoners. . . . Part of our business before we crossed this river was to tear up railway track and the way we made it fly was a caution. . . . We expect we will have as hard fighting as we had in the Wilderness and at or near Spotsylvania C.H. but I hope it will not be of 12 or 15 days duration again. I hope we can get their Army in Richmond and then beseige the place.[23]

Richmond may have been close in terms of geography, but its ultimate capture was still distant in terms of time. In any case, Richmond itself was not the primary objective—that remained the destruction of Lee's army and of the South's capacity to continue the armed struggle. Many battles still had to be fought before that could be accomplished. Cold Harbor was to be the first.

After a brief rest at Hanovertown Court House, the regiment and the rest of the division edged its way, perhaps only a mile or two each day, along the road until they reached a point only ten miles from Richmond and two from Savage's Station. Here, in the early afternoon of May 31, the enemy artillery opened fire, and a gun battle ensued in which the rebels lost a large number of men. At six thirty, the order came for an attack, and the regiment went in. It was accompanied by the Second Connecticut Heavy Artillery, a regiment which had hitherto been engaged in manning the defenses of Washington and had never before been under fire.[24] Major Poole recorded what happened in his diary:

We passed over an open field a few rods, then through a pine grove about 20 rods, and the balance of the way over open fields, the entire distance being less than half a mile. As we emerged from the woods the rebels opened fire and our men commenced dropping. The enemy's fire being too severe for the 2nd Connecticut, they broke up in great confusion, retreating through our lines, so that we became the front line. The loss of the 2nd Connecticut was over 400, including the Colonel, who was a brave officer and fell at the head of his regiment riddled with rebel bullets. Our line continued to advance in good order until we had reached within thirty rods of the rebel works, when an order came to fall back to a small ravine in the rear, but before the order could be obeyed, the rebels had discharged their heaviest fire fearfully thinning our ranks. . . . The regiment returned, to the ravine, and threw up breastworks on the crest of a small ridge.[25]

This curtain raiser to the main battle had cost the regiment seventy-five casualties. Lieutenant Wooster was killed outright, and Poole himself received injuries which resulted in the loss of his left arm.

That night the rest of the army arrived at Cold Harbor, together with Grant and Meade. The fighting of the previous day had forced Lee to extend his line further south to protect his flank, inevitably thinning the line. Grant saw his opportunity and ordered an immediate attack, but the men could not be got ready in time and the attack was postponed until the third. This delay proved disastrous. Lee took the twenty-four hour breathing space to reinforce his defenses. Within an hour of the attack, seven thousand Union soldiers lay dead or injured on the field—losses on the Confederate side were no more than a quarter of that figure.

Wells, though slightly wounded, was able to write an account of his experiences in the first few days of the battle. His family must have been relieved, if not reassured, by his letter of June fifth:

Dear Folks at Home,
I am still alive and I am thankful that I am so and that I am well as usual. Some say that we are about 8 or 9 miles from Richmond and about 16 miles from White House Landing which is on the Pamunkey River. We have not had much rest since the 6th of May and have been under fire a good part of the time. It has been marching and fighting and maching about all of the time.

10. Battle of Cold Harbor

We reached this place about noon the 1st of June and formed in 4 lines of battle ready to move on the enemy's works. Our Batteries took position and opened and at 5 o'clock P.M. we moved forward and were soon under a murderous fire. The men commenced to fall very fast. We were in an open space while the enemy were covered. Our regiment started in the charge in the 4th line of battle and when we arrived near their works we were in the first and only effective line of battle (Plate 10). Some regiments did not behave as they might and we had to go over there and some broke. Our regiment done well I think. When we advanced to the last little rise of ground in front of the enemy's line and found we could go no further with any success, we were ordered to fall back a short distance and lie down. We done so, and held the ground that we had gained. Our Batteries throwing shot and shell over our heads some of the shell from our batteries exploding prematurely and wounding some of our own men. As soon as it was dark, shovels and spades and picks were passed along and we dug a rifle pit and it afforded us considerable shelter. Early in the morning of the 2nd we started forward again but advanced only 3 or 4 rods. Twas no go but we held the ground gained. Men had to lie down again and tools were passed out to the few that was left of the front line and they had to dig a shelter the best way they could, they could hardly get back or raise up but had to dig as they were lying. We are now about twenty rods from the enemy and have rifle pits dug. Our Batteries with a few exceptions are about 100 rods in rear of us. We have to keep well down. Some men got wounded or killed going back after water; if they catch sight of a head above the works a bullet is sure to whistle uncomfortably close. On the night of the 2nd I was struck on the head by a bullet, it seemed to glance on the top of my head. It bled some but it is a slight wound. I am thankful that it was no worse. There is continual sharp shooting all day long. We have been under fire since the first of June in this one place. I don't know when they will relieve us. We are the first line, it is little sleep that we get. I don't know whether we will advance further at this point or not. I am writing this in our Pit and the sharp shooters bullets are flying over us quite lively. Our division has lost heavily. Do not know yet how many. Our regiment has lost about 75 killed and wounded in the last fight. Sand Carrington was slightly wounded in the head by a piece of shell. Uriah Trapp, James Robinson of H Co. were wounded. I hope to write you again, you must excuse my haste, but there is no knowing where we will be attacked. Men all keep their belts on and guns loaded and capped. Our sharp shooters are very busy. Give my love to all, write all the news, Good-by for the present.

Love to All
Herbert.[26]

One of the sharpshooters mentioned by Wells in his letter was Thomas B. Scott of Company B, who had only recently been detailed for this duty. Scott had had some qualms about the morality of sharpshooting, and explained in a letter to the *Journal* that he did "not think it right in ordinary times to resort to sharpshooting during a battle, but as the rebels seem determined to murder our wounded and those that are carrying them from the field, there is no other way for our commanders but to do as they do." Evidently some of Grant's ruthlessness was beginning to rub off on his men. In the same letter, Scott quotes with approval remarks by Confederate prisoners describing Grant as fighting "like a bull dog," and the letter ends with some derogatory remarks about the army's former hero, McClellan.[27]

By the date of Scott's letter, June 8, the battle had become more or less a stalemate. Scott found himself at this point in exactly the same position as the regiment had been on the first. No one dared move for fear of being picked off by rebel marksmen; they hid in the rifle pits listening to the artillery battle going on over their heads. By the twelfth an elaborate system of trenches in parallel lines had been constructed, as described by D:

We have here three parallel lines of works, the front one nearly up to the point of our charge on the night of June 1st, the work having been built under a heavy fire of musketry and artillery from the enemy, and under protection of a like fire from our own side. This is properly a double trench, so that a large number of troops can be used to repel any attack, and redans for guns are thrown up at intervals so as to sweep any advance of the enemy, or to co-operate in any movements.

About one hundred yards to the rear is our second line—a strong work; and two hundred and fifty yards further back a strong line of batteries well protected by earthworks, with the reserve infantry in works close behind them. In some places all these works are in double lines, to facilitate the massing and protection of troops, while the lines are connected by gaps and covered ways, so that the troops can be relieved without exposure.[28]

The intricacy of the trench system at Cold Harbor, and the static warfare associated with them, was in marked contrast to the restlessly mobile type of campaigning employed earlier in the war. It also, of course, presaged the kind of fighting to be used against Petersburg later that year and, half a century later, the trench warfare of the First World War.

In his campaigns of the early summer of 1864, General Grant had succeeded in developing a new method of waging war and also in injecting the Northern army with a new and bitter determination. While he had yet to inflict outright defeat on the rebels, his army had moved slowly but relentlessly nearer to the Confederate capital. But all this had been accomplished at the most staggering cost—fifty-five thousand Northern casualties, equivalent to half the fighting strength of the army when the campaign first began. The first stage of Grant's 1864 campaign was over—it was to be followed by a second, only slightly less expensive, but ultimately more successful.

IV · THE ROAD TO VICTORY

Cold Harbor, then, marked the end of the first phase of Grant's final campaign and the beginning of the second. In the battles of the Wilderness, Spotsylvania, and Cold Harbor, Lee appeared to have been the gainer. The Confederates had not been defeated, and they had lost fewer men. All Grant's attempts to outflank his wily opponent had failed. Nevertheless, the Northern army emerged from these bloody encounters far stronger in men and resources than the overstretched Conferate troops, and they still held the initiative. As on the two previous occasions, Grant did not pause after Cold Harbor but immediately put into action a plan which might, if all had gone as intended, have brought the war to a speedy and decisive conclusion.

Basically, this plan involved moving the Army of the Potomac to an area south of the James River, where it would be poised to threaten Petersburg and the rail link with Richmond. For this to be accomplished, the army had to be withdrawn from Cold Harbor without giving Lee a clue as to its ultimate destination. This part of the plan was accomplished skillfully. To mask the army's withdrawal, Grant mounted a number of diversions. Sheridan was sent off with the cavalry to the north of Richmond to link up with Hunter's forces in the Shenan-

doah Valley, while Butler was ordered to strike at Petersburg where Confederate defenses were known to be well under strength. The attack on Petersburg was a failure—a series of blunders and missed opportunities ensured that the city would have to be taken by a lengthy seige instead of a quick, straightforward assault. The crossing of the James, however, in which the 122nd participated, was a complete success.

The regiment was pulled out of its trenches at Cold Harbor at 9:00 P.M. on June 12; after crossing the Chickahominy, it arrived at Charles City Point, on the north bank of the James, at midday on the fourteenth—much to the surprise of another unit that had left six hours earlier and arrived eight hours later.[1] Assisted by the Sixth Corps, the 122nd supplied the rear guard of the army as it crossed the James on the sixteenth. That night they set off from City Point to Bermuda Hundred, and from there to Point of Rocks, roughly midway between Richmond and Petersburg.[2] They finally fetched up in camp about five miles nearer Petersburg. There they settled into breastworks similar to those they had abandoned at Cold Harbor, though further from the enemy, and stayed there for the next four weeks.[3]

That they found themselves immobilized in this way was

FROM MEMORY.
W.E. RUGGLES.
122ᵈ N.Y.

((((IN FRONT OF PETERSBURGH, VA.))))))
JULY 4ᵗʰ 1864.

11. In Front of Petersburg—July 4th, 1864

owing to the Union's earlier failure to take Petersburg when it lay open to attack. Between June fifteenth and seventeenth, the North was offered three successive chances to capture the city; on each occasion the opportunity was missed. Although greatly outnumbered, Beauregard successfully fought off all three assaults. Each time, the Union army hesitated to press home the attack, until, on the morning of the eighteenth, reinforcements from Lee's army arrived to swell the depleted Southern defenses and make the city secure against all but a protracted and costly seige. Wells, with the regiment outside Petersburg, was both disappointed at the North's failure to take the city and thankful for the respite from fighting that the seige afforded. "Our Corps," he explained to his family on June 27,

has been up to Petersburg (or in our works near that place) but we have since moved further to the left, and are on the left of 2nd Corps. It is very quiet in front of our Division now for a wonder, but up on the right they are popping away the most of the time on the skirmish line. Petersburg might have been taken over but when our army moved around here of course Lee moved his army in the fortifications at the city and the result is that the enemy hold the place yet notwithstanding the Syracuse Journal said that Petersburg was taken. Some works near the city are taken but we have not got the place yet. For the first time in a good while we have our tents up in shape of a camp, but are liable to move any hour. I hope we will rest some now for we have had a pretty rough time of it since we left Brandy Station. Firing along the line takes place more or less night and day. We have Breastworks here. We have lost a great many men during this Campaign and must lose a great many more before we get Richmond. We have to charge them out of their works. I dont think Grant ever saw

such fighting before, and he finds a larger body of men and a worse place to take than Vicksburg. If we could only fight them in the open field we would soon wipe them out.[4] (Plate 11)

If Petersburg could not now be taken by direct assault, the obvious tactic for Grant to take was to cut its supply links with Richmond. The focus of Northern attention was the Weldon Railroad, which linked Petersburg and Richmond to the vital port of Wilmington further south. An attack on this railroad provided the 122nd with a welcome diversion from the boredom of the seige. On July 1, D sent this report to the *Journal*:

Day before yesterday we broke camp and moved about six miles south to the Weldon Railroad, which we immediately proceeded to destroy. We and one other small regiment got on the track, all took hold on one side, and at the word of command from our senior officer, who had command of the working party of the Brigade, over went the track. It was the "U" rail, and the rails all coupled by connecting bars, and a very little force kept it going over for some two hundred and fifty yards, when it broke at a weak place. We then took of the ties, put the rails on the top so that the burning of the ties would heat the rails in the middle and let the ends bend down by their weight, and so become useless until re-rolled. Then a breastwork was cut in the grade of the road, and so that was spoiled. Although we expected a fight, we were happily disappointed, and last night we came back to the point where we now remain.[5]

The attack on the railroad was evidently enjoyed by all, as it offered a chance to strike at the enemy without running much risk of being attacked. To destroy lengths of the line was comparatively easy—it was much less easy to occupy the route and ensure that the Confederate supply lines remained cut. This did not prove possible until August. In the meantime the regiment became involved in a much more desperate and potentially dangerous engagement—fending off Early's audacious foray into the North, a move that carried him to the gates of Washington itself. To attack the Northern capital had not, in fact, been the original intention of this remarkable and dramatic stroke—it could never have resulted in the capture of Washington. Early's raid had been inspired by desperate necessity: the paramount need to maintain contact between Richmond, Lee's army, and their vital sources of supply in the farmlands of the Shenandoah Valley—Lee's bread basket. Attacks on the Weldon Railroad already menaced one set of Southern supply lines, the other was now endangered by the Union advance down the valley in early June, led by General Hunter. Lee's response to this second threat was prompt; he dispatched Early with a contingent of twelve thousand men to deal with it. The move met with unexpectedly easy success—Hunter retreated without attempting to fight and, aware that his own supply lines were now vulnerable, pulled back to the west across the mountains, leaving the valley wide open.[6]

Early did not miss his chance. He crossed the Potomac on July 6, brushed aside Lew Wallace's attempt to bar the way, and by the eleventh was on the doorstep of the capital. Despite the strength of the defensive works, these were almost unmanned, apart from a nondescript collection of clerks and supernumeraries. Some of those involved were convinced that "had an assault been made on the morning of the 11th, when invalids, militia and departmental clerks were almost the entire force to oppose them, there is not the remotest reason to doubt but the tried and stubborn veterans composing the old corps of Stonewall Jackson would have swept into the city like an avalanche."[7] But the Northern command, though slow to react, had not been totally idle. To oppose the "tried and stubborn veterans" of the Confederacy, they called up their most experienced, available troops—the men of the Sixth Corps (which included, of course, the 122nd). The regiment arrived in Washington at 2:00 P.M. on the eleventh and marched immediately through the city along Seventh Street, then out along the Seventh Street road to Fort Stevens. Here the regiment found the front, and "troops of citizens in greater or less degrees of demoralisation were getting to the rear as rapidly as possible. The rebels were said to be 'just out thar,' and the skirmish line within five hundred yards of Fort Stevens, the yip! of rebel bullets into, and over the Fort, and the wounded going back, showed that they were indeed 'that.' " A member of Company E described his perception of the battle, which was distinguished, amongst other things, by the presence at one point of the president himself.

Saturday afternoon we were ordered out with the rest of the brigade, as we supposed, to relieve the first brigade, that were on picket, but we had different work to do. We advanced along the 7th avenue road, and massed the brigade on the right of the road, just behind the picket line. The Seventh Maine was ordered to charge up the hill, and take some houses that were occupied by the rebs. They piled their knapsacks, and started in splendid order. As soon as they came in sight of the rebel skirmishers, the latter "skedaddled" as fast as they could, leaving everything in the pits. We were ordered up—immediately after, on the double quick, and deployed as skirmishers. As we advanced our Company (C) was the first company on the right of the road, (their place always being on the right) and the rest of the regiment deployed on the left. When we got up on the hill we found the Seventh had taken the houses, and we were advanced further than any other part of the line. The firing now became very heavy and the rest of the regiment moved to the left and got separated from us. They halted before they got to the houses, but we kept on, not knowing that they had stopped, passed the houses, and over an open field, to a wood, twenty rods from the houses. There we got shelter behind the fence and stumps, halted and looked around to see the condition of things, and it was there we found we were far in advance of the rest of the line, but the rebs did not seem to be in much force in front of us. We remained there some time, until we feared they had a cross fire on both flanks, then the First Sergeant ordered us to fall back to the house, (we have no commissioned officers.) We did go, and we found they had a cross fire on us still, but we laid low and held our ground until we were relieved. We had one man shot.

The rest of the regiment had more lively times. When they got to the top of the hill, they found the enemy in heavy force, so that they could not advance as far as we did, but got behind a fence and opened on the enemy a destructive fire. In a short time the rebs moved to the left to try and flank us, but we moved after them. Our regiments coming up prolonged the line. In a short time the rebs formed in two lines of battle, and charged us, but it was "no go"; such destructive vollies were poured into them, they could not stand it. They broke and ran, but rallied again and came up as before. Our regiment (122nd) got out of ammunition, but held their ground for twenty minutes. We then fell back, rallied again, charged them without ammunition and drove them

back again. We were then supplied, and we gave them all they wanted. The fire was kept up until nine o'clock, when the rebs fell back, and this morning were not to be found, but the field is strewn with dead and wounded. We had no light artillery with us, only the heavy guns in the fort, and they were miserably worked. The President was in one of the forts, watching the progress of the battle, and every hill top that could be reached by the citizens was crowded (Plate 12). I suppose they think it was a splendid sight, but we poor fellows could not see much fun in it. The regiment lost four killed, one captain and two privates wounded—twenty-five in all.[9]

The defense of Washington had lasted a day and a half—by daylight on the thirteenth the Confederates had abandoned the field. If there had ever been a real threat to the capital, the arrival of the Sixth Corps decisively thwarted it—some Southern prisoners alleged that an attack had never been intended, and in a sense that was true. The original Confederate plan, as we have seen, was to safeguard Southern supply lines in the lower Shenandoah Valley; therefore, an attack on Washington, even if successful, could not have been consolidated. But even the threat of capture struck a severe blow at Northern pride and, in what was a crucial election year, at Lincoln's personal political standing. To repair that political damage, Northern victories were required.

One factor in this alteration in Northern military fortunes had arisen from Early's foray against the capital. Grant and Lincoln were convinced that the Shenandoah Valley must be blocked to the South—it must no longer be allowed to provide the Confederate army with supplies or to exist as an access

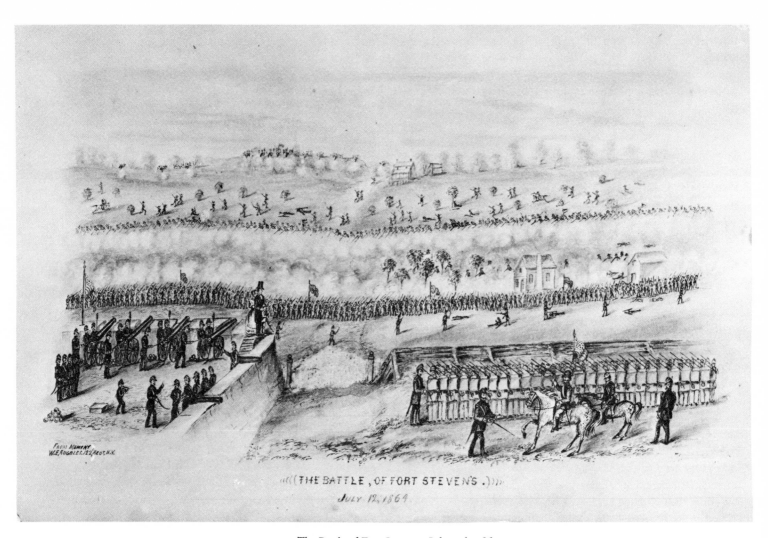

FROM MEMORY
W.E. RUGGLES. 122 REGT. N.Y.

((((THE BATTLE, OF FORT STEVEN'S.))))
JULY 12, 1864.

12. The Battle of Fort Stevens—July 12th, 1864

route into Northern territory. To accomplish this objective, Grant appointed Sheridan to command of the middle department. Sheridan's task was to defeat Early once and for all and to destroy anything in the valley which might be of use to the enemy. This task he embarked upon with vigor.

Among the fifty thousand or so troops assigned to Sheridan at this time were the Sixth Corps and the 122nd.[11] After taking part in the successful defense of the capital, the regiment did not return to the seige of Petersburg but was engaged for the next few weeks in the pursuit of the rebels, without at first succeeding in forcing a stand-up battle. A minor skirmish occurred near Charlestown, Virginia, on August 30, when the Union cavalry screening the regiment's front began to fall back before Rhodes' and Gordon's Confederate divisions. As the cavalry retreated behind the infantry picket lines, the Sixth Corps moved up to offer the rebels a fight. That was not what the rebels were after: "they left on the elongated double-quick when they found our main lines were moving for them, and the cavalry, sent right out, only saw glimpses of horizontal grey coat-tails."[12] Heavily outnumbered, Early saw nothing to be gained by accepting the challenge and withdrew to a strong defensive position at Fisher's Hill. Sheridan initially declined to attack him—as if living up to Early's own estimation of him as a commander "without enterprise, and possessed [of] an excessive caution which amounted to timidity."[13] Early must soon have changed his opinion. Revitalized by a visit from Grant, Sheridan met Early at Opequon Creek, or the third battle of Winchester, and defeated him soundly (Plate 13). Once again the 122nd was in the thick of battle. On September 18, they left their camp near Berryville and struck out across country on what was described as a "reconnaissance in force."

We moved about four miles and went into line about three quarters of a mile from the Opequon Creek, the rebel skirmishers having shown themselves. They soon fell-back across the creek, and our skirmish line pushed them back close to their main line. The Division massed in a piece of woods out of sight of the enemy, and a brigade of cavalry was sent on our left flank, when Cowan's Battery, (1st N.Y. Independent) took position and opened. For some time no reply was elicited, and some curiosity was entertained as to the whereabouts of the John Henries. But about 2 p.m. our fire got so annoying that the enemy put twelve guns rapidly into position and opened upon us with shell and spherical case. Their shots went over our guns, but we happened to be in range, and it was a pretty warm section of the country for a few minutes. They soon got the range of our battery, and it limbered up and went to the left on a gallop, the enemy training their guns on it, but giving us the benefit of their fire, as the range became high the instant it was changed. In this way their fire swept from the right to the left of the whole Division, cutting great antics, and raining fragments of shell, case, splinters and limbs among us. The losses were, however, very slight, when the severity of the fire is considered.

Meantime our sharpshooters had been thrown across the creek, and had deployed and were troubling the enemy severely. A detachment of grey-backs was sent on their flank and they charged our fellows, causing a very rapid rally of our chaps on our side of the stream. This was effected without loss, and the rattle of the skirmishers was kept steadily going. Soon after the Orderly Sergeant of the sharp shooters was struck through the breast and in-

13. The Battle of Winchester

stantly killed. He was from the 98th Pennsylvania. The enemy now conceived the brilliant idea of sending a regiment out on the flank of our skirmish line and charging it, and as we formed the arc of a circle, this move would bring the charging party back nearer to their own side, but they went, and the commander of our cavalry on the flank, seeing the move, let them go on, keeping his command massed and hidden in some woods. Just before they got all ready, he quietly swept round them in column, and dashed up, coolly ordering their commander to "Surrender if you please." The rebel Colonel started and looked for a place to make a dash, but he only saw a double line of seven-shooters ready to open all around him, and he did what any sensible man would do in the circumstances, he handed over his sword and his command. They proved to be the 8th South Carolina regiment, and were taken entire, colors, field-staff and all. The regiment was an old one and only numbered 250 men—about the size of ours you will see. Our cavalry on the right also took some prisoners. I do not know how many. At dark we withdrew, having fully accomplished all we were sent out for. The rebels followed our skirmishers as soon as they left, but if the Johnnies are not governed by Scripture in their treatment of prisoners, they imitate Peter in one respect—they follow afar off—when they chase the fighting Sixth; they did not come within range nor fire a shot, and we had no trouble with them, but reached camp about nine p.m. Our loss in the Division was one man killed, two officers and six men wounded, and the battery had one officer wounded—Captain Cowan, a sharp-shooter hitting him through the point of the hip at a distance of about three-fourths of a mile, but inflicting only a flesh wound, not at all dangerous. The rebel Colonel of the regiment taken said he was sorry to be taken "But," said he, "I'll tell you, gentlemen, this Southern Confederacy is about played out. We have got our last man into the field, and there seems to be no end to yours."[14]

Losses on both sides had been heavy—perhaps as many as five thousand Union men, and four thousand Confederates.[15] The 122nd had thirty-four killed and wounded.[16] Moreover, as the Confederate colonel had observed, Southern losses could not be replaced, Northern losses could. At the end of his report on Winchester, D had noted with approval the readiness with which the latest call for new recruits had been answered (though he may have exaggerated the enthusiasm of the response). Casualties aside, there was no doubt after this battle where the victory lay. Winchester ended in a rout of the Southern army, a rout which the Northern troops immediately followed up. Early withdrew to his stronghold on Fisher's Hill to lick his wounds, but this time he relied upon its strength in vain. Two days after Winchester, Sheridan arrived before the Confederate position on an almost sheer escarpment at Fisher's Hill and on the twenty-second ordered the whole line into the attack (Plate 14). The 122nd was in the second line of battle, but as soon as they neared the rebel works, the men made a charge. The flag of the 122nd was one of the first to mount the works; the cost was one man killed and about a dozen wounded. The rebel lines broke, and the Confederate army scattered.

D himself had not been present at this battle but, arriving shortly afterward, was surprised with the strength of its natural and man-made defenses, and the seeming impossibility of ever dislodging an enemy from it. His description of the battle was perhaps excusably exultant.

The fight began on the 21st, after our army had chased the rebels to that point. Our forces advanced for a position for an assault, and the rebels made determined fighting to prevent the deploy-

14. The Attack on Fisher's Hill—October 24th, 1864

ment of our men. But our skirmishers firmly pushed them, and got as well posted as possible. Early on the 22nd our whole line pushed forward and were fiercely met by the enemy. Our fellows had their blood up, and soon the cheers on the right told that the rebel flank was turned, and our lines marched straight at the enemy's center and left, up a hill almost perpendicular, every foot of which was swept by rifle pits on the crest, and by a rebel battery on a knoll; and which was obstructed by small trees cut down so as to interlace the branches. But all this could not stop them. Up they went, clambering and clinching, yelling and firing, right into the works and routing the rebels, taking seventeen guns and caissons, and in a few cases horses. Our colors and those of the 43rd New York Vols. entered the works first, side by side. It was "nip and tuck" between old Sergeant Chase and the other color bearer, but Chase does not allow boys to beat him in such places. Our regiment took four of the guns for their share, but kept right on after the rebels, who were flying in the utmost confusion, and when on the level ground Chase gave the regiment some very tall running to keep up with the colors as they dashed after and into the flying rebs. The regiment was complimented by General Bidwell in the following terms: *"I believe the 122nd would charge through hell if they were ordered to do so."*

Our army followed the enemy closely all the way up the valley . . . fighting at various points, but the rebels always running when a general engagement was offered. Many of their wagons broke down, and prisoners were taken on the way. A large hospital was left at Mount Jackson by Gen. Early, and the Confederate surgeons produced his order for them to remain, which Gen. Sheridan at once confirmed . . .

Take it all around, the idea prevails hereabouts that one Gen. Jubal E. Early got pretty thoroughly used up in the late series of operations.[17]

Not for the first time in the history of men and armies, the triumphs of yesterday almost became the defeat of tomorrow. Early may have lost the day at Fisher's Hill, but he was by no means yet a spent force. Quickly assembling reinforcements, he was soon back up the valley and, during Sheridan's temporary absence in Washington, came close to undoing all the North had won in mid September. On October 19, exactly one month after Winchester, Early launched a surprise attack on the Nineteenth and Eighth Corps at Cedar Creek. The attack turned into a rout: Union forces fell back in confusion, leaving behind twenty pieces of artillery and a large number of prisoners. Fortunately the redoubtable Sixth Corps, which had been placed in the rear of the line, was able to cover the retreat of their fellows by falling back slowly to Middletown and fighting fiercely all the way. According to the first lieutenant of Company L, Andrew Wilkins, at Middletown

We halted and reformed our line, throwing up temporary breastworks of rails etc., and held the rebels back until the scattered fragments of the Eighth and Nineteenth Corps could be brought back and reformed on our right. We had just succeeded in getting in to good shape to resist their further advance when Gen. Sheridan, who had been absent in Washington two or three days, arrived on the ground and rode along our front lines. At the appearance of the hero of Winchester and Fisher's Hill, for whom the men of this army have a love almost amounting to veneration, and in whom they repose the utmost confidence, the whole line resounded with cheers, and many a man exclaimed "Here comes fighting Phil; we'll sleep in our old camp tonight!"

The rebs, flushed with victory and confident of success, made charge after charge on our lines, but were sternly repulsed. About

15. The Battle of Cedar Creek—October 19th, 1864

two hours before sunset, the long-expected and hoped for orders came to advance the whole line. We charged in splendid style under a terrible fire and had advanced to within a short distance of the rebels, when the left of our line was momentarily forced back. The right, however, held their ground behind a stone wall and soon the left was rallied and formed on the same line. Again we charged, and the right, having succeeded in forcing the enemy back, their whole line broke in the wildest confusion, closely pressed by our gallant boys.

We pursued them to Cedar Creek, two miles from Strasburg, beyond the entrenchments from which the Nineteenth Corps were driven, when night, and sheer exhaustion of the men, put an end to the contest, and we returned to our old camp. The cavalry, however, continued the pursuit, and with what success, the cheering from the camps about us at all hours of the night informed us. In the morning we learned something of the result, but not until this afternoon did we know the full extent of our glorious success. The enemy were last night driven beyond Fisher's Hill and today the cavalry have been pursuing them up the Valley beyond Woodstock. Thus far we have recaptured all our artillery and prisoners and have taken in addition over forty pieces of artillery, all their trains, and a large number of prisoners. About noon, Capt. Clapp and Lieut. Wells saw near Sheridan's headquarters forty-eight pieces (including our own recaptured) and since then I learn that twelve pieces were taken at Front Royal, while endeavouring to escape through Luray Valley, and others near Woodstock up the Shenandoah . . . Our defeat has thus ended in glorious victory. All honor to our gallant leader, "Irish Phil."[18]

Cedar Creek was indeed something of a personal triumph for Sheridan. Arriving at a critical moment, he had rallied his stricken army and completely turned the tables on Early. This battle effectively marked the end of the war in the Shenandoah Valley. Early retreated to the south and was never able to threaten the Northern army again. Only the last act, around Petersburg and Richmond, had still to be played in this theater.

But Sheridan also owed a considerable debt to the stalwart Sixth Corps who had prevented the earlier reverse turning into a full-scale rout. In this stubborn defense, and in the subsequent advance, the 122nd had played a key part. As usual, they had paid for it: four of its men were killed, including the well-liked Major Brower (Plate 15). More than thirty others were wounded, amongst them the commanding officer, Lieutenant Colonel Dwight.[19] The Rev. I. O. Fillmore, visiting the regiment on behalf of the Christian Commission, noted sadly that only about sixty members of the original 122nd still remained on active duty. "Thus the brave fellows melt away."[20]

Cedar Creek, the last major battle in the Virginia theater that year, was followed by a long harsh winter of relative inactivity on both sides. Writing from Camp Russell near Winchester at the end of November, Herbert Wells had little to report, other than that he was still alive and well, and anxious for news from home.

I hardly know what to write to you—we are lying still at present and have been entrenching our camp or our lives . . . There are various rumors of what we are to do or where we are to go this winter. We may make another move or the enemy may attack us, as they are supposed to be heavily reinforced, but I hardly think they will risk it.[21]

Wells was right. Far from being reinforced, Lee's army was gradually but inescapably dwindling in size as the rain and

16. In Front of Petersburg—March 25th, 1865

cold, and the evident hopelessness of their situation spurred his men to desert in ever increasing numbers. There was no need for Grant to make a move—the bitter winter was doing his work perfectly well for him, and he was content to sit tight, improving his fieldworks and letting his men recoup ready for the final spring offensive. In December the regiment was moved from Camp Russell to Washington, from there on the steamer *Mary Washington* to City Point, and finally by rail to the fortifications before Petersburg.[22] But even here, at the last Confederate bolt-hole apart from Richmond itself, there was little to do but sit out the winter and wait. In January Wells wrote,

There is no news of interest here just now. We have some Picket firing on our right and left, but none in front of our Division. We sometimes have snow and then rain which makes the going very bad. The railroad from City Point runs within 1200 yards of our camp, so we do not have to haul our supplies by waggon very far. When we first came here it seemed as if we were to have a big fight and that we were to attack the enemy's works but now it looks as if Grant was going to let us rest a few weeks. I think we deserve a rest after doing the work we have the last summer.[23]

If Grant was content to let his men rest, Lee was not. By early March Confederate forces were so reduced that each mile of their long defensive line was backed by little more than one thousand men. At the beginning of that month Lee contacted Grant with an offer to discuss terms for peace, but the latter was firmly instructed by Lincoln "to have no conference with General Lee unless it be for the capitulation of Gen. Lee's army," and this overture was ignored.[24] Lee then decided on one last, desperate move—he planned to break out of Petersburg with a surprise attack to the east of the city, then slip southwest to join Johnston, in the hope that together they might defeat Sherman and then return to deal with Grant. The plan had virtually no chance of success, but the move against Fort Stedman on March 25, did result in temporary capture of the fort.

The 122nd was amongst those involved in countering Lee's move. Early on the morning of the twenty-fifth, the men were ordered to pack up and be ready to move at short notice. They were drawn up in line behind the works, kept waiting until about one o'clock, then marched out toward the left of the line before forming up and moving against the enemy. The rebel pickets drew back to their front line of entrenchments, but these the regiment easily carried. Union troops were able to push ahead a quarter of a mile to the main enemy defenses before being withdrawn. Then a rebel attempt to outflank them on the right brought the 122nd and First Maine Veteran Volunteers back into action. Exposed to heavy musketry fire from the front, they were raked by artillery on the left and rear. Among the casualties was the regiment's commander, Colonel Dwight, who was shot in the head and instantly killed[25] (Plate 16). The unfortunate Dwight had led the regiment for much of the war, but while Colonel Titus had been in command, Dwight had not received a rank commensurate with the job. Finally promoted to full colonel in February, 1865, he had been able to enjoy the promotion for less than a month.

The honor of leading the regiment to its final victory at Petersburg lay then not with Dwight but with his successor,

FROM MEMORY.
H.E.RUGGLES. 122 REGT. N.Y.

((((((IN FRONT OF PETERSBURGH.))))))

BREAKING OF THE LINE.

17. In Front of Petersburg—Breaking the Line

Horace H. Walpole. Walpole had enlisted as a captain when the regiment was first formed and was made a lieutenant colonel in Dwight's place in February. A private letter from Walpole described for the readers of the *Journal* the last days of the regiment's long campaign in Virginia:

After a terrible experience of marching and fighting, I sit down to give a detailed account of our experience during the past most glorious and remarkable week. At about eleven o'clock, on the night of April 1st, my regiment (122nd) was ordered under arms, to go in support of our pickets in front of the enemy works. I moved out to the picket lines, and was placed in position as support, by detachments, along a line of half a mile. I had hardly got my men posted before an aid came up and ordered me to join, with my command, my brigade, which was massed for an assault at Fort Welch; so we joined it and lay, until the least glimpse of day appeared, when the bugles sounded the charge, and we made a grand rush for the enemy's breastworks, they pouring in their shells like hail (Plate 17). They fell back before us, and we carried the works with a yell that would have aroused the "seven sleepers." The rebels fled, pell-mell, over the country, with our good boys chasing after them, capturing them, or killing them if they would not halt or surrender. Thus we broke their lines and then swept round to their right wing, about four miles, and turned back, marching to the left towards Petersburg, driving everything before us until we came up nearly to the suburbs of the city, where we rested during the day, in war like attitude (Plate 18). I was detailed as division "officer of the day," and had six hundred pickets under my command. I deployed my men as skirmishers, and advanced three hundred yards in front of our line of battle. Just as day was dawning I was ordered to advance my line toward the town quickly, which I did, charging at a double-quick, and

did not halt until my men were in the streets of Petersburg. We were the first men in the city, and the Mayor came out with a flag of truce in his carriage and surrendered the city to the old Sixth Corps. We then took up the pursuit of the retreating enemy; arrived at "Sailor's Creek" on the 7th; had a skirmish near the Appomattox Courthouse the rebels flying and burning everything they had, on the 8th; marched all day on the 9th, and heard the news of Lee's surrender on the 10th.[26]

Wells, too, described these hectic few days in a letter home that was more exuberant than usual:

Since my last we have made our final attack upon the enemy's formidable works and carried them. This was Sunday April 2nd, a big Sundays job. The cutting in two of the rebel army southwest of Petersburg caused the evacuation of the said place and also of Richmond. Monday morning the pursuit of Lee's army commenced. We had got him out of his fortifications and all felt confident of his ultimate destruction. Sheridan with his cavalry would get in his flanks—cut his trains and bother him in every way possible—(At the time of Lee's surrender he could not march 3 miles either way without getting into a fight. He could not reach Lynchburg with his army). His army got short of provisions—the men disheartened and were deserting in large numbers. He undertook to make a stand one afternoon at Little Sailor Creek in order to check us until dark so that he could get off his train. Our Corps being near at hand the impetuous Sheridan rushed in the 1st and 2nd Divisions as they had got up. They had to charge through the creek and swamp where the mud and water was up to the waist and there up the hill on which the rebs were posted. Johnny fought well but it was no use. They broke before the 6th and Custar [*sic*] coming up in their rear many threw down their arms. It is said that some eight or nine thousand prisoners were

18. In Front of Petersburg—April, 1865

taken along the line that day. The next morning we were in hot pursuit and Johnny could find no rest. It was continual skirmishing from the time we left Petersburg. Destroying the rebel trains—taking prisoners etc. It was sort of a running fight in which Cavalry were mostly engaged and when the Cavalry could not force them further then up came the infantry and Lee concludes that he cannot stand them until he reaches Lynchburg and he flies again. They look out for Sheridan and the Cavalry.

Well the 9th of April we were marching along as fast as our wearied limbs would carry us, hearing the booming of the Light Artillery (attached to the Cavalry) ahead and calculating that about 3 o'clock P.M. would bring us into the fight. Afternoon came—we filed out of the road into a field stacked arms and rested—were told to cook coffee, supposed it was to refresh ourselves before the battle—but the firing just ahead ceased. What did it mean—various rumors flew around—but nobody knew. Men looked at each other and tried to guess the cause. Finally we were told to go into camp for 2 or three days—Then the men were certain that hostilities had ceased for three days—then the question arose—what will be the result. Finally the official news came, Lee had surrendered with his army—how the boys cheered—how the hats and caps flew into the air—the batteries fired salutes, the men were fairly besides themselves with joy—2 hours before we had expected to fight—but now how different. Well you have read it all.[27]

Lee's surrender at Appomattox Courthouse did not, of course, mark the end of the war, though that end was not long in coming—nor did it mark the end of the 122nd's term of active service (Plate 19). After Lee's surrender the regiment marched back to camp near Burkesville, where they lay quietly for a week, carrying out all the usual camp duties except drill.

The health of the men was reported as good and the weather splendid. To Burkesville were brought all the captured Confederate cannons and small arms before being shipped to Washington—a collection which aroused some considerable interest amongst the Union men. "The artillery, 80 pieces in all, is the most mixed collection of guns we ever saw—some of them must have been in use when Adam was a boy—some are of the best English make. There are several cords of small arms of all kinds and descriptions, from a small pistol up to the best Sharp's Rifle."[28] For a time rations were scarce, but there was no shortage of rumors—the prevailing opinion being that they would all be home by the first of June, perhaps sooner.

There was still some work to be done. After a week at Burkesville the regiment marched again—this time to Danville to help close off the last gap open to Johnson's army as it wrestled with Sherman. After spending a month at Danville, they returned to Richmond, where they were reviewed through the streets by General Halleck, and then to Washington. Here, on May 23, the entire Army of the Potomac, one hundred thousand strong, including the Sixth Corps and the 122nd, took part in a grand review before the new president, Andrew Johnson. They were followed the next day by Sherman's army, a force of similar size—the whole review offered the most spectacular demonstration of military might of the whole war. On June 23, the 122nd received orders for mustering out. The same day they started for home. On June 27, 1865, the regiment was finally officially discharged.[29]

The story of the 122nd Regiment New York Volunteers ends where it began—in its home city of Syracuse. As they had

((((APPOMATTOX, VA.))))

THE 122º REGT. N.Y. AT THE SURRENDER OF GENL. LEE.

APRIL 9TH 1865.

19. Appomattox, Va.

done for the men of the 149th, the city's inhabitants prepared a welcome for its returning heroes. On June 27, the city was ready and waiting. The bridges over the canal at Warren Street and Salina Street had been decorated with the national colors and branches of evergreen to commemorate both those who had returned and those who never would. The four entrances to Fayette Park were similarly decorated, as were the principal residences surrounding it. In the center of the park was placed the stand from which the welcoming ceremonies would take place, while along the south side were ranged the tables where officers and men would be entertained, "tastefully filled up, and profusely ornamented with bouquets and small flags, and literally loaded with good things for the honored guests of the occasion." The last word may be fairly given to the Syracuse *Journal,* which had so faithfully reported the regiment's activities throughout the long and bitter war.

Another gala day in Syracuse! The people celebrate the return of the third regimental organisation which went out from our midst during the past three years. They rejoice that in the day of restored Peace and Union, the brave and honored soldiers who have achieved this proud and memorable result, are returned to their homes. On every hand the insignia of welcome and honor are displayed. The flag of the Union, and its colors in various tasteful decorations, twined with evergreens and bearing fitting inscriptions, are everywhere to be seen, and the universal demonstration gives the returned heroes the completest evidence of the warmth of the people's love for thm, and of the heartiness of the greeting extended to them.

The day, after the refreshing rain, is all that could be desired. The attendance of interested spectators, both from the city and from the country at large, is very large. The preparations for the reception and entertainment of the returned veterans are of the most perfect and generous character. The general committee have made the decorations at the bridges in the principal thoroughfare and at the place of formal reception and entertainment all that could be wished. The citizens generally have entered with the greatest zest into the making of such displays at their business places and residences as befit the event of the day, and attest the depth of feeling entertained for our country's defenders. . .

The One Hundred and Twenty-second has seen as much active and severe service as any other regiment from Central New York, and its roll of lamented heroes is long and honorable. It has taken a prominent part in all the campaigns of the Army of the Potomac under Burnside, Hooker and Meade. At Fredericksburg, Gettysburg, Rappahannock Station, in the defense of Washington, and finally in the campaign through the Wilderness and in front of Richmond. In many battles and in many skirmishes this regiment has done its whole duty. It has a proud and honorable record, and its surviving members may well rejoice in the contemplation of a full and honorable discharge of the highest duties the patriot owes his beloved country.[30]

V · LIFE AND DEATH IN THE THIRD ONONDAGA

A Regiment of Citizens

The American Civil War has frequently been described as the "first modern war." At the very least, it was a war which involved an entire society. In a democratic country with full adult white male suffrage, the people had a voice in the political issues of war and peace that was unprecedented since the days of the Greek and Roman city-states. The economies of the Union and the Confederacy were closely geared to the war effort. The inhabitants of both sections, soldiers and citizens, found not only their future destinies, but their day-to-day lives, deeply affected by the fact of war.

Indeed, during this war, the very distinction between soldier and citizen became blurred. The feature that, above all, distinguished the Civil War armies from the armies of the European powers, was that they were citizen armies. The regular army of the United States, as it existed on the eve of war, numbered no more than about sixteen thousand men—a totally inadequate force with which to quell the rebellion of the vast South.[1] Once the firing on Fort Sumter had convinced government in the North that secession could be put down only by force, the need to expand the military might of the Union—suddenly and massively—led to a curious decision. This decision was not, as might perhaps have been expected, to recruit into the existing regular army, but to make national use of what had previously been a state institution—the state militia. In April, 1861, believing that the emergency would be short-lived, Lincoln called upon the states for seventy-five thousand militia to serve for three months.[2] The militia, hitherto a social or ceremonial organization rather than an effective military force, was, in addition, a volunteer force. The principle of voluntarism, despite the introduction of conscription in the North in March, 1863, remained at the heart of Northern recruitment policies. The regular army was maintained throughout the war as a distinct organization, though occasionally it provided instructors or seconded officers for the new volunteer regiments.

The principle of voluntarism was exploited most extensively in the formation of these volunteer regiments. The new volunteer army was first called into being by Lincoln's proclamation of May 3, 1861, which asked for forty-two thousand volunteers in forty regiments, to serve for three years.

Such was the enthusiasm for war service in the states, that this call was vastly oversubscribed. The forty regiments, by early July, had become 208. By the time Congress reconvened on the fourth, the total strength of the Union army had exceeded three hundred thousand. Not content with merely approving the terms of Lincoln's proclamation, Congress authorized him to ask for five hundred thousand more and, after the First Bull Run debacle, yet another half million. By the end of 1861, the total that had been recruited was approximately six hundred and fifty thousand.

The problems which faced the administration, at least up to this point, were not those of raising men, but of providing for them. The lack of supplies, arms, and equipment could not be made up with corresponding speed. A War Department that, at the outset, employed a staff of less than a hundred, could not hope to create much order out of such chaos. Secretary of War Cameron was quite unequal to the task, and it was not until the appointment of Edwin Stanton in January, 1862, that matters began to improve. One of Stanton's early decisions was to slow down recruitment; in April, he suspended the recruiting service briefly. This provided a breathing space, though when recruitment resumed in June, it met with a noticeably subdued response.

Stanton's reorganization of the War Department contributed significantly to the Northern victory, yet even he could not eradicate all the weaknesses in the recruiting system and the overall military organization which had crept in during the hectic early months. Recruitment continued to be organized by the state authorities, ensuring that appointments to officer rank were frequently influenced by political rather than military considerations. Once regiments were raised, no provision was made for them to be supplied with new recruits to make up for losses—instead, new regiments offering new opportunities for commissions were raised. Most volunteer regiments raised early in the war had, by the end, dwindled to a mere handful.[3]

The 122nd Regiment New York Volunteers, raised in the fall of 1862 in response to Lincoln's new call for three hundred thousand more men, was typical of such volunteer regiments.[4] It was raised from a single small locality—Onondaga County—and was composed entirely of volunteers with little or no previous military experience.

The regiment was commanded by Colonel Titus who, with the chaplain, Major Davis, Captain Brower of Company A, and Lieutenant Tracy of Company I, was one of the very few officers to have seen any previous war service. Titus' early career included service in the militia and part ownership of a general store, but at the outbreak of war he had been running a small lumber business. At the news of Fort Sumter, he immediately abandoned it and, we are told, "literally tumbled his operatives into the street—stopped his steam engine and put out the fires, locked the doors and threw the keys away—and then hunted for the regiment that would soonest march to the protection of the National Capital." Titus was described by an admiring contemporary as "a tall, gray-haired, blazing-eyed, grave but mortally earnest man," a fine soldier and horseman who distinguished himself in the early engagements of the war as adjutant on the staff of General Peck. The unanimous choice of the Military Committee to command the new regiment, Titus remained nominally in command until the last few months of the war, though for the last year at least he had been occupied with other duties. In May, 1864, he was appointed assistant provost general of New Jersey, and much of his time was taken up with courts-martial and commissions of inquiry.[5]

During Titus' absences, command devolved upon his second in command and successor, Lt. Col. Augustus W. Dwight. Dwight excelled as a regimental officer: he was careful of his men and proud of their achievements, which he reported from time to time to the *Journal*. Slightly injured at Winchester in September, 1864, he suffered a severe wrist wound at Cedar Creek and in March, 1865, only days before the end of the war in Virginia, he was killed outright by a Confederate shell.[6]

Dwight, like most of the senior officers in the regiment, had been a lawyer from the city of Syracuse. The adjutant, Capt. Andrew Smith, and Quartermaster Lester were also lawyers, as were several of the captains.[7] This group formed a clique of whom Herbert Wells was later to complain: "There is a certain class in this regt. that are rather inclined to run the machine themselves. They are mostly Syracuse officers."[8] "It is suggested," commented the Syracuse *Journal* with heavy humor, "in behalf of the regiment, that it has the law on its side, whatever the result of its battles."[9]

What was true for the officers, held also for the enlisted men. Numbering close to a thousand volunteers, seven-eighths of these claimed to be farmers, a few of them were owners of substantial properties worth eight to ten thousand dollars.[10] Their complete lack of military expertise quite failed to dampen the enthusiasm of the *Journal*. "Nearly all the men," it was reported, "are farmers and mechanics—men inured to the most severe labor—men who have wielded the sledge and the scythe, and whose well developed limbs are well calculated to bear up under the most rigorous exactions, privations and dangers of the battlefield."[11] Even if the new recruits were as hardy and tough as the *Journal* claimed (and in view of the generally lax medical examination procedures throughout the Union army, this seems unlikely), fit men need to be trained before they can fight effectively. Such training the regiment was obliged almost entirely to do without. Enrollment of recruits had begun in mid-July and was completed one month later. By early September officers and men had set off for "the seat of the war." In those few weeks there had been little time for training other than some musket drill, in which the men reportedly became "quite proficient . . . and showed their ability to perform the various evolutions with commendable precision."[12]

The 122nd Regiment, like its two sister regiments, had been recruited during a wave of patriotic enthusiasm for the Union cause, and little difficulty was had bringing the regiment up to strength in a very short time. But as the war dragged on, with few decisive victories to maintain civilian morale, voluntary enlistment fell away, and both the Union and the Confederacy were reluctantly obliged to resort to conscription. Conscription was seen as undemocratic, in direct conflict with those political principles which both sides, from their different standpoints, were pledged to defend. It was also highly unpopular, with the result that the Northern Conscription Act, which allowed the draftees to offer a substitute, or to buy exemption on payment of $300, was largely ineffective. Wells, for one, was critical of the $300 loophole, as he was of "fireside soldiers":

I have been waiting patiently to hear from the draft in Onondaga Co. I wish to know who is drafted. I almost wish there were no

$300 clause about it, then all that were drafted would have to come. If all pay their 300 there will be another draft made and by and by some one will get sick of paying. I think that clause will be struck out if we do not get men enough the first draft. Then "Home Guard" look out. Some storekeepers will find talking fight at the fireside (or in their stores) quite a different thing from real fighting in the field. They wont be over anxious for this or that Genl. to "Onward to Richmond." Now our Army of the Potomac ought to be filled up immediately for the next and perhaps last Grand Battle will be fought between the two armies of the Potomac. Lee will ask for so many men, perhaps the next day the draft will be made and in a short time he has his men. While we have hardly commenced drafting. They force the thing through. We wait for some reason or other. In the next battle the strength of the South will be combined against our Army of the Potomac. Then will be the Grand Battle. Either the downfall of the rebellion or its continuation for a longer period of time. So I say give us the men immediately, cut down traitors wherever they may be found and let us go through with it.[13]

Wells' concern that he be sent fresh recruits at what he considered to be a critical juncture in the war is understandable, as is his impatience with the deficiencies of the Conscription Act of March 1863. Conscription had initially been intended as a device to make good losses in existing regiments—the volunteer could choose his regiment, but the draftee could not. In practice it did not always work out like this, despite the fact that from the middle of 1862 onward, the initiative in recruitment clearly belonged to the federal government. The states, formerly active in the formation of local regiments, became little more than mere recruiting agents.[14] The 122nd's steady decline in numbers as death, injury, sickness, and desertion took their toll, does not suggest that conscription was effective in keeping up its numbers.

According to one account, owing to sickness and disease, the regiment lost a total of three officers and eighty-five enlisted men—this amount almost equalled the number of those killed or mortally wounded in action.[15] The chief killer seems to have been typhoid; however, its victims did not have to be dead to be rendered unfit for duty. At any one time there were always some members of the regiment too ill to march, and some perhaps who merely pretended to be. "The health of our regiment," reported a soldier in October, 1862, "is quite as good as that of any in the brigade. We have a number of sick, and the average number of shirks, who, like the boy, are a little too sick to work, and just about sick enough to go fishing, but none are dangerous."[16] Despite the optimistic tone of this report, the regiment had in fact already buried one Porter Austin, a victim of typhoid who had aggravated his condition by drinking a quart of fresh cider, and by early November, twenty-three sick men had been sent to the hospital at Harper's Ferry. Three officers, Captains Kent, Chamberlin, and Walpole, were unfit for duty, and Chamberlin eventually resigned on account of ill health.[17] Possibly the state of the regiment's health did seem satisfactory in comparison with others. Another correspondent, writing in early November, described "the sanitary condition of our regiment" as *good.* "Four men have been buried besides Capt. Gilson, and there are only about thirty that are in the hospital, or ought to be, while the 121st, which arrived one day before us, has already buried fifteen, and has about 200 in the hospital."[18] Evidently, the seriously ill were routinely sent off to one of the general hospitals, while the mild cases were left behind. By the end of the month there had been three more deaths, and five captains were sick and away from their commands.[19] Two additional deaths from typhoid followed in December.[20] Judging by contemporary standards, the 122nd seems to have been well served by its medical officers, and the accounts of sickness were usually accompanied by tributes to the effort and skill of the doctors.

Perhaps because the regiment soon became involved in an almost unbroken succession of military operations, reference to illnesses other than those caused by injuries seldom occurs after 1862. In contrast, casualty lists were published regularly after that date, often specifying the nature of the wound, and its degree of severity. A numerical table of battle losses is to be found in the Appendix. One example of a casualty report will suffice to illustrate the flavor of such accounts:

On the 10th [of June, 1863] about two hundred and fifty of the men were out on picket duty, and encountered a body of rebels— John F. Connor, Co. B was struck by a round ball from a hunting rifle, in the right thigh, the ball passing diagonally through and coming out just above the knee—a severe and painful, but not dangerous flesh wound.

Charles Everingham, Co. G minnie ball through the right arm. Severe flesh wound, the ball curving by the elbow joint, and not breaking the bone—a singular fortunate case.

Dwight S. Hall, a round ball from a hunting rifle, in the outside of the right foot in the hollow joint above the ball, and coming out just under the instep, on the inside of the foot. The bones, curiously enough, were uninjured. The wound was painful but by no means dangerous.

In another movement, the rebels were encountered, and Lieut. M. L. Wilson of Co. A received a slight wound in the knee—

these were all the casualties up to the time of the return of the regiment across the Rappahannock and the march back to Stafford Court House.[21]

The regiment was not always so fortunate. In each of eleven engagements between December, 1862, and Appomattox, total casualties of killed, wounded, and missing attained double figures: Gettysburg, Cold Harbor, and Cedar Creek were three of the worst such occasions. Most disastrous of all was the battle of the Wilderness, in May, 1864. Total casualties numbered a staggering 119. The aggregate of losses throughout the history of the regiment came to 429.[22]

Another important cause of decline in numbers, though one that understandably received little public attention at the time, was desertion. Between August, 1862, and the final muster out in June, 1865, some 180 members of the regiment deserted—a figure that represented almost 16 percent of total enlistment. Though substantial, this proportion was considerably smaller than losses by death, injury, or disease, and it could even be argued that desertion was not an unmixed evil. The largest exodus came at the beginning of the regiment's history and may well have had the effect of ridding the unit of unsuitable manpower. In August, 1862, ten new recruits deserted; in September, thirty-seven, and in October, twenty-three. On only three occasions after that did the monthly desertion rate rise to more than a handful—in January, 1863, and again in June and July of the same year.[23] These sudden increases are easily explained. The January figures reflect the physical exhaustion brought about by Burnside's "Mud March," those from June and early July correspond to the rigorous march to Gettysburg. More unexpected, perhaps, are the substantial figures for the latter part of July, following Gettysburg, a battle that historians (though not necessarily the combatants themselves) have seen as an important turning point in Union fortunes. It is interesting to note that the battle in which the regiment suffered the heaviest losses in killed and wounded—the Wilderness—was not followed by a corresponding increase in the desertion rate. Monthly desertion figures for 1864 were low by any standards, and by 1865, desertion, though not unknown, was almost negligible. If a useful conclusion can be drawn from this, it might be that physical exhaustion, rather than the horrors of battle, was the most compelling cause of desertion. While the decline in desertion during the last months of the war could be explained by the bolstered Union morale as the tide finally turned in the North's favor, a more satisfactory explanation might be that those who had survived this far were the most inured to physical stress and discomfort. Such men were least likely to lose heart and desert.

By the summer of 1864, barely two years after the 122nd had been formed, the regiment was in an alarming state. An anxious correspondent described the situation in great detail:

Our present number, including officers, musicians, hospital nurses, pioneers and all men, sick and well, for whom we draw rations with the regiment, is 224. This does not include the Quartermaster, Quartermaster's and Commissary's Sergeants and teamsters, who are with the trains. Of the former number, twelve are officers, as follows: One Lieut. Col., one Major, three Captains, four First Lieutenants and one Second Lieut., one Chaplain and one Surgeon, which last two are nominally present, though of course they are non combatants. Of this number Captain Marks and Lieut Wells have been wounded, but are getting all right and have not left their commands, though officers have gone to Washington for less severe wounds, or else some of the medical department are much mistaken, and I do not think they are. . . .

Our pioneers number ten and our musicians nine, our hospital nurses six. Add to these twelve officers and eight men sick with us, who are excused by the Surgeon from duty, and you have an aggregate of forty-three to deduct from the total of two hundred and twenty four, which brings our number of muskets considerably below two hundred.

When it is remembered that we started out with over four hundred [sic] men, one field, one staff and nineteen line officers, and that one field, two line officers and fifteen men have joined us on the march, it will be seen that nearly two-thirds of our men and nearly three fourth's of our line officers, and our only staff officer, who is a combatant, have been killed, wounded, or taken prisoners. Some idea of the severity of our duties and labors may thus be formed.[24]

Neither these duties and labors, nor the list of casualties suffered by the regiment, was yet completed. By October, 1864, the 122nd scarcely existed. Following the battle of Cedar Creek, a visitor from the Christian Commission reported that "Lt. Col. Dwight told me his regiment lost about four in killed and between thirty and forty in wounded. This was a severe loss, when you take into account the small number of the regiment that was left for duty. There are only about sixty of the old 122nd left now. Thus the brave fellows melt away."[25]

The Regiment at Rest

The life of a soldier, it is said, consists of long periods of boredom punctuated by short periods of hell. Although the

122nd Regiment was particularly active and took part in its fair share of battles, major and minor, it spent only a small proportion of its war service in actual combat. The rest of its time was taken up with life in camp, marching, and counter-marching. Life, even when not engaged in battle, was often tedious, hard, exhausting, and, owing to the threat of disease, highly dangerous. Combat was all of these, except tedious; that it made up for by being terrifying. On the other hand, army life had its lighter side, and the Union soldier was, on occasion, able to see the humor of his situation.

When not actually on the march, the regiment spent much of its time in camp. These camps were constructed according to a regular, almost stereotyped plan—a system that had certain obvious advantages. Each new camp would be sufficiently like the previous one that confusion was kept to the minimum. The regular arrangement of its streets made it easy to keep clean and contributed to the general sense of order and discipline essential to the command structure of an army. Such a camp could be set up quickly, even by relatively inexperienced troops. In October, 1862, the 122nd put together its camp near Cherry Run, Maryland, in less than a day:

We have been in our camp about eighteen hours, and it looks like a little village. Streets swept and tents in parallel rows; fires for cooking in a line ten paces to the rear of the back row of tents; officers' tents in a line ten paces further back; and headquarters thirty paces back of the centre of the line; a guard all around, well pretty *sojer* generally.[26]

Any fool, Field Marshall Montgomery used to say, can be uncomfortable. The ability to build a "little village" from noth-ing in a short space of time could mean the difference between relative comfort and misery. In December, 1862, the regiment built a new camp near King George's Courthouse in far from pleasant circumstances; in this instance, the experience of camp planning and construction proved unusually useful.

Last Thursday we marched from our last camp to the mouth of the Potomac creek, and the next day to this place. We arrived in a pelting rain, which turned to snow soon after we had dived into a thick pine forest, filled with undergrowth, for a camp, and the comforts of our position were not those of an exalted character. Wet to the skin, and chilled by the cold wind as it whirled and whistled the snow from the Northeast around us, we got up our shelter tents, and by great efforts got some fires going in part of them, and then we were soon comparatively all right. That night it cleared off cold, and the next day we managed to get our blankets and clothes dry and get into comfortable shape.

Our place of abode *was* a thick forest; it *is* a pretty well cleared space, with numerous piles of brush lying around. The company streets are fixed up quite tastefully with evergreens; one has a regular triumphal arch over its entrance, and many of the boys have log houses already built. How long we shall stay no one knows, but the boys work on the true soldier's plan—"making yourself comfortable when you get a chance."[27]

The basic form of shelter erected in these company streets was, of course, the tent. Early in the war, two designs of army tent had been in common use—the Sibley, and the Wedge. The Sibley tent was in the form of a tall cone, supported by a central pole, and was intended to accommodate about twelve men; the Wedge had a simpler design, being little more than a rectangular sheet of canvas laid across a horizontal pole and pegged down to the ground on either side. Additional flaps could be fitted across the ends for further protection. Both designs had their disadvantages, but the main one in each case was that the tents were so bulky that they could only be carried in the baggage train. As it was often difficult for the train to keep in close contact with the advancing troops, the men might well find themselves trying to build a camp without tents. The need, obviously, was for a tent which could be carried by each individual soldier. For this purpose the half-shelter tent was devised. Like the Wedge, or A tent, the half-shelter consisted of a simple rectangle of canvas made habitable by stretching it across a bar—lashed perhaps to two rifles stuck, bayonet first, into the ground. One man's "half-shelter" could be attached to another's by cords, making a small cabin just large enough for two.[28] There is no mention, in the annals of the 122nd, of any tent design other than the half-shelter, or the A tent.

In more permanent camps, the tent could be used simply as a roof covering for a sturdy cabin built of logs or wood from an abandoned house. Herbert Wells described a cabin of this kind that he and a fellow officer occupied in a camp near Bell Plains in December, 1862. The hut was about six and one-half feet square, made of logs and topped with their A tent. Inside was a bunk about eight inches off the floor and covered with springy cedar boughs and brush. Over this mattress they spread one rubber and one woolen blanket, covering themselves with two more woolen blankets and their overcoats.[29] Wells frequently included descriptions of his cabins in letters home, believing, no doubt, that the details of their construction would be of interest to his father, a millwright. Something of Wells' own enthusiastic personality shines through in these letters:

I wish you could see my shanty. It is nearly 12 feet long and 6 feet wide on the inside—it is built of 3 and 4 inch joice to about 4 feet high and my pieces of shelter tent make a roof of about $\frac{1}{3}$ pitch making it about $7\frac{1}{2}$ feet high at the peak, so you see I have plenty of room. I have boarded up the front end with pieces of cracker boxes leaving a doorway, but I haven't made a door yet. Across the back end and about 2 feet from the ground I have built a bunk about 3 feet wide of boards and barrel staves with a 3 inch hickory pole for the front edge and have it well filled with hay. I take and spread my rubber blanket on the hay—use my woollen blankets for a covering—my coat for a pillow—so you see I have a splendid couch. I have as good a house as any officer in the line.[30]

Wells was evidently particularly adept at building cabins, though this one was his most ambitious. How galling it must have been, after expending so much care and effort, to receive the order to move and be obliged to dismantle a comfortable home. How much more galling, as must so often have happened, to then have the order countermanded. This was the experience of the 122nd on October 25, 1862, according to D:

Wednesday night at twelve o'clock an orderly dashed up to Col. Titus' quarters, and gave the order to move at daylight. Some one was for giving the order to move at once, but he was too old a soldier to be caught so, and the men were allowed to sleep till daylight, and then called up and the order given. In twenty minutes all were ready, and we waited on our arms, for the word "March!" Our friends at home have but little idea how we look under such circumstances. The men had struck and rolled their shelter tents with their blankets. The officers had sent off theirs in the wagons and the muskets were stacked in a long line, behind which the men lay "in place rest"—overcoats on and blankets over their shoulders, while the officers stood around in front and rear, ready to spring to their places. The field and staff officers were standing around "convaynient," their horses saddled and by their sides, and in that peculiar condition of watchfulness which attends an inclination not to be caught napping.—Thus the day wore on, and as the day was cool and the fall wind swept chilly through the valley we occupied, the order was given to the men to make themselves as comfortable as possible without taking anything off, and the officers imitated them. Several laid down and went to sleep, others went to making coffee, and the Colonel entertained Messrs. Austin and Quick, of Onondaga, who had been joyously received in camp, while the Lieut-Colonel rolled himself up in his long cavalry overcoat and went to sleep on a grassy bank, holding his horse by the bridle.[31]

Waiting, often for long periods without explanation, has always been a soldier's lot. Senior officers confer and make decisions, and the decisions are finally translated into action. One has the feeling that even at this early stage in its war experience, the regiment had become used to waiting and took it as a matter of course. Although Ruggles and Ostrander produced no drawing of this particular scene, one can see a similar situation in their picture of some men of Company B at Mine Run (see Plate 6). This description, together with the picture, reminds one of how the men must have looked, what equipment they carried, and clothes they wore, as they waited, or marched, or fought.

The single most important item of equipment possessed by any soldier, at any time, is his personal firearm. A wide variety of small arms was used by both sides in the war, but on the Union side the standard issue was the Springfield or Enfield rifle musket. These were reasonably accurate muzzle-loaders that shot the cone shaped Minié or "minnie" balls. When fired, they expanded under the force of the explosion, gripping the rifling inside the barrel.[32] Early in its career, the 122nd was issued Enfield rifles of British manufacture, which were similar to, though heavier than, the American Springfields. The only other small arm mentioned in relation to the regiment was the Sharp's rifle—an accurate, long-range, breechloading rifle with a telescopic sight that was issued to the marksmen of the "Berdan's sharpshooters."

Although primarily meant for use as a firearm, the Enfield was fitted with a long bayonet. Bayonets were useful accessories. In addition to their intended use, they served as cooking knives, and as candle holders; they were also capable of cutting through undergrowth and, together with an inverted rifle, useful for holding up one end of a shelter tent. Ammunition for the musket (an issue of forty rounds was usually made before an engagement) would be carried in a cartridge pouch or in the haversack, along with the soldier's few personal possessions, and rations. On the march, he would carry not only a knapsack, but also blankets, and his half-shelter tent. The cost of all this impedimenta may be gauged by the bill presented to William Ruggles for losing it—$25.46.[33] Losses were commonplace, as most men entering battle, whether ordered to or not, would take the precaution of discarding anything which might interfere with their freedom of movement.

In the early stages of the war, the provisioning of military equipment caused considerable difficulties. The huge rush of volunteers had taken the authorities by surprise. Appropriate administrative and manufacturing capability had not been developed, and dishonest contractors provided poor quality uniforms and other items whose shoddy construction and materials soon caused them to wear out. Occasional shortages occurred but, in general, the Union managed the problem of equipment with much greater efficiency than did the Confederacy. The men of the 122nd were reported as being "fully uniformed and equipped" as early as September 1862.[34]

Oddly, perhaps, providing the men with food seemed to create more frequent problems than providing equipment. It is notable that in its first journey from Syracuse to "the seat of war," the regiment relied a good deal for food on local charitable organizations like the Volunteer Relief Association.[35] By October, the shortage of rations had become quite acute: "We are in pretty good condition, but have been short of rations much of the time, owing to the limited amount of transportation allowed. Much of the time we have only had eight or ten hard crackers, or 'hard tack,' for two days rations."[36]

A lack of food supplies kept the regiment at Stafford Courthouse until late November. The problem seems to have been more one of communications than supply, and once the road up from Acquia Creek had been properly corduroyed, rations began to pour in faster than they could be eaten. Transportation difficulties plagued the army and disrupted food supplies to the end—even after Lee's surrender, the 122nd found itself short of food, simply because it was proving "impossible to transport a sufficient quantity over the road for the wants of the army . . . But who cares—the rebellion is busted and we all hope soon to enjoy the comforts of home."[37]

In 1862, the comforts of home lay in the distant future. But difficulties over food supply must not be exaggerated. Adequate supplies of basic foodstuffs—hardtack, salt meat, dried vegetables, and coffee—were usually available for the men. These were prepared and cooked either by men detailed as company cooks, or by the soldiers themselves. Wells seems to have found these arrangements perfectly satisfactory. "Lieut. C. and myself," he told his parents, "eat 3 times a day and have plenty to. We buy our provisions at the Brigade Commissary's, such as hard bread (or hard tack as the boys call them) sugar, coffee, tea, pork, fresh beef, salt beef, molasses, sometimes potatoes, sometimes dried apples and peaches. They don't always have all these things at the same time, but enough so we can live comfortably."[38] Sometimes the items available for sale could be supplemented by foraging, or even animal husbandry. For Christmas dinner, in 1862, Wells' fellow officer Capt. Smith "found" a couple of ducks to add savor to the season. Wells himself, by the winter of 1864, seems to have set up almost a small holding round his cabin:

Who says I have not got a home! I have no wife—no cow—no rig—but have got a pack horse—one rooster—and three hens or chickens. The best part of the whole concern is one of the hens has commenced to lay eggs, and by and by I shall have a good mess for breakfast without paying 60 or 80 cts. a dozen and half of them rotten at that.[39]

Extras, like tobacco or whiskey, usually had to be bought; prices, for those times, were high. Smoking tobacco fetched

$1.25 to $2.00 per pound from the quartermaster in late 1862—later it was to become almost unobtainable except by barter with the enemy.[40] Spirits, likewise, were expensive and scarce, though occasionally, in a burst of generosity, the army distributed a small ration: "We drew a ration of whisky day before yesterday," one noncommissioned officer told the *Journal,* "four spoonsful each! Was not that a big drink! It was the first we have drawn, and it was fun to see the men trying to trade crackers sugar or coffee for whisky. I have a little the best of the boys on that, for I am 3rd Sergeant now, and I have to draw all the rations for the Company and deal them out, and I had a chance to *smell* of the whisky before they got it."[41]

On a soldier's pay—thirteen dollars a month for most of the war, and sixteen dollars from May, 1864—there was little opportunity, even if they had been available, to buy many luxuries, or even many necessities.[42] For these, men of the 122nd were very dependent upon two additional sources—charitable organizations and the folks at home. The regiment had particular cause to be grateful to the U.S. Sanitary and Christian Commissions—two remarkably efficient and effective institutions which, although they have not escaped contemporary and subsequent criticism, between them raised mountains of supplies, built hospitals, ran convalescent homes, and dispersed comforts of all kinds to the men of the Union armies.[43] They attracted this encomium from a member of the regiment:

Clean clothes, lemons, ice, jellies, wines, liquors, stationery, stamps, towels, soap—everything—without money and without price; and the best of care, worth more than all else. The two Commissions

have saved thousands of lives. They never sell anything. I never knew a cent's worth sold by them, but a sick or wounded man has only to come under their notice, and he is supplied instanter.[44]

In addition, the local inhabitants of Onondaga played their part in sending gifts to their regiment, though sometimes it required a direct appeal in the local press to mobilize their charity. In the wintertime, there was a great need for mittens, either because these were not an item of regular army issue, or because supply could not keep up with demand. The *Journal* of October 29, 1862, carried the following request:

Let me call the attention of our friends to one thing that we want very much—mittens with a finger for the forefinger. The boys cannot get gloves if they want them, and cannot afford to pay two or three dollars per pair for sheepskin ones, even if they were procurable. Has the liberality of Onondaga already been sufficiently taxed? If not, I assure you that nothing is more needed, and nothing would be more gratefully received. Any packages of the kind sent to the Colonel at Washington D.C. or Hagerstown Md. will meet those for whom it is intended, and the contact of fingers with frozen firelocks, on these nipping mornings and cold days of fall and winter will be made very much more agreeable.[45]

This call for mittens was renewed annually. It did not fall on deaf ears. In a large Christmas parcel sent to the regiment for Christmas, 1863, the inclusion of a consignment of mittens provoked a special word of gratitude:

Then the mittens were a godsend. At dress parade the Sergeants have to report men absent without leave, and men sometimes get off after wood and water and get caught by the assembly too far away. But on the parade that night every man was on hand, looking as tickled as if he had a nicely silvered pewter quarter in his pocket and a circus was coming in at the other end of the town. The long line, firm and motionless, showed not a naked hand, and the report was "All present and accounted for." Ladies, we thank you, and will try to pay you in *fitin*.[46]

Naturally, a particularly important and welcome source of gifts for each soldier was his own family. If Wells' letters were typical in this respect, it was usual for a soldier's letters home to include a request for some item which would help soften the rigors of campaigning. Writing on December 10, 1862, Wells reminded his parents that in his last letter, "I wanted Father to send me a pair of Buckskin gloves by mail, some pepper, postage stamps, I would like a knit smoking cap for a night cap, if it would not be too much trouble and just get a good piece of rhubarb root and do up in the gloves or cap and send by mail."[47] In the same letter, Wells spoke of the difficulty of getting boxes sent from home from Washington to the regiment. Delays were considerable and perishable goods duly perished; stealable items were stolen. These hazards prompted the following letter to the *Journal*:

Now friend *Journal,* one word to our anxious friends at home. Don't try to send us gingerbread and custard pies, broiled chickens and currant jelly, strawberries and cream, or boiled eggs on toast, by Express—If you do they will *spile*. A load of boxes came up the other day, containing almost everything from a charlotte ruse pudding to a boot jack, and not one third of the whole had kept from being entirely spoiled.

Articles of clothing, dried fruit and love letters will keep—but grapes, gin and ginger snaps always mould by the way. One sol-

dier of the German persuasion had a package of three gallons of the last named article but one, sent him by some sympathizing friend of the Vaterland probably, and the said package had been entirely excavated on the way—narry a drop left. The dutchman had received advice of its shipment per letter, and opened the box with eager hand, glistening eyes and watering mouth, seized the demi john, uncorked it and himself, threw his head back, took a fair squint at the sun over the bottom rim, and was about to give the first "glug" when—Mr. Editor, let us draw a veil over the agony of outraged humanity, with the simple remark that Teutonic expletives were plenty in that quarter.

More than two thirds of the other packages had been rifled of similar articles, eatables and drinkables having been selected to keep them from spoiling, which the former were pretty sure to do.[48]

The provision of food and shelter was obviously of the first importance to any soldier; thus, camp building and cooking accounted for a considerable part of his daily affairs. In addition, there were other military duties to be performed—roll calls, training, and drill—though the infrequency of references to these activities suggests either that they were so mundane as to be taken for granted or, in fact, occurred only infrequently. We do know, from the company muster books, that a more or less accurate tally was kept of each individual soldier's presence on or absence from duty, but on only one occasion after the initial period of regimental training is there any mention of drill—this occurs during the regiment's brief respite at Warrenton in the fall of 1863.[49]

It is not surprising that it is the unusual event which figures most often in letters home, rather than the everyday. We do get some idea, however, of how the regiment spent its leisure moments—mainly, one gathers, in reading news from home in the columns of the *Standard* or the *Journal* or by celebrating festivals such as Christmas or Thanksgiving. The following description of Thanksgiving in 1862 provides a vivid picture of how that traditional event was modified to suit army conditions:

Thanksgiving day in the army is not celebrated by the usual outpouring of thanks and improving of good things in the way of gastronomic experiment—'cause why? The turkeys and chickens all die soon after an army comes into a locality or, at least, you don't see 'em around, which must be owing to the atmospheric insalubrity, or the wrigneck matical fever, or the pressure of the atmosphere on the peasbeater; as per example, *a* apple, *a* eyeball, *a* oyster. At any rate, no turkey. But our Major did buy a tough old veteran though the other day, and he has been chained up with a strap around his leg for several days, and today he's gone, and gone *up* and *down* in the headquarters dinner, I reckon. But we did have a service in our brigade at the general headquarters, and after the four clergymen present had tried their hands, and got off a *very* mild infusion of a service, General John was invited and urged by one of them, in the name of all present, to say something. He complied rather reluctantly, but General John never does anything ill, or by halves. He said that he should address the audience entirely in a secular and not in a theological point of view, and then, with "It has been said that bayonets think" for a text, he spoke for half an hour in his silver toned and massive evidence and logic in favor of using every means and resource of the rebels, niggers and all, to beat them in our struggle. The officers in his brigade call him the "Silver Syllabled Cochrane."

How he can blow a man up! and all the while his words sound like the rippling of silver rivulets over a bed of pearl shells.

It is a most lovely day, and if you at home, with your *goodies,* can mix them with a day like this, you are indeed fortunate.[50]

Marching into War

Such happy experiences as the celebration of Thanksgiving provided a rare and welcome relief from the monotony of camp life and the unrelenting tensions of war. Camp life itself was only an interlude. Extended periods in camp were usually confined to the winter months. For the rest of the year, the regiment was most often on the move, marching and countermarching, in the seemingly endless dance to outmaneuver Lee and his generals in the Virginia theater.

Historians with an interest in the technological side of war tend to emphasize the importance of steampowered transportation as a factor in the North's ultimate victory. The railroad and, to a lesser extent, the river steamboat could be and were used to transport men and materials across the country. But the railroad suffered from severe limitations—the lines were vulnerable to attack, and their location did not always fit in with military operations. For front line troops like the 122nd, by far the most usual method of movement was marching, and even the huge baggage and ammunition trains which carried essential war supplies to the front were mule trains, not railroad cars. While it is true that the regiment's first movement from Syracuse to Washington in the fall of 1862 was carried out by a series of train journeys, this was almost the last time that it travelled in this way as a unit.

Marching, then, remained the normal method of moving the regiment from place to place. After battle, it was the most exhausting feature of army life. The regiment had an early taste of this in October, 1862, on the march to Hancock:

One week ago today we marched to Hancock, twenty-seven miles in twenty-three hours—a pretty good forced march we call it—and the next day, as we had just got our tents pitched and things kind o' snug, an order came to march. We fell in, and about sunset got to this place [Cherry Run, Maryland]. The night was one of those described as "midnight without moon," as like a stack of black cats in a dark cellar at midnight, and we stumbled along on the "follow my leader" principle, the best way we could . . . When here we turned into a lot and turned down on the ground, and slept at an awful rate till the next morning.[51]

Not surprisingly, several of the men complained of blistered feet, and perhaps a dozen stragglers fell out on the march, but the physical effects do not seem to have been too severe.[52]

In the long run, the physical effects of hard marching were perhaps less damaging than the effects on morale. On the Hancock forced march, spirits were kept up by singing (a popular song was "Old John the Baptist Went A-fishing Clams" to the tune of "Glory Hallelujah"). But on these long marches there was a real danger of pushing the men beyond the limits of their endurance, and, consequently, seriously undermining their will to continue. The best known example of this was the notorious "Mud March" of January, 1863, when General Burnside took the gamble of continuing to campaign in the winter months. His entire army became thoroughly bogged down in the mud in the process (Plate 2). One soldier described the scene for the *Journal*:

Before we had proceeded far, we overtook artillery stuck fast in the mud. To one twelve pounder was attached sixteen horses, but they could not stir it an inch. Those of us who had laughed at "Virginia mud" as one of the humbugs of last winter's campaign soon found out our mistake, for a muddier lot of fellows than we were after we had marched half a mile, could hardly be found. We marched about three miles, and halted in a piece of woods for dinner. All along our route we saw pontoon bridges, artillery and ammunition wagons sticking fast in the mud. At one place twelve horses were hitched before a pontoon bridge wagon, while on each side ropes were attached which were manned by a hundred strong soldiers, vainly trying to get the wagon up a hill. The soil in this part of Virginia is a reddish clay, and makes the richest kind of mud. Through this mud mules stood no sort of chance, and we passed many on the way that had sunk down in the mud and died.[53]

At other points in their campaigning, the regiment was to suffer the hardship of other long and hard marches (notably just before Gettysburg) but nothing touched the "Mud March." Its effects went far beyond mere physical exhaustion.[54] In one correspondent's opinion "this expedition has been worth more to the rebels than our repulse at Fredericksburg. We have lost more men this time by desertion than we lost by death and wounds at Fredericksburg. Our regiment has not lost many men, but the complaint is universal—that the men are deserting by scores."[55]

The physical and psychological effects of the "Mud March," however damaging, could not compare with those of actual battle. And yet documentation of this area of military experience by newspaper correspondents is not completely satisfactory. There are perhaps two reasons for this, both of which are connected with the fact that letters to the local press were, naturally, intended for publication. Correspondents, and their editors, would be anxious not to cause unnecessary distress to readers with relatives in the regiment. Early in the war, at any rate, most writers declined to go into too much detail about battle scenes—as one put it "its horrors cannot be known except they are seen."[56] Similarly, correspondents were reluctant to own up to any personal or regimental weakness. Their accounts, which may tell a good deal of what they saw, tell little or nothing of what they felt.

For information on this point, private letters are the most informative source, though, even here, an unwillingness to upset the family at home often inhibited the writer. Herbert Wells' early letters, for example, say little about his actual battle experience, though he often expresses his gratitude at having so far been spared. In the last year of the war, however, the strain was evidently beginning to tell, and Wells began to complain of the effects of battle fatigue. Most notably, he found that men were beginning to lose track of time. "Sometimes," he confessed, "one does not know whether it is Sunday or Monday, and if he asks he may get a correct answer or he may not. I recollect telling you that the big fight at Spotsylvania was on the 13th May. It was on the 12th and I think I told you in my last letter that I was wounded on the 2nd June it was on the 3rd. You see when a man is up most of the time nights and is marching or fighting most of the time and tired out—beat through he is not so apt to be correct as if he were rested out."[57] By January, 1865, Wells was near complete exhaustion; for the first time, he spoke directly of what battle was actually like for those taking part. For weeks the regiment desperately, and with scarcely a break, had been fighting in the Shenandoah Valley campaign. In January, along with the rest of the army, it was investing Petersburg. Although the end of the war was only three months away, the regiment, depleted, exhausted, had no way of knowing this. "I think," Wells wrote home,

we deserve a rest after doing the work we have the last summer. You will probably know that to attack works where you have to tear down two or three rows of sharpened stakes or limbs of trees with the brush trimmed off, and the prongs sticking out just high enough so you cannot leap over the buts buried or pinned to the ground so that it is hard work to tear them out so you can get over and all this while the musketry and Grape and Canister being poured into you is no delightful work. I have been in places before now when the lead and iron would cut through the air so that it seemed as if the air was in a continual sharp rush. Something coming at one which if it hits kills or wounds. Imagine our feeling, well so it goes.[58]

This last minute mental shrug cannot disguise the depth of Wells' war weariness. He survived the war to return to his old trade at Frazee's mill, living until 1891. Others were not so lucky.

VI · THE CAUSE, COPPERHEADS, AND BUTTERNUTS

Enough has been said to prove, if proof were necessary, that life in the 122nd Regiment was both difficult and dangerous. The regiment was closely involved in most of the major engagements in the Eastern theater from just after Antietam to the close of the war. Casualties, both in battle and from disease, were high, and a soldier's chances of surviving untouched were small. Yet this was a volunteer regiment: every man in it had chosen to enlist. It is legitimate to ask why. What forces impelled men to volunteer for such hazards? Was it commitment to a cause, and if so, what was that cause? Was their motive the preservation of the Union, suppression of rebellion, the abolition of Southern slavery, or something less exalted but equally compelling?

There are few hard facts that explain why so many eager recruits swarmed to join the 122nd and the other Syracuse regiments in the late summer of 1862. Many, no doubt, joined in the firm conviction that rebellion must be put down, and the security of the government preserved. Some may have felt, even before Lincoln's Emancipation Proclamation, that this was a war to free the negro, and end slavery. Certainly there is evidence from the regiment's later years which would support both these suggestions. But most recruits probably joined because they were swept along on the wave of emotional patriotism engendered by the embattled state of the North, and Lincoln's call for troops. At such a time it would have been more difficult to stand against the pressure to enlist, than to be carried along by it. The number of men who deserted almost immediately testifies to the weakness of a purely emotional decision.

If many new recruits were uncertain why they had joined, and for which cause they were fighting, they found out quickly. At the first important regimental occasion—the ceremony in August, 1862, at which the regiment was presented with its battle flag (patriotically worked in costly materials by the ladies of Lafayetteville)—the principal speech explained to the soldiers in the clearest terms what cause they had been called to defend. The speaker was Mrs. M. E. Gage:

Mr. President, it has been said, "all that man hath will he give for his life"; but at the present time there are hundreds and thousands of men who willingly take their lives into their hands and march boldly forth into battle, for there are things dearer than life, there are things without which life would be valueless, there are things rather than lose which, we would lose life itself.

And what is this for which men so willingly hazard their lives?

It is not territory, nor power, nor the subjugation of a people, but it is to uphold liberty, and maintain the government. It has been sometimes said by some traitors, that the poor men fight for the benefit of the rich, but this is not true, for side by side with the poor man in the ranks of the army, stand rich men, whose wealth counts by hundreds of thousands, and who sprang to arms as privates upon the President's first call for aid.

The United States is emphatically the poor man's government. The rich can buy immunity and obtain favour under any form of government, but in no other land on the globe but this, do rich and poor stand on a political level. The man who lives in a log hut,—the man who this year is a log-splitter, may next year sit in the Presidential chair. Every poor man who fights in the army fights for himself,—he fights to sustain his own rights, and more than that, the fate of unborn millions of poor men will be decided in this war.

In the hands of every soldier lies the destiny of some other being; but for us all, and for the nations of Europe, Asia and Africa. What will be your fate—what will be the fate of us all if the North is defeated, for the war of the North and the South is a war of principles. On the one hand, Liberty and the Union, and the poorman's rights forever, and on the other Slavery and the aristocratic dominion of a few, over both the black man and the poor white man.

Let the soldiers, when they are on the battlefield, remember what I say now. You are fighting for your own liberty, and let every blow be dealt with a stalwart hand, for should liberty fall, despotism will arise in its stead, and houses, or lands, or money, or even life itself, will not be worth what they now are.

Let Liberty be your watch word and your war cry alike. Unless liberty is attained—the broadest, the deepest, the highest liberty for *all*—not for one set alone, one clique alone, but for men and women, black and white, Irish, Germans, Americans, and negroes, there can be no permanent peace.

There can be no permanent peace until the cause of the war is destroyed. And what caused the war? Slavery! and nothing else. That is the corner stone and key-stone of the whole. The cries of down-trodden millions arising to the throne of God. Let each one of you feel the fate of the world to be upon your shoulders, and fight for yourselves, and us, and the future.[1]

Flag presentation ceremonies of this kind were commonplace, and all of them must have had their share of patriotic speeches.[2] But Mrs. Gage's speech was a particularly fine one, and no soldier who gave it proper attention can have been left in any doubt about the cause for which he had volunteered to fight. But this did not necessarily mean that all soldiers shared the opinions of Mrs. Gage, and it is the general view that throughout the Union army, enthusiasm for the cause of negro freedom was matched by racial prejudice against blacks; many feared the effects in the North if abolition should bring about a great migration of freedmen from the South.[3]

Of these fears and prejudices in the 122nd, there is little sign—indeed, opinions about abolition or the negro race are conspicuously rare. The best indication of where the regiment's sympathies lay is provided by its members' attitudes toward the 1864 presidential election, where the contest was between Lincoln and McClellan, the president versus the popular general, the emancipator against the advocate of compromise.

It might not have been surprising if the regiment, or at least a substantial proportion of it, had come out in support of its former commander in chief. McClellan had been a popular leader, and the resentment felt in the army at large over his sacking by Lincoln has already been noted. In the regiment itself, a more detached view seems to have prevailed—perhaps because the 122nd's service with McClellan had been so short, and their contact with him slight. In fact, the regiment's support for the president apparently did not waver. Most members of the 122nd had no sympathy for those who opposed him. For example, a good deal of ill-feeling was caused in the regiment by the presence of the 75th Regiment of the National Guards as military escort at the funeral of an officer from the 122nd, Lieutenant Wilson. The objection to this particular unit was

that there were many who composed this escort who were well known to be open and avowed sympathizers with Jeff Davis, and bitter and unscrupulous enemies of the government. Prominent amongst these was one who, but a short time since, gave the following toast at the hotel of N. G. Foster: "Here is hoping that every man who enlists under old Abe Lincoln may get killed." Another one, an officer and a leading spirit among them, has frequently declared his preference for Jeff Davis, brazenly avowing his determination to fight under him if required to fight at all. Others among them are in the habit of uttering sentiments as treasonable as these. Such being the spirit that activates and controls the majority of these would-be heroes, it was a matter of much chagrin and regret often and forcibly expressed that it should become necessary to employ such men to escort the honored remains of a brave and loyal officer to his final rest among the glorious dead.[4]

Men whose feelings about Southern sympathizers were as strong as this were unlikely to favor compromise. The news of the failure of the plan to oust Lincoln as the Republican presidential candidate in the fall of 1864 was welcomed by those who possessed a clear perception of current issues. "To any man of reflection it must be evident that the only way to end the war, suppress the rebellion, and restore the country to a peace which will amount to anything but a renewal of the war with tenfold rigor and bitterness, is to continue the present administration and suppress the rebels."[5] A vote for Lincoln was a vote to continue the war. As soldiers engaged in some of the most bitter fighting they had yet known, they must have felt some temptation to vote for "Little Mac." But a vote for McClellan was a vote to abandon what they had fought for so long; it was a vote for the South. After the election was over, and Lincoln returned in triumph, Herbert Wells recorded a minor incident which made this quite clear.

On the Skirmish the other day when the rebs were reconnoitring our present position, some of the men sung out "Hurrah for Old Abe"—the rebels responded by singing out "Hurrah for Little Mac"—Just occasional talk that's all, but it shows plainly that they were more in favour of Little Mac than Abe. They thought he was the man for the Yanks to vote for.[6]

Herbert Wells had no time for compromise, or for Copperheads. From the start, he had seen the war as a fight to the finish and had urged the strengthening of the regiment, and the army, as the only way of resolving the conflict quickly and decisively. His opinion is particularly valuable for it provides confirmation and support for the views published in the columns of most local newspapers. The *Journal* in particular never wavered in its opposition to McClellan or its support for Lincoln. In October, 1864, it contributed to the election campaign by publishing some verses lampooning McClellan, verses which merit full quotation:

"HURRA FOR MCCLELLAN"

Hurra for McClellan! the Brilliant and Brave!
The bold little Statesman! the gem of the nation!
The pet of the army! the choice of the slave—
Owner! pledged to *uphold and resist* confiscation.

He's in favor of Peace—little Mac is you know—
He's in favor of War—he's opposed to coercion—
Believes in maintaining the Government, though
By peaceable means and by warlike exertion.

He believes in the olive branch and in the gun—
Boat,—office and spades and the powers of Chicago—
That white men have rights, while black men have none—
In Vallandigham, Seymour, and "honest Iago."

Come, go for McClellan; remember his care
Of the rebel White House! Remember Antietam!
How politely he bowed to the chivalry there,
When Hooker, the fool, couldn't help but defeat 'em.

Come boys, we'll unite with one common accord,
Nor let such a grand opportunity pass us,
To render the hero a fitting reward
For Chickamahominy and for Manassas.

He'll stop all this fighting—relieve Farragut—
Evacuate Vicksburg—leave Richmond—give Grant a
Long furlough—beast Butler and Sheridan too—
Call Sherman away and surrender Atlanta.

He'll pardon Jeff Davis, Bragg, Longstreet and Lee—
Pay off all the debts that the South has contracted—
Return all the slaves that pretend to be free,
By the spurious laws that the North has enacted.

Then how grand and how glorious our Union will be—
The eyes of the nations all resting upon her—
The land of the brave and the home of the—slave—
With all one could wish, save—Peace, Union and honor.

D. A. M.[7]

Compromise was synonymous with surrender. The point was made with great clarity and feeling by George Devoe, a member of the 122nd who had been brought up as a strict Democrat, but who now rejected the Democracy in the South as well as in the North:

We need not refer to history to learn the ways and features of war, for it is right before us, threatening the foundation of the greatest government that ever existed. And what makes it doubly distressing is the fact of its being brought about by an aristocratic class of men who prefer slave labor to free, and who, after a persistence of nearly four years in their attempt, find an opposing resistance which has gained on them so far that defeat and subjugation stares them almost out of countenance. Who envies their situation at this present time? An awful responsibility rests upon somebody. And great will be their lamentation when, after the eighth of November, they will find Abraham Lincoln still our President for another term. Compromise is out of the question. They must surrender unconditionally, and acknowledge the authority and obey the demands of the United States Government and the laws. As a last resort they are making desperate efforts to thwart the movement of the army, hoping to influence thereby the coming election. They entertain the foolish idea that their sympathizers at the North will succeed in their fiendish designs by putting up McClellan for President, trusting that his supposed popularity in the army and elsewhere will be enough to secure his election. But, deluded people, how mistaken they are. Northern traitors cannot draw me into a trap by any such means as they have devised, and I assure you there are enough others who think the same to roll up a heavy majority for Abraham Lincoln when the appointed time comes.[8]

Devoe was quite right, of course, and the vote for Lincoln in the army was overwhelming.[9] There was no further talk of compromise, and within six months of Lincoln's reelection, Southern resistance finally came to an end. On April 9, 1865, Lee finally surrendered his army at Appomattox, and the task of the 122nd was almost done. But one final blow was still to fall. Within the week, Lincoln himself was dead. The regiment and the country mourned. "Last night," wrote Wells in a letter to his family, "we heard of the murder of Lincoln. The men all feel like taking vengeance on someone. That foul murder has hurt the *rebel cause* more than the losing of twenty thousand men to them. I wish the soldiers had the murderer and all those that sympathize with him to deal with as they saw fit. We are anxious to get a late paper with all the particulars. You don't know how we feel about it here."[10] A bitter ending to a bitter struggle.

But was it so bitter? The men of the 122nd may have fought with determination and courage, they may have been united in their support of their president and their government, they may have detested the Southern cause against which they struggled. It does not necessarily follow from this that they hated their opponents or regarded them with bitterness. The attitudes of experienced soldiers toward their enemy, even in a civil war, are influenced primarily by the behavior of their enemies in the field. Men of the 122nd looked upon the South more with compassion than with detestation; they regarded their Southern counterparts more with respect than with contempt. Only in the later stages of the war, as the desperate straits of the Confederacy weakened its troops' regard for the conventions of military behavior, did the feelings of the 122nd toward the rebels begin to change.

In November, 1862, the regiment found itself camped in Virginia, not far from Stafford Court House. For many, this must have been their first visit to the South, and they were not impressed. "We are now two miles from Stafford Court House," wrote one soldier to the *Journal,*

eight miles from Acquia Creek landing, about ten from Falmouth and fifteen from Fredericksburg, and in a country where they raise nothing in abundance—inhabited by a very poor class of white people. I have come to the conclusion that we have no poor at the North, when I look at the condition of these poor uneducated beings. It would seem as if they must actually starve, for what little they have had has been taken from them without compensation, by both armies, and many of them are left with nothing but a little corn to winter on; for they are not able to purchase, on account of high prices, anything eatable. Salt is $25 per bushel, and sugar, tea and coffee out of the reach of anyone. This class of people are tired and sick of the war.[11]

It was difficult for Northern soldiers not to feel some sympathy for a people in such conditions—robbed by both sides

20. Kelly's Ford, Va.—March, 1863

and ruined by the chronic inflation that undermined the Southern economy almost as much as the physical damage wrought by war. But not all of the South, or even of Virginia, presented the same aspect. In Warrenton, the regiment was pleasantly surprised by the appearance of the town, though less so by the welcome of its inhabitants. Warrenton was described to the *Journal* as "a pretty place—very pretty at a distance, and the best I ever saw in Virginia anyhow, but the women are secesh all over. Over half of them are in mourning for somebody killed in the war, and the rest for the delapidated state of the Southern Confederacy. They are the most venomous little she rebels you ever saw. At first they could hardly keep their faces from scowling when they looked at us, but now they are some better."[12] No doubt Northern chivalry has not been totally without its effect on the ladies of Warrenton.

Chivalry, indeed, was a word with some relevance to the behavior of both sides toward each other, at least in the early years of the war. The South prided itself upon its canon of gentlemanly behaviour—Northern men refused to be outdone. In addition, for much of the war, there was a feeling of comradeship between the soldiers of both sides, based perhaps on the suspicion that what really distinguishes the man in the rifle sight from the man whose finger lies on the trigger, is more the color of his uniform than the color of his opinions. As in so many wars, there were many friendly exchanges between men of both sides. Such an incident took place quite early in the regiment's war service, when stationed near Falmouth, Virginia: "The last day we were in front," one soldier reported,

the opposing lines of pickets got quite jocular. As morning dawned, a rebel officer cried out to our men, "Now boys, be fair, if you won't shoot today, we won't." "Who are you?" said our officer. "The Lieut. Colonel in command of the pickets," was the reply.—"Agreed," said ours, and not a shot was fired by either side from the pickets.

One of the rebel officers proposed to lay aside side arms and have a chat on the middle ground, which offer was declined because against orders, when he threw off his sword and came near our lines and asked all sorts of questions. The men were not so scrupulous, but stole up and got in groups, and our fellows traded coffee for tobacco at a big profit, as the weed is high with us and low with them. They also exchanged buttons, knives etc., and had a high time generally when they managed to escape the observation of the officers. Entire good faith was kept, and though the intercourse was against orders and covert, the cessation from firing met with the entire approval of our officers. The rebel pickets now are quite willing to cultivate friendly relations with ours across the river, but all communication is strictly forbidden, except under regular flags of truce.[13]

A similar incident took place the following spring between pickets at Kelly's Ford, about twenty-five miles from Falmouth. This time supplies of coffee and tobacco were exchanged across the river on small boats made out of wooden planks with rag-sails[14] (Plate 20).

Such exchanges were obviously something of an embarrassment to those in authority. Were they to turn a blind eye to friendly relations between soldiers of opposing sides, or were they to enforce military discipline? The situation sometimes threatened to get out of hand, as when the 122nd, together with the 23rd Pennsylvania and the 67th New York were on picket, and a rebel soldier cautiously approached, offering to exchange newspapers.

One of the 67th coolly laid down his gun, walked over to the rebel lines, and swapped papers. As he came back he was arrested, having been detected by an officer, and at the instant of his arrest another trade was seen going on between one of the 23rd and a reb. He was also arrested, and at the same time a rebel corporal and a file of men were seen arresting the reb. who had made the trade. Where the line ran through a little hollow, an officer yesterday missed two or three men, and going a little to the front found them engaged with about the same number of rebs very socially and amicably pitching coppers. It seems one side had "stumped" the other, and promised "honor bright," and the "stump" had been accepted, and the pledge violated neither. The officer would not break the word of his men, but rather savagely ordered the rebs back to their line, and placed his own men at once under arrest. But you must not imagine that these men would not fight each other.[15]

Fight each other they did, but with a good deal of mutual respect. Neither side made the mistake of underestimating the skill and courage of the other, though comparisons between them were usually made to the advantage of the teller. "Yon reb," conceded an Onondaga soldier,

is no fool or coward. Keep close, for if you don't fetch him, he won't jump or move for that ball within a foot of him, but he'll fetch you if you give him a chance. The heavy long rifles of the "Berdans"[16] are our advantage, and Johnny knows it, and he is playing it close and quiet. It may sometimes look like cowardice when three or four of them run at the pointing of a Berdan, but

I've seen blue-jackets run under similar circumstances, at an elongated double quick, and men who were as brave as lions and as cool as cucumbers all the while. The only place where we are any better or braver than they are is with the bayonet. The shock, rush, heat and excitement of firing agrees with the impetuous Southern blood exactly, but the cool, deliberate, determined Northern blood drives a line of bayonets the farthest, and bears down Johnny's flashing valor. Hence they always fight in the woods, if possible, and I verily believe that in the open field our men would feel sure of victory in every encounter with ten per cent of superior numbers on the part of the enemy. Nor is this without reason. Our men are stronger and more muscular, though not averaging any taller.—Many of the rebs are fierce looking fellows, but I think the counter poise of equal numbers on the average would be more than ten per cent in our favor. No doubt this is owing to the tendency of the Southern climate and Southern habits to make men thin and spare—the physique of almost all the Virginians, even, where white men labor considerably, and much more so further South, where idleness is the rule from childhood.—Still this is by no means an invariable rule. Many of our prisoners at the storming of the heights, May 3rd, were finely-formed, good-looking, frank fellows, but the very biggest I saw were foreigners impressed into the service.[17]

What impressed many Onondagans, in the earlier stages of the war at least, was the natural courtesy and chivalrous behavior of those Southerners with whom they came into contact. Only a short time after the regiment arrived in Virginia, it happened that the surgeon, Dr. Tefft, was taken prisoner by a small band of Southern guerrillas. His captors for some reason believed him to be a senior yankee officer, possibly even McClellan himself and insisted on taking him back to the main body camped near Berryville. Taken before the commanding officer, the doctor was able to prove his identity, whereupon he was at once released unconditionally, kept all night, and entertained "in the kindest manner," given tent and blankets and the best of everything to eat and drink. The next morning the Doctor was sent on his way unharmed, "without having had an uncivil word spoken to him by anyone." The civility, chivalry, and general good manners of Southerners who came in contact with the regiment were frequently remarked upon. Dr. Tefft described his captors as "a rollicking, devil-may-care set of young fellows," and he had obviously thoroughly enjoyed his involuntary visit.[18] Rebel prisoners, taken after the skirmish near Snicker's Gap in June, 1863, soon "seemed on the best of terms with our men." One of the officers, a Major Mayo from North Carolina, was described as "very intelligent and communicative."[19] The adherence of both sides to the terms of truce was a matter of regular satisfaction.

By the middle of the war, attitudes had changed, largely because the Southerners themselves appeared to have betrayed their former high standards of behavior. Particular anger was expressed at the treachery of guerrillas—"honest farmers"—who pretended allegiance to the government but secretly fought against it. "Hot weather, guerrillas, and blackberries," wrote a correspondent from Warrenton,

are the three principal fruits of production hereabouts. The blackberries are going, the hot weather coming, and the guerrillas fast occupying a sort of intermediate suspensatory condition. You see that these last are a sort of "honest farmers" who have taken the oath of allegiance a few times and got passes and safeguards from the Government.—Well they start out and arm themselves with anything that comes handy—pistols, sabres, carbines, shotguns etc. and being mounted and in citizen clothes proceed to lay in wait for some poor devil of a blue jacket. If they can catch a few after berries, without arms, their valor shines—they take 'em and kill them on the spot, or run them off and wait for a fresh lot . . . But if a body of troops come upon them they plunge into a piece of woods, hide their arms, and "dig" for some house.[20]

The chivalry of the South was ultimately believed to be a sham. The "devil-may-care young fellows" of Dr. Tefft's experience had become "honest farmers," and courteous Major White was replaced by Major Mosby, scourge of unprotected sutlers' wagons, ambulances, and baggage trains. "Matters are much the same in the Valley," readers of the *Journal* were informed in September 1864,

The guerrillas hang around, and the gallant Chevalier Bayard of Southern Maidens, Mosby, continues to dash out upon sutlers, where he can find them unguarded or broken down, and he generally takes them without the loss of a man. Now and then an ambulance or two, full of sick men, is taken by him without loss, and he has been known to surround a load of hats and boots, and a nigger driving the train, and storm the position with all the bravery and recklessness of a Knight-errant of the olden times, storming the enchanted castle in which dwells the imprisoned form of his "ladye-fayre." But with such vulgar things as infantry escorts and squadrons of Union cavalry, the chevalier disdains to meddle.[21]

Not to be outdone, the blue-jackets lowered their standards of behavior to match. A detachment of cavalry sent out after guerrillas, with orders not to bring back any prisoners, caught up with and captured half a dozen of them.

The Captain thought of his orders—he is a stern stiff-necked chap—and he said to the six gray-backed cut throats, "Boys, I'll have to leave you where you are; its against orders to take you along." Secesh began to prick up their ears; "but," turning to his own men, "boys, for fear they will hurt themselves thrashing around, we'll put their feet a few inches from the ground"; and in five minutes they hung dangling where they were the next morning, when some fellows benevolently dug a hole, cut the ropes and let them tumble into it, and *kivered them up*.[22]

Neither the treatment meted out to the wretched guerrillas, nor the terms in which it was reported, did the North much credit.

This change in attitudes may in part reflect the increasingly desperate condition of the South. The Confederacy, its armies dwindling (though not as quickly as its supplies), could not afford to treat Northern prisoners with its former generosity. Charles T. Wyman, captured in the fall of 1863, commented bitterly later on his treatment at Southern hands:

Whether I get home or not matters but little now that I am out of the unhuman hands of the most accursed foes a man ever fought. We were terribly maltreated. That our fare was of the most inferior quality, and small in quantity, I don't complain. Other inhumanities galled and injured us much more. Our fare was a small loaf of unbolted unsifted corn bread, a piece of bacon the size of a horse chestnut, and rice soup. We had barely room to lie down, being packed away as closely as a lot of sardines. No blankets or overcoats, no fires, no warm meals. We were robbed of all clothing except what was absolutely necessary to cover our nakedness—our money, pocket knives, pipes, combs, tin cups, in fact everything.

Only 10 men of 700 were allowed to visit the rear at once. Nor were we allowed to stay on the lower floor. Guards were at the foot of the stairs and in the yard (which is about the size of aunt's parlor) to prevent more than the prescribed number from going below. Towards Spring they tardily issued us blankets and clothing, which our Government sent forward to my knowledge, last Fall. Twenty-six per cent (I have official figures) died during the past six months; 100 cases of smallpox were in our building at one time.[23]

The South's growing inability to feed and clothe its own troops may explain, if not excuse, its failure to do as much for Union prisoners. In battle, too, it became common practice for them to strip desperately needed arms and clothing from Northern dead and dying. Other inhumanities, such as the bayoneting of men of the Eighth Corps in their tents, material shortages could neither explain nor excuse.[24] Small wonder that relations between the soldiers of either side, which had begun so amicably, ended in bitterness and recrimination.

As has been emphasized in this study, the American Civil War was above all a citizens' war. This did not only mean that it was a war that affected the lives of ordinary citizens much more than the European wars of the eighteenth century. It meant also that the very armies were composed of citizens who had chosen to fight. Soldiers on both sides, to an unprecedented degree, were articulate and educated, able to grasp the issues at stake and express their views upon them. On the Union side, the 122nd regiment knew what it was fighting for, and was determined to reject any compromise short of total victory over the South. The cost was awesome, but the objective was fully achieved.

VII · EPILOGUE: THE RUGGLES BEQUEST

In January, 1958, an elderly American woman, Miss Reba Ruggles of Craichie House, in the county of Angus, Scotland, died. Her will was simple. After making provision for her sickbed, funeral expenses, and the painless disposal of her cats and dogs, she left the remainder of her estate to the ancient University of St. Andrews to establish a fund, the "Dr. Agnes Rogers Memorial," for the purchase of books in the fields of psychology and education. This estate consisted of real and personal property of modest value. The real property included, in addition to the house, three small cottages. The personal property consisted of investments in the United States worth an estimated £500, and a few personal effects.[1]

It was these personal effects which provided the starting point of this study. Miss Ruggles, it appeared, had been the younger daughter of William Eugene Ruggles, a private soldier on the Union side in the American Civil War. Upon her death the University of St. Andrews received not only the property previously mentioned, but also some relics from the war that had belonged to her father. No doubt many American families owned similar collections—a private soldier's Bible, stained and dog-eared, a shabby "housewife" with needles and thread, a broken-toothed folding comb, some rounds of ammunition, assorted badges and buckles, and a tattered mass of newspaper cuttings relating to Ruggles' regiment, the 122nd Regiment New York Volunteer Infantry. The assortment was interesting, but scarcely unique.

The one unusual feature was a collection of twenty-three carefully preserved drawings, executed in pencil and ink on identical sheets of artist's board. All but two of them showed scenes from Civil War engagements—in each drawing the 122nd Regiment figured prominently. Each Civil War drawing was identified with a title (often misspelled) and bore on the left-hand bottom corner the words "From Memory, W. E. Ruggles, 122nd NYV." It is true, of course, that drawings, engravings, and photographs of the American Civil War abound—it was, in its day, the best illustrated war in history. Photographers and artists, like the illustrator Alfred Waud, were sent by newspaper and magazine proprietors to cover the campaigns and send back sketches that were then engraved and published. Most of such sketches and engravings were of higher artistic merit than the drawings in the Ruggles collection.

Nevertheless, the Ruggles drawings were in certain respects unusual, even unique. For one thing, they all depicted a single regiment. Collectively, they provided an illustrated history of

21. Noble Ruggles' House, 156 East Washington Street, Syracuse, N.Y.

that regiment's progress from its formation in 1862 to its presence at Appomattox and the surrender of General Lee. In addition, the drawings contained their own built-in mystery: the most cursory examination revealed that each drawing had originally borne a second name. In the bottom right-hand corner of each drawing, traces of a second signature, erased to varying degrees, were apparent. On no single drawing could more than a few letters of the name be deciphered, but careful examination of each made it possible to construct a composite signature. This second signature was eventually discovered to be that of Philip M. Ostrander, 149th Regiment New York Volunteers.

Naturally, the discovery and identification of Ostrander's name raised many questions about the drawings, their authenticity, and their authorship. It could no longer be assumed that Ruggles himself had drawn them, or even that he had had any part in their production. At the time, little was known about either of the men, nothing about any possible connection between them. It was not clear when the drawings had been made, though their condition argued for postwar dating. Nor was it known why they were made. The reasons for the erasure of Ostrander's name could only be guessed at. Before any historical use could be made of the drawings, answers to some of these questions had to be found. The remaining relics in the Ruggles collection had to be carefully scrutinized, and other sources of evidence examined. Gradually, pictures of the two men, William Eugene Ruggles and Philip M. Ostrander, emerged, and their connection with the drawings became clearer.

William Eugene Ruggles

Little is known even now about William Ruggles' life before the Civil War. He was born in Syracuse, New York, on April 19, 1846 and, apart from his period of war service, spent the rest of his life in that city.[2] His father, Noble O. Ruggles, was a carpenter and churn maker, a pillar of the local Wesleyan church, and a supporter of the Liberty Party in the early fifties.[3] His mother, Sarah Shoens (or Shaw) worked as a tailor for a number of employers. From the 1850s onward, they lived at 156 East Washington Street, Syracuse (Plate 21). In addition to William, the Ruggleses had two other sons, Philo and Charles.[4] Philo was later to die at the battle of Rappahannock Station.

When the first shots of the war between North and South were fired at Fort Sumter on April 12, 1861, William was approaching his fifteenth birthday. In July, 1862, at age sixteen, he enlisted, together with elder brother Philo.[5] A poignant reminder of his youth, and that of many eager young Civil War volunteers, is provided by a newspaper cutting in the Ruggles collection—a poem that tells of two volunteers, one sixteen and the other sixty, who both lied about their ages to be allowed to enlist. (It is interesting to note that the other soldier connected with the drawings, Philip Ostrander, claimed to be younger than he actually was when he joined the Union forces.)[6] The young Ruggles was described as a carpenter by trade, and of medium height, with dark hair, eyes, and complexion. The examining surgeon duly pronounced him free from all bodily defects and mental infirmity, and on July 21, 1862, the recruiting officer, Captain Chamberlain, enrolled him in the new regiment being formed in Syracuse, the 122nd New York Volunteers.[7]

Ruggles' life as a private in the Union army was neither uneventful nor very happy. From his enlistment almost until the end of the war, he followed the regiment in all its campaigns. Although he survived, his health was permanently impaired. Bad food and the rigors of war left him with a chronic illness that prevented him thereafter from holding down any job requiring heavy physical labor.[8] There is some evidence that he tried to desert along with several other members of the regiment as early as October, 1862, at Clear Springs, Maryland.[9] Apart from that incident, he was recorded as being on roll (except for a three day tour of picket duty at the end of 1863) until March, 1864.[10] On March 10, when the regiment was stationed at Sandusky, Ohio, he tried to desert again. Apparently hoping to make his way to Canada via Buffalo, he was arrested in Cleveland the following day and escorted back to Sandusky under guard.[11] During this brief spell of freedom he managed to lose all his kit, including rifle, bayonet, knapsack, canteen and half-shelter tent. For these, plus an additional thirty dollars to cover the expense of his arrest, he was billed by the United States government for $55.46. Evidently, that was the extent of his punishment.[12] Desertion, as mentioned previously, was prevalent amongst the armies of both sides. Indeed, one authority claims that there was no time in the history of the Army of the Potomac when it reported less than a quarter of full complement absent without leave.[13] Punishment of deserters varied: several were shot, but usually they were put to hard labor or confined to the penitentiary to work out their unexpired terms. Ruggles had been fortunate to escape punishment of this kind—he was to be less fortunate later.

His next adventure away from the regiment came not through desertion, but by capture. In early May, 1864, the 122nd took part in the bloody battle of the Wilderness. At seven in the morning on May 6, the regiment advanced against the Confederate forces through a thick tangle of small trees and undergrowth but could not break through. The rebels counterattacked with great force. Carrying the Union troops before them, they forced the 122nd back, despite three attempts by that regiment to rally. In the confusion Ruggles disappeared; he was at first reported killed. Although he had, in fact, been captured, he was able to escape, running six miles before catching up with a Union wagon train and rejoining his regiment.[14] As souvenirs of his adventure, he sent his father some Confederate postage stamps and extracts from rebel papers, some of which are to be found in the Ruggles collection.[15] Also in the collection is an extract from an unidentified post-war paper, that contains a Southern officer's account of a young Union soldier who, condemned to death as a spy, had escaped from the gallows by wriggling out of his handcuffs and knocking down the guards.

Ruggles' third and final attempt to desert is surrounded by a good deal of official confusion. On the company muster roll he was entered as absent without leave beginning on April 24, 1865.[16] Desertion at this point, if not excusable, was understandable. The war in Virginia was over. Lee's forces had laid down their arms on the twelfth, and for the 122nd there was no enemy left to fight. Why not go home? But, in fact, the date of Ruggles' court-martial is recorded as March 12, 1865, and unless this is an error, his desertion must have taken place before that date.[17] By sentence of the court, confirmed by higher authority in Washington as late as July 3, it was decreed that the offender was "to forfeit all pay and allowances now due; to be dishonourably discharged, drummed out of camp, and to be confined at hard labour a period of six months at Fort Delaware."[18] Again there is some confusion; no confirmation exists that this sentence was ever carried out. The war was now over on all fronts, and a presidential proclamation of March 11, had offered amnesty to all deserters who returned to their units within sixty days.[19] The adjutant general's office in 1883 confirmed that Ruggles had been mustered out with the rest of his company at Washington, D.C. on June 23, 1865.[20]

William Ruggles returned from the war in 1865 with his health impaired, but otherwise unharmed. Soon afterward, in 1866 or 1867, he married a local girl, Alida Alexander, in the Wesleyan church at Syracuse. Alida bore him two daughters. The first died after only a few weeks; the second, Reba, born on October 29, 1883, survived and became the donor of the Ruggles bequest to St. Andrews University.[21] From 1868 until William's death in 1907, the family lived, almost without a break, at 34 Renwick Avenue, Syracuse[22] (Plate 22). The house was renumbered 212 in the reorganization of 1888–89.

There is no evidence that William ever returned to his old trade as a carpenter, though he held a number of unskilled jobs in the late 1860s before setting up as a cigar manufacturer in 1869.[23] In one of the affidavits sworn by a friend in support of Ruggles' claim for a disablement pension, it is stated that he worked for many years after the war in a meat market in Renwick Avenue,[24] but, in fact, he seems to have worked as a cigar manufacturer in a small way for the rest of his life, occasionally acting also as a safe agent.[25] The pension he claimed in 1881 on the grounds of physical disabilities arising from his war service was ultimately granted, and at the time of his death, amounted to ten dollars per month.[26]

Although William's trade as a cigar manufacturer, even combined with the small pension, earned him only a modest livelihood, he could always live on memories. The overriding interest of his life, apart from his family and his work, lay in his old regiment, and the local branch of the Grand Army of the Republic (G.A.R.)—the Northern veterans' organization. He attended the annual reunions of the 122nd with fair regularity at least until 1888.[27] But he threw himself with even greater enthusiasm into the activities of Lilly Post, one of the two Syracuse branches of the G.A.R., serving on the small committees which placed wreaths on veterans' graves in Oakwood Cemetery and holding other minor offices in the organization.[28] Despite physical weaknesses that obliged him to drop out of parades at frequent intervals, he insisted on marching with the "Continentals"—the ceremonial wing of Lilly Post—decked out with their special uniform based on the officer's dress of the revolutionary war.[29] The Ruggles collection contains some badges and other decorations from his Continental uniform.

But memories are not financially profitable. When Ruggles died of a cerebral embolism on May 27, 1907, he left his wife and daughter almost destitute. At fifty-eight,[30] Alida Ruggles found herself with neither money nor property other than the family home in Renwick Avenue.[31] The frame house, single

22. William Ruggles' House, 34 (212) Renwick Avenue, Syracuse, N.Y.

story at the front rising to two stories at the back, was old and in frequent need of repair. Its value was estimated at between $17 and $18,000, but it carried a mortgage of $700 at 5 percent.[32] Apart from this, Alida's support came from what she could earn herself as a dressmaker, supplemented by any help that Reba, twenty-four, could provide.[33] However, Mrs. Ruggles successfully applied for a widow's pension that, by the time of her death, amounted to thirty dollars a month.[34] She died on September 22, 1927, in Prescott, Ontario, and her body was brought back to Syracuse by her daughter and buried close to William's in Oakwood cemetery.[35] Of Reba herself, little is now known. Before her father's death she had worked as a bookkeeper at Darrow's Creamery in Syracuse; in 1905, she moved to Brooklyn.[36] At some later date she met Dr. Agnes Rogers, a professor of psychology from Scotland, who spent most of her working life in New York. Reba Ruggles became Dr. Rogers' companion and, on the latter's retirement, returned with her to Craichie. When Dr. Rogers died, Reba inherited Craichie House and other property, on the understanding that at her death it would pass to the University of St. Andrews.

Philip M. Ostrander

Philip Ostrander was considerably older than William Ruggles, and although the precise date of his birth is uncertain, it was probably the thirteenth or fourteenth of April in either 1812 or 1813.[37] His parents, John and Anna Ostrander, were both native Americans. At the time of Philip's birth, they were living in Albany, New York.[38] Some time before the Civil War, Philip left Albany and traveled by packet boat to Syracuse where, apart from his period of war service, he lived for the rest of his life.[39]

By profession Ostrander was an engraver. He had already made himself something of a reputation in this field before the outbreak of war. In 1848 he made his first steel engraving in Syracuse—a picture of the Onondaga Indian, Chief Oshahinta, which was used as the frontispiece for Clark's *History of Onondaga County*. Another of his engravings, a view of Syracuse probably executed in 1851, was also used as a frontispiece for a book—M. A. Hand's *From a Forest to a City*, published in 1889. Other examples of his work are now rare. Apparently he engraved campaign badges for the Republican candidates in the 1856 presidential election[40] and was alleged to have been one of only three men considered competent enough to engrave U.S. bank notes shortly before the war.[41] In January, 1918, the Syracuse *Post-Standard* published a copy of one of his drawings depicting the battle of the Wilderness in early May, 1864, a drawing to which we will return later. In the article which accompanied the picture, it was tantalizingly reported that his drawings of Civil War battle scenes were still cherished by his son, Alderman Harry C. Ostrander, and by several veterans of the city so fortunate as to possess them.[42] Unfortunately, inquiries carried out over a number of years have failed to unearth any of these. Only one undoubtedly original drawing by Ostrander is now known to exist—a pencil sketch of *Lookout Mountain, Tennessee*, now in the possession of the Onondaga Historical Association.

Soon after war broke out, Ostrander enlisted in the Union army. On September 15, 1861, he was enrolled in Company G of the 81st Regiment New York Volunteer Infantry. His enlistment papers describe him as an engraver by occupation, about five feet, six inches tall, with fair complexion, blue eyes, and dark hair. He gave his age as forty-two, though he must at the time have been at least forty-eight.[43] (One is reminded of the poem in the Ruggles collection.) Probably on account of his mature age, he was immediately given the rank of third sergeant, a rank which he held as long as he served with the regiment, but he soon found that army life was having a serious effect upon his health.[44] In March, 1862, he fell sick in Washington, D.C.; by May his health had so far deteriorated that on the twenty-eighth he was discharged on grounds of general debility (chiefly asthma) having spent the last weeks of his enlistment in Eckington General Hospital.[45]

In view of this, it is perhaps surprising to find him reenlisting in Company A of the 149th Regiment New York Infantry as early as August, 1862, this time simply as a private soldier.[46] The 149th was a sister regiment to the 122nd, formed at about the same time in the same burst of recruiting zeal. Ostrander's motives for reenlistment can only be guessed at—continued enthusiasm for the cause, unwillingness to stand by while others in his locality rushed to sign up, or possibly, since on this occasion he described himself as a laborer, because the army offered secure employment. Despite his previous medical history (which no doubt he kept quiet about), he received the usual certificate from the examining surgeon stating that he was "free from all bodily defects and mental infirmity which would in any way disqualify him from performing his duties."[47] At this critical stage of the war, when the first flush of enthusiasm to enlist had subsided and the need to expand the armed forces of the Union was pressing, no very searching inquiry into the physical fitness of volunteer recruits was likely to be carried out. As it happened, Ostrander's health held out until the summer of 1863. At the beginning of the year he even secured promotion to corporal, but in June he fell out sick on march, and on July 30, was reduced to the ranks.[48] He recovered and managed to remain on duty for almost a year, but in May, 1864, he was taken ill again and had to be transferred to the military hospital in Chattanooga, Tennessee.[49] Although, unlike so many others who contracted wartime illnesses, he survived, he never again took an active part in the war and was finally mustered out with the rest of his company on July 12, 1865, near Bladensburg, Indiana.[50]

Unlike Ruggles, Ostrander had been married for several years before his first enlistment. On February 24, 1844, he had married Eliza Collett in New York.[51] Between 1845 and 1869 they had seven children, none of whom, it would appear, inherited their father's artistic talents to any degree, though they all became skilled tradesmen in a variety of occupations. The third son, Henry (Harry) Charles Ostrander was a successful builder who became a well-known alderman in Syracuse. West Ostrander Street in that city is named after him. Philip, after his discharge in Indiana, rejoined his family in Syracuse where he took up again as an engraver. Initially he worked at home but later moved his business to premises in the center of the city. Unlike the Ruggleses, the Ostranders moved house quite frequently over the next twenty years. The most settled period of their lives was from 1874 to 1881, when they lived at 70 Taylor Street, and Philip carried on his trade downtown in Wieting Block.[52] The chronic diarrhea and persistent malarial fever that he had contracted in the service, however, never disappeared entirely, and he was frequently unable to work for long periods. On the basis of this disability, Ostrander applied for an invalid pension in February, 1883. There is no record that his first claim was successful; he did reapply five years later.[53] This second claim was still pending when he died on May 1, 1888, at the age of seventy-six, survived by his widow Eliza, and six of their seven children.[54]

Ruggles, Ostrander and the Civil War drawings

The discovery of Ostrander's name, or at least the remains of it, on the drawings raised many questions—principally, of course, who really made the drawings, and why was the Ostrander signature erased?

From all points of view it seems most probable that Ostrander, the only professional artist of the two, either was the true artist or took the major part in the creation of the pictures. The artistic style of the drawings is very similar to that of the one known original Ostrander—the sketch of *Lookout Mountain*—though not close enough to be conclusive. An interesting contribution to the debate is provided by the picture of the Wilderness reproduced in the Syracuse newspaper in 1918. This picture is claimed to be by Ostrander—it is also quite obviously an engraving of the same scene in the Ruggles drawings. The accompanying newspaper article states that Ostrander was a participant in the battle. Yet it is quite clear, both from the campaign history of the 149th Regiment, and from Ostrander's own military record, that he was not.

This discrepancy raises similar problems with regard to all the Ruggles drawings, barring one. Each of the pictures in the Ruggles collection relates to a scene in which the 122nd Regiment, and therefore Ruggles himself was directly involved. In only one of these battles, Gettysburg, was the 149th also a participant: by coincidence, both regiments happened to find themselves fighting side by side in the vital engagement in defense of Culp's Hill. This engagement was, in fact, the only one during the entire war that brought the two regiments together in a battle. It is difficult to see how Ostrander, unaided, could have produced a series of drawings showing a regiment of which he was not a member, in battle scenes to which he was not a witness. Nor is it easy to understand why he should have wished to do so.

Attention, therefore, switches back to Ruggles. Of the two, he was the only one with the relevant experience, and the only one likely to want a collection of drawings of the 122nd. As noted earlier, many of the drawings are inscribed "From memory, W. E. Ruggles 122nd NYV." Perhaps the words "From Memory" should be taken literally—Ruggles provided the recollection of the scenes, and transmitted these, by word of mouth or perhaps by sketch, to his collaborator. If he did so, his powers of recall were remarkable. There is an unusually close correspondence between the details of each drawing, and the actual scene as it exists today, allowing for changes such as the growth of trees or the building of new roads or buildings. The picture of Sugarloaf Mountain, for example, shows in the background the church at Poolesville, Maryland (see Plate 1). This is St. Peter's Episcopal Church, completed in 1847 and still standing today. In almost every respect—overall shape, the construction of the steeple, and so on, it is today as it was in the picture. The only slight differences are in the number of windows and the orientation of the church in relation to the village. For a soldier, who passed only briefly through the area before moving on to fight in many furious and bloody engagements, to remember the scene in such precise detail was a remarkable feat.

The most likely explanation of the drawings seems, then, to be that they were the outcome of collaboration. If so, then they were most surely produced after the war, not during it—a conclusion that is supported by the generally good condition of the drawings, and the similarity of materials used to produce them. It is difficult, though not impossible, to imagine Ostrander carrying the materials of his trade from battlefield to battlefield. It is beyond belief that he should have done so in order to illustrate scenes to which he was not an eyewitness.

If Ruggles and Ostrander collaborated on the drawings, then when did they do so, and for what purpose? It is true that their regiments did fight together at Culp's Hill, but it hardly seems likely that they spent the frantic hours beating back the Confederate attack discussing future plans for an artistic partnership. The meeting between them must, in any case, have taken place after the war. How did this come about? There is evidence that Ruggles worked for some years after mustering out in a meat market on Renwick Avenue. Such an occupation must have brought him into contact with other local veterans, and their wives. Also, his enthusiastic membership in the Grand Army of the Republic must certainly have kept old friendships alive and initiated new ones. Neither of these two circumstances offers any lead to a connection between Ruggles and Ostrander. On the one hand, as already noted, there is reason to doubt the accuracy of the claim that Ruggles worked in a meat market—the local city directories make no mention of such an occupation for Ruggles. On the other hand, Ostrander does not seem to have shared his partner's enthusiasm for veterans' reunions and parades.

There are, however, two further circumstances that may provide the necessary link between the two men. The first is that, for a short period, the two families lived close to each other. The Ruggleses, it will be recalled, lived at 34 Renwick Avenue, Syracuse. In 1883, the Ostranders moved to number 28, only three houses away—even after 1885, when they moved away again, this continued to be listed as Ostrander's business address.[55] That a meeting took place between them sometime in the years from 1883 to 1888, when Philip Ostrander died, seems highly plausible.

There may also have been a second link. William Ruggles, it has been mentioned, was a cigar maker, if only in a small way. At this time he worked from his home in Renwick Avenue; only occasionally was he able to take business premises elsewhere in the city. In 1883, the year that his family moved to Renwick Avenue, Ostrander's third son, Harry, changed his occupation from clerk to cigar maker, and though he soon gave it up for work in a livery stable, his younger brother, Bertram, became a cigar maker in 1885[56] after apprenticing himself for a year.[57] No business premises relating to these young men were listed in the city directory for the period, but it seems likely that a business connection between them and William Ruggles could have existed.

Neither of these circumstances, of course, proves beyond doubt that the Ruggles–Ostrander meeting took place at this time or through such a connection. Of the fact that a meeting did take place at some time, the drawings themselves are adequate proof. There is nothing about the drawings inconsistent with the proposition that they were produced after 1883, and they certainly must have been completed by 1888. But none of this explains why they were produced.

Once again, there can be no final and conclusive answer to this question. The first assumption, in such a case, might be that financial gain of some kind was involved. This could well have been the explanation for Ostrander's participation in the project. He was, after all, a professional. Ruggles may very well have paid him for making the original drawings, and the existence of a second version of the Wilderness picture may suggest that he made more than one copy of others, either in order to give them away to friends and relatives, or simply to sell them. The financial motive is less strong in Ruggles' case, though he may well have taken a share in any of the proceeds. He may, of course, have tried to sell the originals, though, if so, obviously without success. A more satisfactory explanation, and one that corresponds more closely with what we know of William Ruggles, may be quite different. One thing known for certain about Ruggles' life after the war is the great part played in it by the activities of veterans' organizations. Ruggles, not surprisingly, kept many mementos from his life during the war, even including a piece of stone and a tree splinter picked up on the field of Gettysburg. Yet if the war had been both arduous and exciting—the one great adventure of his life—it had not been without its inglorious moments, and its ending had been particularly unfortunate. The commissioning of the drawings, involving both a detailed recollection of the excitements of war, and the production of a permanent record of his part in it, must have been a thoroughly satisfying experience. Although Ruggles was poor, the financial value of the drawings would have been secondary in this case.

If this argument satisfactorily accounts for the making of the drawings, it could also account for the erasure of Ostrander's name from them. Ruggles, it might be suggested, not only wanted credit for having fought in the war, he wanted sole credit for the drawings themselves. In view of what has already been said, this is a more difficult argument to sustain. If other versions of the drawings existed in the neighborhood, and one certainly did, it might have been difficult to claim as one's own work pictures known to be almost identical with those drawn by another. On the other hand, it might have been Ruggles' intention to keep them firmly in the family, in which case the rubbing out of the artist's name would have been for the benefit, not of his wife, Alida, surely, who must have known of the collaboration, but of his daughter Reba, born three years before Ostrander died.

Speculation on this point may be intriguing; it can never be satisfied. The drawings, however, remain, as do the other relics of William Ruggles' Civil War adventures. Between them they offer more than just a glimpse of one man's war. Combined with additional relevant evidence, they provide both the starting point and the essential framework of this study of a regiment at war—the war history of the 122nd Regiment New York Volunteer Infantry.

Ruggles and Ostrander, Titus and Dwight, all the members of the 122nd Regiment, have long passed away. There was, it could be said, nothing unusual about any of them, and the history of the regiment was not unlike the history of many others. Other men fought and died for the same cause; other regiments were formed along similar lines, used the same equipment, engaged in the same battles, and, the struggle over and the war won, their remnants likewise mustered out with honor.

Yet the history of the Civil War, like the history of any great event in the affairs of men, is also the history of the men themselves—the sum of individual experience. The story of Ruggles' Regiment brings into clear focus not only the great issues of a great war, but also its human, and inhuman, face. In the breathing spaces between battles, Herbert Wells calmly builds his beloved cabins and tends his livestock. Union and Confederate men exchange coffee and tobacco across a creek. The terrible suffering and devastation of the war are occasionally lightened by the sight of Alfred Waud scurrying after his horse, or an unfortunate German deprived of his expected supply of gin. We learn of both the cruelty, and the chivalry of war.

The story of the 122nd was not unique—neither was it indistinguishable from that of other regiments. Few others surpassed its bloody battle record, the extent of its casualties, the part it played in key actions in the Virginia theater. It is fitting that that story should be recalled and recorded.

APPENDIXES

APPENDIX A - REGIMENTAL LIST

Name	Age on Enlistment	Enlisted		Company	Rank[a]	Discharged/ Died		Remarks
Abbey, William P.	18	30 July	1862	C	Corp	18 April	1863	discharged for disability
Abbott, William	18	26 July	1862	F	Pte	9 June	1865	wounded at Wilderness and Petersburg
Abrams, Daniel F.	18	2 Aug	1862	H	Pte	20 Dec	1862	
Adams, Oscar	18	18 Aug	1862	D	Pte	22 Sept	1864	deserted
Adkins, Loriston	31	4 Aug	1862	B	Corp	2 May	1865	wounded 14 July 1864
Agan, Hiram	18	6 Aug	1862	C	Sgt	23 June	1865	wounded at Gettysburg
Aird, William B.	44	6 Feb	1864	E	Pte	17 April	1865	transferred to V.R.C.[b]
Albring, James	44	4 Aug	1862	K	Pte	19 July	1864	died in hospital
Alderman, John	37	12 Aug	1862	K	Corp	23 June	1865	wounded at Wilderness
Allen, Andrew	44	30 July	1862	D	Pte	3 Jan	1863	discharged for disability
Allen, Henry	18	14 Aug	1862	H	Pte	1 July	1863	deserted
Allen, Morgan L.	34	16 Aug	1862	G	Pte	7 July	1863	deserted
Allen, William H.	21	30 July	1862	C	Pte	25 Jan	1864	discharged for disability
Amidon, George	18	11 Aug	1862	D	Pte	23 June	1865	wounded at Cold Harbor
Amidon, Henry F.	24	12 Aug	1862	D	Corp	23 June	1865	
Amidon, Jr., Lewis	22	27 July	1862	D	Sgt	23 June	1865	wounded at Cold Harbor
Amidon, William H.	22	11 Aug	1862	D	Pte	23 June	1865	wounded at Wilderness
Anderson, William J.	24	28 July	1862	B	Sgt	23 June	1865	wounded at Cold Harbor
Annable, Dwight	19	15 Aug	1862	D	Pte	15 Dec	1863	transferred to 1st Ind. Battery
Anthony, George H.	29	13 Aug	1862	F	Pte	30 Dec	1862	
Ashfield, William	21	6 Aug	1862	E	Pte	27 June	1865	wounded at Gettysburg, transferred to V.R.C.

[a] The rank entered in Column 3 denotes the highest rank achieved by that individual during his term of enlistment.
[b] Veteran Reserve Corps.

Name	Age on Enlistment	Enlisted		Company	Rank	Discharged/ Died		Remarks
Atkins, William J.	18	14 Aug	1862	F	Pte	6 Feb	1863	
Auborn, William	21	1 Aug	1862	B	Pte	19 Oct	1864	killed at Cedar Creek
Austin, Oscar	20	6 Aug	1862	D	Sgt	26 Feb	1865	captured at Wilderness
Austin, Porter	22	2 Aug	1862	H	Pte	19 Oct	1863	died of typhoid
Axten, George	22	26 July	1862	F	Pte	3 April	1863	died of dropsy
Babcock, Henry F.	18	5 Aug	1862	I	Corp	23 March	1864	transferred to V.R.C.
Babcock, William R.	24	15 Aug	1862	K	Sgt	1 July	1863	deserted
Bailey, Jonah	37	14 Aug	1862	C	Corp	23 June	1865	
Baker, Edward V.	21	12 Aug	1862	F	Sgt	23 June	1865	wounded at Cold Harbor
Baker, Elijah	18	1 Sept	1864	F	Pte	23 June	1865	
Baker, Thomas	17	26 Feb	1864	B	Pte	23 June	1865	
Ball, Anthony	22	16 Aug	1862	K	Pte	23 June	1865	
Banning, Lewis	21	31 July	1862	A	Corp	12 Oct	1864	died of wounds
Barker, Loran W.	29	12 Aug	1862	D	Pte	4 Oct	1862	deserted
Barker, Theodore P.	21	12 Aug	1862	D	Pte	4 Oct	1862	deserted
Barnard, David	19	13 Aug	1862	G	Pte	30 Sept	1864	transferred to V.R.C.
Barnes, Henry	22	11 Aug	1862	H	Pte	23 June	1865	captured—6 May 1864, paroled 13 Dec 1864
Barnes, Oscar A.	19	6 Aug	1862	C	Pte	23 June	1865	
Barnett, George A.	18	29 July	1862	F	Pte	26 July	1865	wounded 2 April 1865
Barney, Edwin S.	25	25 July	1862	I	Sgt	23 June	1865	wounded 1 June 1864
Barrow, William C.	19	2 Aug	1862	D	Pte	27 June	1865	wounded 1 June 1864
Bartlett, John	27	6 Aug	1862	D	Corp	15 June	1865	
Bateman, William	18	7 Aug	1862	G	Pte	23 June	1865	wounded 1 June 1864
Bates, George C.	18	12 Aug	1862	K	Pte	23 June	1865	
Baxter, Charles	18	7 Aug	1862	E	Corp	23 June	1865	
Beach, Alan J.	20	16 Aug	1862	G	Pte	24 March	1863	
Beach, Andrew W.	34	14 Aug	1862	F	Corp	23 June	1865	
Beaden, Richard H.	18	1 Aug	1862	K	Pte	23 June	1865	
Behan, John	44	5 Aug	1862	C	Pte	14 Sept	1862	deserted
Behan, William	23	15 Aug	1862	H	Pte	23 June	1865	wounded 1 June 1864
Bell, Charles H.	23	13 Aug	1862	G	Pte	1 July	1863	deserted

Name	Age on Enlistment	Enlisted		Company	Rank	Discharged/ Died		Remarks
Bell, Elijah P.	36	12 Aug	1862	G	Pte	18 July	1863	discharged for disability
Bell, James	25	9 Aug	1862	I	Pte	23 June	1865	wounded 7 Nov 1863
Bell, John	20	9 Aug	1862	G	Corp	28 Sept	1863	discharged for disability
Bellinger, Charles J.	18	30 July	1862	C	Pte	28 Oct	1862	deserted
Bennett, Elias	44	29 July	1862	F	Pte	24 Aug	1864	died of disease
Bennett, Ethan A.	19	14 Aug	1862	B	Corp	23 June	1865	wounded 1 June 1864
Bennett, Joseph G.	37	5 Aug	1862	F	Pte	4 July	1865	transferred to V.R.C.
Bentley, Garner	30	4 Aug	1862	E	Pte	3 July	1865	transferred to V.R.C.
Bentley, John	38	4 Aug	1862	A	Pte	12 July	1864	killed at Fort Stevens
Benton, Silas W.	18	7 Aug	1862	F	Corp	23 June	1865	
Bertrans, Pierre	22	9 Aug	1862	I	Pte	31 Aug	1862	deserted
Bessy, Joseph	42	29 July	1862	F	Pte	6 Feb	1863	discharged for disability
Bessy, Warren	39	29 July	1862	F	Pte	17 Dec	1862	died of disease
Bethel, Prince E.	20	28 July	1862	B	Pte	28 June	1863	deserted
Bettinger, George W.	21	30 July	1862	C	Pte	23 June	1865	
Billings, Lucius H.	22	13 Aug	1862	I	Sgt	6 May	1864	killed at Wilderness
Bingham, B. F.	19	2 Aug	1862	H	Sgt	23 June	1865	wounded, Winchester and Petersburg
Bingham, Jonathan J.	24	12 Aug	1862	B	Pte	23 June	1865	wounded at Wilderness 6 May 1864
Bisbow, Charles	21	31 July	1862	K	Pte	20 April	1865	AWOL
Bishop, William A.	26	4 Aug	1862	A	Pte	11 Dec	1863	discharged for disability
Black, James	27	15 Aug	1862	F	Sgt	23 June	1865	wounded at Wilderness 6 May 1864
Blair, Albert G.	18	23 July	1862	K	Pte	13 May	1863	transferred to adj. gen.'s office
Blake, Judson	35	8 Aug	1862	I	Corp	23 June	1865	
Blake, Stephen	20	9 Aug	1862	B	Pte	16 July	1863	died of wounds
Blakeman, Peter V.	22	5 Aug	1862	A	Pte	25 May	1863	discharged for disability
Blakeslee, George H.	28	6 Aug	1862	K	Pte	13 April	1864	deserted at Sandusky
Blanch, John	22	25 Jan	1865	A	Pte	31 Aug	1865	wounded 2 April 1865
Blanchard, Clark	44	6 Aug	1862	F	Pte	20 Dec	1862	
Blossom, Peter A.	28	14 Aug	1862	G	2/Lt	3 Dec	1862	
Booth, Elliot L.	39	12 Aug	1862	D	Sgt	12 July	1863	deserted
Boucher, Charles	18	2 Aug	1862	E	Pte	23 June	1865	
Boucher, George	18	9 Aug	1862	L	Pte	3 July	1863	deserted

Name	Age on Enlistment	Enlisted		Company	Rank	Discharged/ Died		Remarks
Bouttelle, Edward H.	18	12 Aug	1862	H	Corp	23 June	1865	
Bow, Florintine	25	4 Aug	1862	I	Pte	3 Sept	1862	deserted
Bowen, George W.	29	26 July	1862	C	Sgt	28 Oct	1862	left sick at Berlin, Md.
Bowen, James H.	21	6 Aug	1862	B	Pte	29 June	1863	deserted, Poolesville
Bowley, Daniel	23	7 Aug	1862	B	Pte	15 May	1865	discharged for disability
Bowman, Darius	26	2 Aug	1862	H	Pte	23 June	1865	
Bowman, John H.	19	31 July	1862	I	Corp	18 May	1863	discharged for disability
Bouce, Lyman B.	34	8 Aug	1862	I	Pte	29 Jan	1863	deserted at Falmouth
Bradley, Josiah	32	11 Aug	1862	B	Pte	13 Feb	1863	deserted at Falmouth
Brady, Patrick	24	1 Feb	1865	A	Pte	23 June	1865	
Brand, Henry C.	18	7 Aug	1862	B	Pte	23 June	1865	
Brand, Jacob	35	15 Aug	1862	E	1/Lt	1 Feb	1864	
Brand, Yates R.	29	9 Aug	1862	H	Corp	23 June	1865	
Breed, Benjamin L.	21	6 Aug	1862	G	Pte	1 June	1864	killed at Cold Harbor
Breese, Robert	18	4 Aug	1862	C	Sgt	23 June	1865	
Breese, William	38	4 Aug	1862	C	Pte	3 April	1865	discharged for disability
Brintnall, Charles	27	1 Aug	1862	I	Pte	1 Sept	1862	deserted
Britton, Hiram A.	35	12 Aug	1862	I	1/Lt	23 June	1865	
Brooks, Charles	19	9 Aug	1862	C	Pte	30 Nov	1862	died of fever
Brooks, Norman D.	19	13 Aug	1862	I	Pte	23 June	1865	wounded at Wilderness
Broom, David	20	6 Aug	1862	F	Pte	11 March	1864	died of disease
Brott, Peter	32	6 Aug	1862	B	Pte	15 July	1865	wounded at Rappahannock Station
Brower, Jobey M.	39	6 Aug	1862	A	Major	19 Oct	1864	killed at Cedar Creek
Brown, Addison	22	5 Aug	1862	A	Pte	7 April	1863	discharged for disability
Brown, Charles L.	20	8 Aug	1862	D	Pte	1 June	1864	killed at Cold Harbor
Brown, Edmund	32	6 Aug	1862	F	Pte	9 May	1863	deserted near Falmouth, Va.
Brown, James S.	21	9 Aug	1862	F	Pte	8 Oct	1863	deserted
Brown, John A.	31	9 Aug	1862	H	Pte	23 June	1865	
Brown, Joseph	21	2 Aug	1862	H	Pte	23 June	1865	
Brown, Samuel	21	5 Aug	1862	D	Pte	23 June	1865	
Brownell, Jonathan J.	28	9 Aug	1862	B	Pte	31 May	1865	discharged for disability
Brunt, Henry	21	14 Aug	1862	I	Pte	22 Sept	1862	deserted

Name	Age on Enlistment	Enlisted	Company	Rank	Discharged/ Died	Remarks
Buck, Nathan	26	25 July 1862	A	Sgt	23 June 1965	wounded at Winchester, Sept 1864
Buckley, William	27	15 March 1864	D	Pte	13 Oct 1864	died P.O.W. at Andersonville
Bugat, John	35	28 July 1862	K	Pte	23 June 1865	captured at Wilderness, paroled
Burdick, Edward	32	22 March 1864	D	Pte	27 July 1864	deserted
Burlington, Benjamin	20	26 July 1862	F	Corp	23 June 1865	
Burlington, James W.	23	1 Aug 1862	F	Sgt	18 March 1865	discharged for disability
Burns, Thomas	40	11 Aug 1862	E	Pte	23 June 1865	
Burns, William	40	7 Aug 1862	C	Pte	25 March 1863	discharged for disability
Burton, James	37	15 Aug 1862	F	1/Lt	19 Sept 1863	discharged for disability
Bush, Henry	21	26 July 1862	K	Pte	30 Dec 1862	
Butler, James	21	8 Aug 1862	D	Corp	absent at muster out	wounded at Fisher's Hill
Butterfield, Hiram	25	31 July 1862	G	Pte	7 July 1863	deserted
Button, Simeon S.	44	29 July 1862	K	Pte	13 April 1864	wounded at Gettysburg
Buxton, William L.	21	5 Aug 1862	F	Pte	28 Aug 1865	wounded at Spotsylvania
Buzzell, Ruel P.	18	30 July 1862	C, K	1/Lt	23 June 1865	wounded at Fort Stevens
Cady, Augustus	24	4 Aug 1862	A	Pte	26 Aug 1865	died in hospital at Washington, D.C.
Cain, John	21	7 Aug 1862	K	Pte	10 July 1863	died of wounds at Gettysburg
Callaghan, John	20	29 July 1862	I	Pte	20 Dec 1862	deserted at Berlin, Md.
Callaghan, John L.	21	19 Jan 1865	H	Pte	23 June 1865	
Cameron, Joseph E.	—	28 Aug 1862	C	1/Lt	3 Dec 1862	
Campbell, David R.	36	6 Sept 1864	E	Pte	23 June 1865	
Cane, Michael	20	17 Jan 1865	B	Pte	absent at muster out	wounded at Petersburg
Cardell, William R.	22	28 July 1862	A	Pte	23 June 1865	
Carlin, Michael	40	11 Aug 1862	D	Pte	23 June 1865	
Carlisle, Charles F.	18	28 July 1862	B	Pte	15 May 1865	wounded at Wilderness, discharged for disability
Carpenter, William H.	22	14 Aug 1862	I	Pte	28 Aug 1862	deserted
Carr, Joshua	30	12 Aug 1862	D	Pte	28 Sept 1862	deserted
Carrier, Samuel B.	23	13 Aug 1862	F	Pte	6 Nov 1862	deserted
Carrington, Samuel P.	32	23 July 1862	A, D	Capt	23 June 1865	wounded at Cold Harbor

Name	Age on Enlistment	Enlisted		Company	Rank	Discharged/ Died		Remarks
Carroll, Charles A.	27	25 July	1862	A	Musician	23 June	1865	
Carson, Randall	25	6 Aug	1862	C	Corp	14 March	1863	
Cary, Samuel	42	1 Aug	1862	K	Pte	23 June	1865	
Case, Sidney	28	13 Aug	1862	D	Pte	3 July	1865	transferred to V.R.C.
Casey, Daniel	18	7 Aug	1862	G	Corp	3 July	1863	killed at Gettysburg
Casler, Andrew	27	12 Aug	1862	C	Corp	23 June	1865	
Casler, George H.	21	15 Aug	1862	H	2/Lt	23 June	1865	captured at Wilderness
Casson, John	25	7 Aug	1862	K	Pte	1 July	1863	deserted
Cates, Charles B.	39	4 Aug	1862	D	Pte	23 Jan	1862	discharged for disability
Caughlin, Michael	18	30 July	1862	A	Pte	23 June	1865	wounded at Petersburg
Chamberlain, Webster R.	29	14 Aug	1862	B	Capt	24 Feb	1863	
Chandler, George B.	20	30 July	1862	C	Pte	23 June	1863	
Chandler, Harvey P. B.	18	22 Feb	1864	C	Pte	12 July	1864	killed at Fort Stevens
Chapman, George	24	13 Aug	1862	H	Corp	22 May	1865	wounded at Wilderness–Cedar Creek
Chapman, Harrison C.	20	28 July	1862	F	Pte	27 July	1865	transferred to V.R.C.
Chapman, Harvey	23	15 Aug	1862	H	Pte	24 June	1863	deserted
Chapman, Thomas D.	18	1 Aug	1862	C	Corp	3 July	1865	transferred to V.R.C.
Chappel, Henry	22	2 Aug	1862	H	Sgt	23 June	1865	captured at Wilderness
Chase, Amasa	44	30 July	1862	C	1/Lt	23 June	1865	
Chase, George W.	18	30 July	1862	C	Pte	absent at muster out		wounded at Wilderness
Cherry, Theron	24	2 Aug	1862	H	Corp	23 Dec	1862	
Chittenden, George	29	14 Aug	1862	G	Pte	23 June	1865	
Chrisler, Philip L.	28	9 Aug	1862	F	Pte	30 May	1865	wounded at Wilderness
Christian, Wright	21	11 July	1862	F	Pte	23 June	1865	
Chrysler, David	19	14 Aug	1862	D	Pte	23 June	1865	
Church, Morris H.	32	16 Aug	1862	I, B	Capt	4 Jan	1864	wounded at Fredericksburg
Clapp, Alonzo	32	6 Aug	1862	A, K	Major	23 June	1865	died in hospital
Clark, Charles	22	4 June	1862	I, G	Capt	23 June	1865	
Clark, David W.	33	5 Aug	1862	C	Corp	23 June	1865	
Clark, Jerome H.	21	24 July	1862	E	Sgt	23 June	1865	
Clark, Joseph	32	4 Aug	1862	K	Corp	31 Oct	1862	transferred to U.S. Infantry

Name	Age on Enlistment	Enlisted		Company	Rank	Discharged/ Died		Remarks
Clement, Alexander	26	9 Aug	1862	G	Pte	18 Jan	1863	deserted
Clements, Ephrain	19	13 Aug	1862	F	Pte	1 Dec	1862	discharged for disability
Clements, Henry	44	13 Aug	1862	G	Pte	– June	1865	transferred to V.R.C.
Clute, Alonzo	22	11 Aug	1862	G	Pte	6 Nov	1863	
Coburn, Charles	20	19 Feb	1864	E	Pte	– Sept	1864	died as prisoner at Andersonville
Coburn, Henry	35	11 Aug	1862	E	Pte	23 June	1865	
Colahan, Francis	23	15 Aug	1862	H, K	Capt	15 May	1865	
Colburn, George W.	24	5 Aug	1862	D	Pte	29 June	1865	transferred to V.R.C.
Colburn, Isaac	28	3 Aug	1862	D	Corp	23 June	1865	
Cole, Ezra	19	28 July	1862	B	Pte	16 Sept	1863	deserted
Cole, Hiram	18	15 Aug	1862	I	Pte	1 June	1864	killed at Cold Harbor
Colegrove, Warren	38	1 Aug	1862	C	Pte	22 Jan	1864	died in hospital, Sandusky, Ohio
Colihan, Patrick	19	1 March	1865	K	Pte	25 March	1861	killed at Petersburg
Collins, Eugene	27	27 Jan	1865	A	Pte	23 June	1865	
Colony, Carnegy H.	33	8 Aug	1862	G	Pte	18 Jan	1863	deserted
Conger, George H.	19	8 Aug	1862	G	Pte	17 Dec	1862	died of typhoid
Connor, John F.	21	11 Aug	1862	F	Sgt	17 May	1865	wounded at Petersburg, discharged for disability
Conway, John J.	35	11 Aug	1862	B	Pte	28 Nov	1863	deserted
Conway, John W.	27	5 Aug	1862	B	Pte	3 Feb	1863	discharged for disability
Cooney, Michael	36	4 Aug	1862	B	Pte	8 Nov	1863	wounded at Rappahannock Station, died of wounds
Coons, Joseph	27	25 July	1862	D	Corp	23 June	1865	wounded at Wilderness
Coover, William	40	2 Aug	1862	A	Pte	23 Feb	1863	discharged for disability
Corbett, John	24	20 April	1864	E	Pte	13 June	1865	deserted
Corbin, Charles H.	28	9 Aug	1862	G	Pte	21 Sept	1862	deserted
Cornue, Dan	35	28 March	1864	D	Pte	10 June	1865	discharged for disability
Cornue, John S.	36	3 Dec	1862	—	Q/M	23 June	1865	
Cossitt, Davis	36	14 Aug	1864	D	Capt	15 Dec	1864	wounded at Fort Stevens, discharged for disability
Cox, Edward	44	11 Aug	1862	H	Pte	23 June	1865	
Cox, Lyman	18	3 Sept	1864	H	Pte	23 June	1865	

Name	Age on Enlistment	Enlisted		Company	Rank	Discharged/ Died		Remarks
Crain, Charles H.	19	7 Aug	1862	C	Pte	1 July	1863	transferred to V.R.C.
Crampton, James	28	11 Aug	1862	B	Pte	23 June	1865	wounded and captured at Wilderness
Crampton, Thomas	29	12 Aug	1862	B	Sgt	23 June	1865	
Craver, George W.	37	15 Aug	1862	K	Pte	15 Feb	1864	wounded at Gettysburg—transferred to V.R.C.
Criss, Andrew	32	11 Aug	1862	B	Pte	23 June	1865	
Crittenden, Joseph	22	7 Aug	1862	D	Pte	23 June	1865	
Crozier, James	21	12 Aug	1862	G	Pte	25 April	1865	deserted
Chrysler, Alfred	21	30 July	1862	D	Sgt	1 March	1863	discharged for disability
Chrysler, Cornell	32	28 Aug	1862	D	Capt	24 Feb	1863	
Cummings, Dennis	21	6 Aug	1862	C	Corp	23 June	1863	
Cummins, George	27	4 Aug	1862	F	Pte	13 Jan	1863	died of typhoid
Cummins, Nicholas	29	25 July	1862	D	Pte	15 Nov	1863	transferred to V.R.C.
Cutliffe, Samuel D.	19	15 July	1862	B	Sgt	23 June	1865	wounded at Cold Harbor
Dakin, Timothy J.	45	7 Aug	1862	I	Pte	22 Feb	1863	discharged for disability
Dallman, Thomas C.	19	14 Aug	1862	I	Sgt	13 May	1865	wounded at Fort Stevens, discharged for disability
Daniels, Austin E.	29	6 Aug	1862	I	Principal Musician	23 June	1865	
Daniels, Stephen W.	26	31 July	1862	E	Pte	23 June	1865	
Darling, Charles H.	21	6 Aug	1862	K	Pte	absent at muster out		wounded at Spotsylvania Court House
Darling, Enos Orin	27	7 Aug	1862	D	Pte	20 Oct	1862	deserted
Davey, Irving W.	20	26 July	1862	F	Sgt	23 June	1865	wounded at Cold Harbor
Davidson, James	18	3 Aug	1862	K	Sgt	23 June	1865	
Davis, Abit	24	12 Aug	1862	B	Pte	11 Feb	1863	died of typhoid
Davis, John C.	32	19 Aug	1862	K	Pte	18 Sept	1862	deserted
Davis, Joshua R.	—	28 Aug	1862	—	Major	15 Jan	1864	wounded at Gettysburg—discharged for disability
Davis, Parker	18	9 Jan	1865	B	Pte	23 June	1865	
Davis, Porter	22	13 Aug	1862	F	Pte	23 June	1865	

Name	Age on Enlistment	Enlisted		Company	Rank	Discharged/ Died		Remarks
Davis, R. Brower	21	11 Aug	1862	G	Sgt	6 June	1865	
Davis, Von Buren	24	12 Aug	1862	D	Sgt	3 July	1865	transferred to V.R.C.
Day, Henry W.	24	2 Aug	1862	K	Pte	31 Oct	1862	deserted
Day, Leander E.	18	12 Aug	1862	I	Corp	1 June	1864	killed at Cold Harbor
Day, Luman	23	27 July	1862	D	Corp	20 April	1864	died
Dean, Charles	18	27 July	1862	I	Pte	23 June	1865	
Dean, W. Addison	31	1 Aug	1862	A	Wagoner	5 Sept	1863	wounded at Marye's Heights, discharged for disability
Deindl, Johann	36	12 Aug	1862	I	Pte	1 Nov	1864	died of scurvy at Andersonville
De Long, Charles	23	26 July	1862	K	Pte	31 Oct	1862	deserted
Denicke, Valentine	38	14 Aug	1862	D	Pte	25 June	1864	wounded at Wilderness—died of wounds
Devlin, William	28	27 Jan	1865	E	Pte	23 June	1865	
Devoe, George H.	19	7 Aug	1862	I	2/Lt	23 June	1865	
Dickey, Albert	18	30 July	1862	A	Pte	23 June	1865	
Dillingham, Darius	21	13 Aug	1862	I	Principal Musician	4 Nov	1864	discharged for disability
Dillingham, Lucius	25	16 Aug	1862	I, A	Capt	23 June	1865	transferred to U.S. Signal Corps
Donaldson, David	29	12 Aug	1862	E	Sgt	6 May	1864	killed at Wilderness
Donnelly, Thomas	17	2 May	1864	E	Pte	1 July	1865	wounded at Cedar Creek
Donoghue, Robert	25	7 Aug	1862	G	Sgt	6 May	1864	killed at Wilderness
Donovan, Michael	20	5 Aug	1862	A, D	2/Lt	23 June	1865	
Donovan, Timothy	27	9 Aug	1862	H	Pte	23 June	1865	
Doran, James	38	16 Aug	1862	E	Pte	30 June	1863	deserted
Doty, John	35	16 Aug	1862	G	Sgt	23 June	1865	
Douglas, Alanson	18	30 July	1862	A	Pte	23 June	1865	
Dow, Lyman W.	21	13 Aug	1862	H	Pte	1 July	1863	deserted
Dow, Merrill P.	24	15 Aug	1862	H	Pte	20 Sept	1864	died at Andersonville
Dow, Philetus	35	12 Aug	1862	H	Pte	23 June	1865	
Downer, Benjamin	18	25 July	1862	A	Pte	4 Feb	1863	discharged in hospital
Drake, Philip	21	15 Aug	1862	G	Corp	23 June	1865	
Drury, Stephen	21	6 Aug	1862	D	Pte	15 Sept	1862	deserted

Name	Age on Enlistment	Enlisted		Company	Rank	Discharged/ Died		Remarks
Dunham, Simeon	36	14 Aug	1862	F	Pte	25 Jan	1863	deserted
Dunn, Joseph	18	11 Aug	1862	E	Pte	20 May	1865	wounded at Wilderness and Petersburg, discharged for disability
Dunning, Charles L.	27	8 Aug	1862	A	Pte	23 Oct	1863	discharged for disability
Dunning, Czar	18	8 Aug	1862	G	Sgt	2 Feb	1863	
Dunton, Charles L.	21	13 Aug	1862	F	Pte	25 Jan	1863	deserted
Durrant, Charles E.	25	2 Aug	1862	H	Pte	23 June	1865	wounded at Cold Harbor
Durst, Nicholas	22	15 Aug	1862	I	Pte	2 Nov	1862	died of typhoid
Dutcher, Philo	40	5 Aug	1862	C	Pte	23 June	1865	
Dwight, Augustus W.	35	8 July	1862	E	Col	25 March 1865		wounded at Cedar Creek, killed at Petersburg
Dwight, Granville S.	18	15 Aug	1862	I	Pte	28 June	1865	transferred to V.R.C.
Dwight, John M.	24	16 Aug	1862	I	Capt	17 Sept	1864	wounded at Wilderness—discharged for disability
Dwyer, Thomas	21	12 Aug	1862	K	Pte	1 July	1863	deserted
Ealden, Robert	18	8 Aug	1862	I	2/Lt	23 June	1865	
Ealden, William	20	8 Aug	1862	I	Pte	absent at muster out		
Earll, Daniel F.	27	5 Aug	1862	K	Pte	20 April 1864		deserted
Easton, Isaac	44	11 Aug	1862	F	Pte	23 Feb	1863	
Eaton, Alonzo	18	12 Aug	1862	D	Pte	absent at muster out		
Eaton, Charles A.	25	1 Aug	1862	C	2/Lt	19 June	1865	
Eaton, Demster	21	11 Aug	1862	B	Pte	6 Feb	1863	discharged for disability
Eaton, Frank A.	18	11 Aug	1862	C	Sgt	23 June	1865	
Eberling, Jacob	44	18 Aug	1862	E	Pte	13 Nov	1863	transferred to V.R.C.
Edds, Thomas	20	26 July	1862	F	Pte	17 May	1865	wounded at Wilderness—discharged for disability
Edwards, DeWitt C.	40	12 Aug	1862	B	Pte	16 Dec	1862	discharged for disability
Edwards, George	30	7 Aug	1862	K	Pte	15 March 1864		transferred to V.R.C.
Eggleston, Charles	21	1 Sept	1864	F	Pte	23 June	1865	

Name	Age on Enlistment	Enlisted	Company	Rank	Discharged/ Died	Remarks
Eggleston, John H.	21	7 Aug 1862	E	Pte	22 May 1865	wounded at Wilderness—discharged for disability
Elder, William	29	5 Aug 1862	A	Pte	11 May 1863	died of disease
Elderkin, Henry S.	19	9 Aug 1862	H	Pte	absent at muster out	
Eldridge, Charles H.	21	28 July 1862	E	2/Lt	23 June 1865	
Elliot, James G.	18	29 July 1862	A	Corp	9 Nov 1863	wounded at Rappahannock Station, died of wounds
Ellis, Van Buren	20	7 Aug 1862	D	Pte	4 Feb 1863	died
Ells, Emmons C.	18	4 Aug 1862	A	Musician	23 June 1865	captured 13 June 1863
Ellsworth, Benjamin	35	11 Aug 1862	D	Pte	23 June 1865	
Elson, George	23	8 Aug 1862	K	Corp	23 June 1865	
Emerick, Richard	25	4 Aug 1862	A	Corp	16 June 1863	wounded at Petersburg
English, Domnick	22	15 Aug 1862	H	Sgt	23 June 1863	
English, Lucius D.	24	8 Aug 1862	G	Corp	22 Dec 1862	discharged for disability
Eno, Drayton	27	14 Aug 1862	G	1/Lt	3 Dec 1862	
Enos, Charles H.	18	8 Aug 1862	D	Musician	23 June 1865	
Esinger, Joseph	44	6 Aug 1862	D	Pte	absent at muster out	
Evans, Milton B.	21	24 July 1862	B	Pte	6 Nov 1862	deserted
Evens, Washington L.	23	15 Aug 1862	G	Pte	1 July 1863	deserted
Evingham, Charles	21	13 Aug 1862	C	Pte	30 Sept 1863	deserted
Evingham, John	21	12 Aug 1862	C	Pte	5 Dec 1863	transferred to First Independent Battery
Fabings, Joseph S.	21	5 Aug 1862	B	Pte	23 June 1865	
Fagan, Edward	22	13 Jan 1865	B	Pte	23 June 1865	
Failing, Josiah	19	2 Aug 1862	A	Pte	absent at muster out	wounded at Wilderness
Farifield, William	34	12 Aug 1862	B	Wagoner	23 June 1865	
Fanning, Patrick	41	4 Aug 1862	C	Pte	3 July 1863	killed at Gettysburg
Fargo, Azariah	39	7 Aug 1862	C	Pte	5 Dec 1862	died of fever
Farmer, John	44	14 Aug 1862	G	Pte	31 May 1865	

Name	Age on Enlistment	Enlisted		Company	Rank	Discharged/ Died		Remarks
Farmer, William	22	13 Aug	1862	G	Pte	18 Jan	1863	deserted
Farrell, James	19	1 Aug	1862	A	Sgt	23 June	1865	
Fay, Frank	18	4 Aug	1862	A	Pte	23 June	1865	
Fellows, Seath	18	25 July	1862	A	Pte	27 May	1864	wounded and captured at Wilderness, died of wounds as prisoner
Felton, Charles Y.	36	6 Aug	1862	K	Sgt	22 June	1864	died of wounds
Ferrall, Nicholas W.	21	8 Aug	1862	G	Pte	1 July	1863	deserted
Fickus, Frederick	43	25 July	1862	I	Sgt	23 June	1865	
Field, Charles H.	19	11 Aug	1862	D	Corp	23 June	1865	
Finch, Philander	35	18 July	1863	E	Pte	23 June	1865	
Fish, George B.	18	11 Aug	1862	H	Pte	23 May	1865	transferred to V.R.C.
Fisher, George E.	20	31 July	1862	A	2/Lt	23 June	1865	
Fisher, Otis L.	32	13 Aug	1862	F	Sgt	24 June	1863	discharged for disability
Fisk, James	18	15 Aug	1862	I	Pte	23 June	1865	
Fisk, Thomas	35	11 Aug	1862	D	Pte	23 June	1865	
Fisk, William	36	10 Aug	1862	D	Pte	23 June	1865	
Fitzgerald, Dwight	20	11 Aug	1862	D	Pte	4 July	1863	transferred to V.R.C.
Fix, Julius	30	8 Aug	1862	F	Pte	23 June	1865	captured 10 Jan 1865
Fonts, George W.	21	19 March	1864	D	Pte	23 June	1865	
Fountain, David C.	18	23 July	1862	E	Sgt	1 July	1864	transferred to V.R.C.
Fox, Justus	22	8 Aug	1862	K	Pte	23 June	1865	
Fox, Justus H.	44	8 Aug	1862	K	Pte	4 Feb	1863	
Fox, Norman	18	9 Aug	1862	K	Pte	6 Nov	1864	wounded at Winchester—died of wounds
Fradenburgh, Alonzo	19	5 Aug	1862	A	Corp	23 June	1865	wounded at Fort Stevens
Fry, Charles B.	—	30 July	1863	—	Asst/Surg	—		
Fry, Henry	22	6 Aug	1862	F	Pte	20 Feb	1865	captured 10 May 1864—died as prisoner of war
Fuller, Charles D.	21	12 Aug	1862	H	Corp	26 Nov	1862	died at Stafford Court House
Gale, Noah	35	2 Aug	1862	E	Corp	15 Sept	1863	discharged for disability
Gallacher, James	21	30 July	1862	E	Pte	2 April	1865	deserted
Gardner, Thomas	21	28 July	1862	E	Sgt	23 June	1865	

Name	Age on Enlistment	Enlisted	Company	Rank	Discharged/ Died	Remarks
Garlock, Norman	20	9 Aug 1862	K	Pte	2 June 1864	killed at Cold Harbor
Gary, Joseph	42	8 Aug 1862	I	Pte	27 April 1864	discharged for disability
Gaylord, Aaron C.	18	5 Aug 1862	F	Corp	17 July 1864	died of disease
Geaugeau, Napoleon	21	26 July 1862	I	Pte	30 Dec 1862	died of pneumonia
Geissel, John	29	11 Aug 1862	B	Pte	19 Sept 1864	killed near Winchester
Gensiver, Leonard	19	7 Aug 1862	F	Corp	23 June 1865	
Gere, James M.	37	15 Aug 1862	H	Col	23 June 1865	
Ghee, Henry	22	14 Aug 1862	E	Sgt	absent at muster out	wounded at Cedar Creek
Gibson, Herbert	26	29 July 1862	A	Comm/Sgt	23 June 1865	
Gifford, Jason	22	1 Aug 1862	C	Pte	28 Sept 1862	deserted
Gifford, John	18	7 Aug 1862	I	Corp	23 June 1865	
Gilbert, George H.	25	26 July 1862	B	1/Lt	23 May 1864	wounded at Rappahannock Station, discharged for disability
Gilbert, William	18	25 July 1862	E	Sgt	23 June 1865	
Gilfillan, William	26	16 Aug 1862	E	Corp	23 June 1865	
Gilson, George H.	28	3 Aug 1862	E	1/Lt	23 June 1865	wounded at Petersburg
Glass, Seymour H.	29	6 Aug 1862	A	Sgt	19 June 1864	killed at Petersburg
Glass, William G.	38	6 Aug 1862	G	Pte	28 Feb 1863	discharged for disability
Gleason, Eli W.	29	7 Aug 1862	B	Pte	17 June 1863	deserted
Glynn, Edwin F.	20	30 July 1862	F	Pte	23 June 1865	
Goodall, Isaac	30	4 Aug 1862	A	Pte	16 Jan 1863	died of typhoid fever
Goodell, Frank B.	25	12 Aug 1862	K	Corp	26 Jan 1865	wounded and captured at Wilderness —died at Andersonville
Goodfellow, Bates W.	27	12 Aug 1862	H	Pte	3 Jan 1863	
Goodfellow, James	22	7 Aug 1862	C	Sgt	23 June 1865	wounded at Fort Stevens
Goodfellow, Stephen H.	44	30 July 1862	C	Pte	18 May 1865	wounded at Fort Stevens—discharged for disability
Goodfellow, Wesley	19	5 Aug 1862	C	Sgt	23 June 1865	
Goodrich, George S.	28	11 Aug 1862	K	Pte	15 Feb 1864	deserted
Goodrich, William W.	26	23 March 1864	D	Pte	23 June 1865	
Gorham, Miles B.	28	8 Aug 1862	G	Corp	29 June 1865	transferred to V.R.C.

Name	Age on Enlistment	Enlisted		Company	Rank	Discharged/ Died		Remarks
Gorman, James	28	11 Aug	1862	C	Pte	13 May	1865	discharged for disability
Gotches, Guy	21	8 Aug	1862	H, F	1/Lt	26 May	1864	
Graf, Martin	24	28 July	1862	F	Pte	25 Jan	1863	deserted
Graham, Aaron	44	2 Aug	1862	E	Pte	23 June	1865	
Grant, Boswell J.	38	8 Aug	1862	G	Corp	23 June	1865	
Grant, Rufus	—	22 Aug	1863	E	Pte	13 May	1864	discharged for disability
Gratto, Francis	32	15 Aug	1862	I	Pte	23 June	1865	
Graves, Orville T.	18	1 Aug	1862	C	Pte	23 June	1865	wounded at Cold Harbor
Graves, Otis	35	31 March	1864	E	Pte	23 June	1865	
Green, Thomas S.	25	9 Aug	1862	B	Pte	22 Oct	1862	deserted
Griffin, Shipman	18	7 Aug	1862	C	Pte	3 Apr	1863	died in hospital
Griffin, Zeno T.	21	22 July	1862	E	Pte	23 June	1865	wounded at Gettysburg, Petersburg & Wilderness
Grodavent, Joseph	29	14 Aug	1862	D	Pte	23 June	1865	
Groom, Charles	28	9 Aug	1862	G	Pte	25 March	1865	transferred to V.R.C.
Grosbeck, Andrew	21	9 Aug	1862	K	Pte	3 Dec	1862	died of typhoid fever
Guerdot, Joseph	43	11 Aug	1862	I	Pte	2 Oct	1862	deserted
Guernsey, George W.	35	28 July	1862	A	Pte	7 July	1864	deserted
Guernsey, Silas	22	23 July	1862	B	Pte	15 July	1863	deserted
Gurnsey, Willard	22	19 March	1864	D	Pte	23 June	1865	
Gunsalus, Martin D.	40	14 Aug	1862	H	Pte	6 Feb	1863	discharged for disability
Guthrie, Herman W.	25	25 July	1862	G	Pte	25 Aug	1862	deserted
Hackett, Martin	18	13 Aug	1862	K	Sgt	23 June	1865	
Hale, John	19	30 July	1862	C	Pte	23 June	1865	
Hale, Luther D.	30	30 July	1862	C	Pte	22 Sept	1864	killed at Fisher's Hill
Hall, James B.	35	9 Aug	1862	C	Capt	7 Jan	1865	discharged for disability
Hall, Joseph	36	9 Aug	1862	H	Pte	20 July	1863	deserted
Hall, Walter W.	19	5 Aug	1862	B	Pte	3 Feb	1863	discharged for disability
Halsted, Dennison	28	5 Aug	1862	A	Pte	23 June	1865	
Hamilton, Hassel	21	8 Aug	1862	I	Pte	20 March	1863	deserted
Hamilton, John A.	21	15 Aug	1862	C	Pte	18 Jan	1863	deserted
Hamilton, Samuel M.	44	13 Aug	1862	I	Pte			wounded at Cedar Creek, absent at muster out

Name	Age on Enlistment	Enlisted		Company	Rank	Discharged/ Died		Remarks
Hammell, Daniel F.	30	18 July	1862	E	2/Lt	31 May	1865	discharged for disability
Hammond, Calvin S.	42	14 Aug	1862	C	Corp	23 June	1865	
Hammond, George W.	18	7 Aug	1862	D	Pte	22 June	1863	deserted
Hammond, William H.	18	8 Aug	1862	G	Pte	22 March	1865	wounded at Cold Harbor—discharged for disability
Handcock, Armigel	40	6 Aug	1862	D	Hospital Steward	23 June	1865	
Hannon, Patrick	21	17 July	1862	I	Pte	28 April	1863	deserted
Harrington, Daniel	27·	28 July	1862	E	Pte	2 Sept	1862	deserted
Harrington, Horatio	21	10 Aug	1862	D	Pte	19 Oct	1864	killed near Middletown
Harrington, Morris	23	11 Aug	1862	H	Corp	19 Sept	1864	wounded at Gettysburg, killed at Winchester
Harrison, James	30	7 Aug	1862	I	Pte	8 July	1863	deserted
Harrison, John	22	5 Aug	1861	H	Pte	28 Aug	1862	
Harron, Charles W.	20	5 Aug	1862	A	Corp	15 Dec	1862	deserted
Harronn, Hiram F.	32	6 Aug	1862	D	Pte	5 May	1863	
Hart, James G.	32	12 Aug	1862	B	Pte	15 Dec	1862	discharged for disability
Hartnett, John P.	40	14 Aug	1862	B	Pte	27 Jan	1863	discharged for disability
Hassett, John	35	12 Aug	1862	C	Pte	1 Jan	1863	died of typhoid
Hatten, Theodore	24	12 Aug	1862	H	Pte	19 June	1865	accidentally wounded 13 July 1863
Hayes, Horace N.	23	14 Aug	1862	H	Pte	29 Dec	1862	
Haynes, Willson	18	4 Aug	1862	A	Pte	30 March	1864	wounded at Rappahannock Station, discharged for disability
Hazel, William	19	31 July	1862	I	Pte	19 Sept	1864	killed at Winchester
Heath, John	44	30 July	1862	A	Pte	5 April	1864	discharged for disability
Hebard, James P.	28	5 Aug	1862	C	Pte	28 Dec	1863	discharged for disability
Henderson, John	19	9 Aug	1862	G	Pte	6 May	1864	believed killed at Wilderness
Henry, Charles H.	21	4 Aug	1862	B	Pte	10 Sept	1862	deserted
Henry, Chryst	19	4 Aug	1862	B	Pte	18 Feb	1865	wounded at Winchester—discharged for disability
Herrick, William H.	19	5 Aug	1862	B	Pte	15 May	1865	discharged in 1863 but reenlisted, wounded before Petersburg

Name	Age on Enlistment	Enlisted	Company	Rank	Discharged/ Died	Remarks
Herrington, Jenks	44	13 Aug 1862	F	Pte	4 Oct 1862	deserted
Hewes, Oscar P.	19	26 July 1862	B	Pte	23 June 1865	
Hewes, Rufus A.	22	28 July 1862	B	Musician	23 June 1865	captured 13 June 1863—paroled
Hewitt, William	18	2 Aug 1862	H	Pte	5 May 1863	wounded at Fredericksburg—died of wounds
Hickcox, Charles	28	1 Aug 1862	E	Corp	23 June 1865	wounded at Gettysburg and Charlestown
Hicker, George	18	4 Aug 1862	A	Pte	5 April 1863	discharged for disability
Hickey, Peter	22	31 Jan 1865	E	Pte	23 June 1865	
Hilron, Henry	19	25 July 1862	A	Corp	23 June 1865	
Hilts, Charles L.	18	2 Aug 1862	C	Pte	19 Sept 1864	killed at Winchester
Hilts, Christian	36	6 Aug 1862	C	Pte	28 Oct 1862	deserted
Hilts, Hiram G.	27	8 Aug 1862	C	Sgt	3 July 1863	killed at Gettysburg
Hines, Orin W.	21	7 Aug 1862	K	Corp	23 June 1865	wounded at Wilderness
Hingle, Henry	30	23 March 1864	D	Pte	10 April 1864	deserted
Hinkley, George H.	27	30 July 1862	F	Pte	absent at muster out	
Hinman, Myron	18	14 Aug 1862	F	Pte	20 May 1863	discharged for disability
Hitchcock, Albert D.	27	29 July 1862	F	Pte	4 Jan 1863	deserted
Hoag, Harlem	27	4 Aug 1862	C	Pte	13 April 1863	transferred to Fifteenth Cavalry
Hoatland, Robert	33	5 Aug 1862	B	Pte	23 June 1865	
Hodge, Austin	27	9 Aug 1862	E	Pte	15 March 1864	wounded at Fredericksburg— transferred to V.R.C.
Hodges, Thomas	32	8 Aug 1862	D	Pte	5 July 1863	died of black vomit
Hogeboom, David L.	23	7 Aug 1862	E	Pte	12 July 1864	killed at Fort Stevens
Holcomb, Luther	21	13 Aug 1862	K	Corp	31 May 1865	discharged for disability
Holenbeck, Joseph	33	13 Aug 1862	B	Pte	6 Sept 1862	deserted
Holkings, James H.	19	13 Aug 1862	B	Corp	23 June 1865	
Hollenbeck, Mathias	25	30 July 1862	E	Pte	absent at muster out	
Hollenbeck, William H.	23	15 Aug 1862	I	Pte	23 June 1865	
Holman, Charles H.	36	11 Aug 1862	G	Pte	6 May 1864	killed at Wilderness

Name	Age on Enlistment	Enlisted		Company	Rank	Discharged/ Died		Remarks
Hotaling, Deloss	26	9 Aug	1862	C	Pte	23 June	1865	
Hotaling, Stephen	27	30 July	1862	A	Pte	23 June	1865	
Houghkirk, Benjamin	18	13 Aug	1862	E	Pte	16 March	1864	wounded at Fredericksburg— discharged for disability
Houghtaling, Charles	21	10 Aug	1862	C	Pte	28 Oct	1862	deserted
Houghtaling, Henry B.	29	13 Aug	1862	E	Pte	—		transferred to V.R.C.
Houghtaling, Jackson	36	19 Aug	1862	E	Pte	30 Sept	1862	deserted
Houser, Alfred	23	6 Aug	1862	C	Pte	—		wounded at Cold Harbor—died of wounds n.d.
Houser, George H.	18	5 Aug	1862	D	Pte	23 June	1865	
Houser, Jacob	28	4 Aug	1862	C	Pte	—		captured at Wilderness—paroled
Howard, George W.	21	2 Aug	1862	A	Pte	23 June	1865	wounded at Spotsylvania Court House
Howard, Isaac H.	19	9 Aug	1862	I	Corp	23 June	1865	wounded at Wilderness—captured 14 May 1864, paroled
Howard, Justin	—	14 Aug	1862	K	1/Lt	3 Oct	1863	
Howe, Jerome	19	26 July	1862	B	Pte	29 May	1865	wounded at Spotsylvania
Howes, Franklin	29	12 Aug	1862	E	Pte	7 Dec	1862	died of disease
Hoxsie, Theodore	31	12 Aug	1862	K	Pte	25 Dec	1862	
Hoyt, Henry H.	24	15 Aug	1862	E	1/Lt	21 June	1864	killed before Petersburg
Hubbard, Abner	23	18 Aug	1862	E	Pte	29 Aug	1865	wounded at Fredericksburg— transferred to V.R.C.
Hubbs, Alexander H.	19	28 July	1862	B	Corp	—		wounded and captured at Wilderness —paroled prisoner at muster out
Hudson, James	36	6 Aug	1862	C	Wagoner	23 June	1865	
Hughes, Augustus	18	30 July	1862	F	Pte	26 March	1863	discharged for disability
Hughes, James	31	20 July	1862	I	Pte	8 Sept	1862	deserted
Hughes, Thomas S.	25	8 Aug	1862	E	Pte	13 May	1865	
Hull, Dwight S.	21	28 July	1862	K	Pte	15 March	1864	wounded at Fredericksburg— discharged for disability
Humphreys, Robert H.	18	4 Aug	1862	F	Pte	3 April	1865	wounded at Cold Harbor—discharged for disability

Name	Age on Enlistment	Enlisted		Company	Rank	Discharged/ Died		Remarks
Hunn, William R.	33	4 Aug	1862	A	Corp	31 March 1865		wounded at Cedar Creek—discharged for disability
Hunt, George	20	5 Aug	1862	D	Pte	15 Sept	1862	deserted
Huntley, William	39	11 Aug	1862	C	Pte	23 June	1865	
Hurd, Asahel	23	28 July	1862	A	Pte	23 June	1865	
Hurdley, Patrick	19	7 Aug	1862	A	Pte	23 June	1865	wounded at Wilderness
Huyck, Isaac	20	4 Aug	1862	A	Pte	11 April	1863	discharged for disability
Hyde, George W.	21	28 July	1862	K	Pte	19 Aug	1863	transferred to Twenty-fourth Cavalry
Ingersoll, William	23	13 Aug	1862	I	Pte	5 July	1863	deserted
Ives, Charles H.	24	12 Aug	1862	D	Pte	31 May	1865	
Ives, Oliver P.	42	11 Aug	1862	E	Corp	23 June	1865	
Jackson, Truman A.	—	18 Aug	1862	E	Pte	18 Nov	1864	captured at Wilderness—died of disease at Andersonville
Jaquin, Charles	26	19 Aug	1862	E	Pte	22 Aug	1862	deserted
Jenks, Walter E.	22	12 Aug	1862	D	Pte	23 June	1865	
Jilson, Harrison H.	39	15 Aug	1862	G	Capt	8 Oct	1862	died of typhoid
Johnson, Henry S.	25	9 Aug	1862	G	Musician	7 July	1863	deserted
Johnson, Nathan	18	20 Aug	1862	K	Pte	13 July	1865	transferred to V.R.C.
Johnson, William R.	39	9 Aug	1862	E	Pte	24 May	1865	wounded at Cold Harbor—discharged for disability
Jones, Andrew H.	20	3 Aug	1862	F	Pte	23 June	1865	
Jones, Daniel	26	9 Aug	1862	B	Pte	1 Oct	1862	deserted
Jones, John	29	9 Aug	1862	H	Pte	1 July	1863	deserted
Jones, John H.	25	31 Jan	1865	E	Pte	23 June	1865	
Jones, John M.	24	5 Aug	1862	A	Corp	25 May	1863	discharged for disability
Jones, Joseph	25	14 Aug	1862	F	Pte	29 May	1864	wounded at Wilderness—died of wounds
Jones, William	21	8 Aug	1862	B	Pte	23 June	1865	
Joyce, Thomas H.	25	10 Aug	1862	D	Corp	23 June	1865	
Jutten, Joseph	22	14 Aug	1862	B	Pte	12 Feb	1863	discharged for disability
Kean, Joseph	20	6 Aug	1862	C	Pte	22 Jan	1863	deserted
Keller, John	21	10 Aug	1862	E	Pte	23 June	1865	

Name	Age on Enlistment	Enlisted		Company	Rank	Discharged/ Died		Remarks
Kelly, Garret	27	6 Aug	1862	K	Pte	1 June	1864	killed at Cold Harbor
Kelly, James	22	22 Aug	1862	K	Pte	11 July	1865	captured and exchanged July 1863, wounded at Spotsylvania, transferred to V.R.C.
Kelly, James	22	1 Feb	1865	A	Pte	4 April	1865	taken sick on march—believed died
Kelly, Patrick	23	14 Aug	1862	B	Pte	7 Nov	1863	killed at Rappahannock Station
Kelly, Thomas	21	15 Aug	1862	G	Pte	23 June	1865	
Kennedy, John	32	2 Aug	1862	C	Pte	12 July	1864	killed at Fort Stevens
Kennedy, Robert E.	29	3 Aug	1862	E	Pte	2 Sept	1862	deserted
Kennett, William C.	22	7 Aug	1862	B	Pte	23 June	1865	
Kent, Noah B.	30	19 Aug	1862	K	Capt	2 Oct	1863	
Kenyon, George B.	19	9 Aug	1862	F	Pte	2 Nov	1862	deserted
Keohnlein, Christian J.	20	7 Aug	1862	E	Pte	23 June	1865	
Kille, John	23	12 Aug	1862	H	Corp	23 June	1865	
Kily, Patrick	36	12 Aug	1862	I	Pte	3 April	1865	wounded at Cold Harbor—discharged for disability
Kincele, Patrick	24	12 Aug	1862	D	Pte	23 June	1865	wounded at Wilderness
Kine, Anthony	33	13 Aug	1862	F	Pte	—		wounded at Wilderness—died of wounds
King, Alexander	21	15 Aug	1862	K	Pte	19 Feb	1863	died of typhoid fever
Kinney, Morris	18	17 July	1862	I	Pte	29 Dec	1862	died of typhoid fever
Kinyon, Charles	42	7 Aug	1862	K	Pte	9 Feb	1865	discharged for disability
Kittler, John	21	8 Aug	1862	G	Pte	23 June	1865	
Kittler, William S.	25	8 Aug	1862	G	Sgt	23 June	1865	
Klaucke, Alexander A.	24	6 Aug	1862	E	Sgt/Maj	31 March	1864	
Knapp, David	18	12 Aug	1862	C	Pte	14 April	1863	
Knapp, Edwin A.	39	19 Aug	1862	—	Asst/Surg	23 June	1865	
Knapp, Melvin J.	28	2 Aug	1862	H	Corp	23 June	1865	
Knight, Horatio	21	4 Aug	1862	B	Corp	23 June	1865	captured at Wilderness—paroled
Knox, Andrew A.	18	3 Aug	1862	K	Pte	27 June	1865	transferred to V.R.C.
Kochenburger, Henry	27	30 July	1862	F	Corp	29 Dec	1862	
Koenig, August	24	19 Aug.	1862	K	Pte	1 July	1863	deserted

Name	Age on Enlistment	Enlisted		Company	Rank	Discharged/ Died		Remarks
Korb, Henry	44	26 July	1862	D	Pte	—		wounded at Wilderness—believed died
La Barge, Joseph	30	19 Jan	1865	H	Pte	23 June	1865	
La Du, John T.	20	11 Aug	1862	H	Pte	23 June	1865	
Lakin, David A.	—	28 Aug	1862	K	Pte	2 Sept	1862	deserted
Lamb, Adin M. C.	35	13 Aug	1862	F	Pte	20 April	1863	
Lamb, Harlow	33	13 Aug	1862	F	Pte	8 March	1863	died of disease
Lamb, Henry	21	6 Aug	1862	F	Pte	20 May	1865	wounded at Wilderness
Lamphere, Alvah	18	26 July	1862	F	Pte	15 Dec	1865	died of disease
Lamphier, Jehial W.	43	15 Aug	1862	G	Pte	23 June	1865	
Lamson, Samuel D.	18	1 Aug	1862	A	Pte	23 June	1865	
Landele, Joseph	44	25 July	1862	H	Drum/Maj	6 March	1863	
Landphier, Charles P.	35	15 Aug	1862	G	Pte	23 June	1865	
Lange, Charles H.	23	1 Aug	1862	B	Sgt	23 June	1865	
Langworthy, Andrew	19	4 Aug	1862	A	Pte	28 June	1863	deserted
La Rue, William H.	—	6 March	1863	E	2/Lt	29 Sept	1863	discharged for disability
Lathrop, Charles	18	1 Aug	1862	A	Corp	28 Jan	1864	died at Sandusky
Lathrop, Charles G.	22	3 Aug	1862	D	Corp	absent at muster out		wounded at Winchester and Petersburg
Lathrop, George H.	18	22 July	1862	I	Pte	5 July	1865	wounded at Gettysburg—transferred to V.R.C.
Laup, George L.	40	11 Aug	1862	B	Pte	28 Aug	1865	wounded at Gettysburg—transferred to V.R.C.
Laurenthal, John	20	26 Feb	1864	C	Pte	23 June	1865	captured 27 March 1865—paroled
Lautermilch, George	30	29 July	1862	E	Pte	28 Jan	1863	discharged for disability
Lawrence, James R.	24	5 Aug	1862	F	Corp	20 May	1865	wounded at Cold Harbor
Lee, Amos O.	20	6 Aug	1862	F	Pte	20 May	1865	
Lee, Edward	18	4 Aug	1862	D	Pte	23 June	1865	
Lee, Lemuel	44	11 Aug	1862	G	Pte	24 March	1863	
Lee, William	21	11 Aug	1862	D	Pte	6 May	1864	killed at Wilderness
Leroy, William	37	26 Aug	1862	F	Pte	17 Sept	1862	deserted
Lester, Frank	31	24 July	1862	C	Q/M	30 Nov	1864	

Name	Age on Enlistment	Enlisted		Company	Rank	Discharged/ Died		Remarks
Lewis, John	18	11 Aug	1862	E	Sgt	23 June	1865	
Lewis, Sylvanus S.	28	8 Aug	1862	E	Pte	13 Sept	1862	deserted
Liechte, Friedrich	37	12 Aug	1862	K	Pte	23 June	1865	captured at Wilderness
Lilley, James F.	18	1 Aug	1862	B	Pte	1 Dec	1862	
Lindner, George	19	6 Aug	1862	I	Pte	23 June	1865	captured Jan 1865—paroled
Lockwood, Calvin	21	9 Aug	1862	H	Pte	23 June	1865	
Long, Patrick	21	23 March	1864	D	Pte	23 June	1865	
Look, Willis H.	17	3 Aug	1862	D	Musician	10 July	1865	
Loomis, Lewis S.	20	6 Aug	1862	I	Corp	6 May	1864	believed killed at Wilderness
Loop, Ephrain M.	19	6 Aug	1862	A	Pte	23 June	1865	
Loop, George	32	6 Aug	1862	A	Corp	23 June	1865	wounded at Wilderness
Loop, Henry	26	6 Aug	1862	A	Pte	23 June	1865	
Loveless, Charles	23	12 Aug	1862	H	Pte	22 Sept	1862	deserted
Lovell, S. H.	28	19 July	1862	I	Pte	28 April	1864	transferred to U.S. Navy
Lowland, Dennis	25	9 Aug	1862	F	Pte	3 Sept	1862	deserted
Lucas, Martin L.	28	8 Aug	1862	I	Pte	4 Sept	1862	deserted
Luce, Roselle E.	18	11 Aug	1862	B	Pte	1 April	1865	wounded at Cold Harbor, transferred to V.R.C.
Lusk, George H.	23	2 Aug	1862	A	Corp	23 June	1865	wounded at Wilderness
Luther, Edward P.	34	14 Aug	1862	D, B	Capt	6 Feb	1865	wounded and captured at Wilderness, paroled. Discharged for disability
MacDonald, Stuart	27	23 July	1862	E, F	Capt	23 June	1865	
Mackin, Patrick	23	29 July	1862	A	Pte	23 June	1865	
Madden, Fergus	24	12 Aug	1862	E	Corp	24 Oct	1864	died of disease
Magee, Andrew	30	5 Aug	1862	A	Pte	23 June	1865	
Mahar, Cornelius	26	9 Aug	1862	G	Pte	21 Aug	1864	wounded, believed killed at Charlestown
Maher, William	19	15 Aug	1862	H	Pte	21 Jan	1863	deserted
Malone, Alfred	32	4 Aug	1862	A	Corp	8 Jan	1863	discharged for disability
Malone, Ransom	22	4 Aug	1862	A	Pte	23 June	1865	
Maltby, William	18	5 Aug	1862	C	Corp	23 June	1865	
Manheimer, Isaac	22	2 Aug	1862	E	Pte	1 June	1863	deserted
Mann, Albert O.	18	23 July	1862	A	Pte	3 May	1863	deserted

Name	Age on Enlistment	Enlisted		Company	Rank	Discharged/ Died		Remarks
Manwaren, Charles	35	11 Feb	1864	D	Pte	18 May	1864	wounded at Wilderness—died of wounds
Manzer, Hubbard	22	15 Aug	1862	H	Sgt	15 Oct	1864	wounded at Wilderness
Marks, Morton	22	2 Aug	1862	H, B	Major	23 June	1865	wounded at Winchester
Marsh, Hudson	18	23 July	1862	B	Sgt	26 Feb	1864	wounded at Gettysburg—discharged for disability
Marshall, Phineas	21	30 July	1862	D	Sgt	20 Nov	1862	died in hospital
Matthews, Joseph	23	11 Aug	1862	H	Pte	absent at muster out		wounded before Petersburg
Maxon, George S.	19	7 Aug	1862	B	Pte	23 June	1865	wounded at Wilderness
Maxson, George W.	26	8 Aug	1862	F	Pte	27 June	1865	transferred to V.R.C.
Maxwell, Herbert A.	18	29 July	1862	K	Sgt	1 Aug	1863	after discharge served in Third Artillery
May, Amos S.	26	7 Aug	1862	F	Pte	23 June	1865	
May, William	24	6 Aug	1862	F	Sgt	23 June	1865	
Mayers, John	31	8 Aug	1862	C	Corp	21 Jan	1863	deserted
McAllister, Clark H.	36	28 July	1862	E	Pte	17 May	1865	wounded at Wilderness and Petersburg
McArthur, George	18	12 Aug	1862	H	Corp	23 June	1865	
McCamley, Francis A.	40	22 March	1864	D	Pte	9 June	1865	
McCamley, Rodman	18	12 Aug	1862	D	Pte	5 July	1863	deserted
McCarthy, Dennis	18	31 July	1862	K	Pte	6 July	1863	wounded at Gettysburg—died of wounds
McCarthy, Edward	22	1 Aug	1862	E	Sgt	2 July	1863	deserted
McCormick, Michael	19	31 July	1862	A	Pte	13 Dec	1863	transferred to First Independent Battery
McCracken, Holland J.	32	9 Aug	1862	H	Pte	23 June	1865	
McCracken, Lewis	22	11 Aug	1862	H	Pte	23 June	1865	
McCumber, William	30	9 Aug	1862	F	Pte	23 June	1865	
McFeeters, Samuel	33	14 Aug	1862	E	Pte	23 June	1865	wounded at Spotsylvania
McGough, Miles J.	26	12 Aug	1862	G	Pte	23 June	1865	
McGrath, Dennis	22	16 Aug	1862	K	Pte	13 June	1865	captured May 1864 at Rapidan River
McGuire, John	24	5 Sept	1863	H	Pte	13 April	1865	discharged for disability
McHale, Michael	22	20 Aug	1862	H	Pte	3 July	1863	killed at Gettysburg
McKay, Duncan	35	6 March	1865	K	Pte	23 June	1865	

Name	Age on Enlistment	Enlisted		Company	Rank	Discharged/ Died		Remarks
McKinley, James J.	31	12 Aug	1862	B	Corp	23 June	1865	wounded at Cedar Creek
McLaughlin, John	26	9 Aug	1862	H	Pte	12 Nov	1862	deserted
McLyman, Colonel J.	31	30 July	1862	C	Sgt	23 June	1865	wounded at Cold Harbor
McMillen, Millen	37	23 Aug	1863	E	Pte	5 July	1865	
McNulty, Terrence	19	17 Jan	1865	B	Pte	23 June	1865	
McQuade, Peter	24	14 Aug	1862	G	Pte	6 May	1864	believed killed at Wilderness
Mead, Arthur J.	—	28 Aug	1862	C	2/Lt	7 Dec	1862	
Mead, David H.	19	9 Feb	1864	E	Pte	19 July	1864	died of typhoid fever
Mead, Frederick A.	18	9 Feb	1864	E	Pte	23 June	1865	wounded at Cold Harbor
Mead, Patrick	18	23 July	1862	H	Pte	19 Sept	1862	deserted
Mehan, Edward	35	30 July	1862	A	Pte	17 June	1865	wounded at Opequon Creek and Petersburg
Melligan, Thomas	30	9 Aug	1862	H	Pte	23 June	1865	
Mercandollar, Herbert	21	14 Aug	1862	I	Pte	14 June	1864	wounded at Cold Harbor—died of wounds
Merriam, Isaac H.	23	13 Aug	1862	I	Sgt	absent at muster out		wounded at Opequon Creek
Merrifield, Alfred W.	23	6 Aug	1862	A	Pte	23 June	1865	
Merrifield, Norman	33	6 Aug	1862	A	Sgt	23 Nov	1863	wounded at Gettysburg—died of gangrene at Lysander, N.Y.
Merritt, Francis H.	19	2 Aug	1862	A	Corp	23 June	1865	
Mersellus, Abram	31	12 Aug	1862	B	Pte	18 July	1863	deserted
Meurs, James	44	12 Aug	1862	K	Corp	24 Dec	1863	discharged for disability
Mickles, Lovell	18	5 Aug	1862	K	Sgt	1 Aug	1863	
Miles, James	25	30 July	1862	C	Pte	23 June	1865	wounded at Gettysburg
Miller, Abram	43	22 July	1862	I	Pte	23 June	1865	
Millions, Chauncey K.	21	15 Aug	1862	H	Pte	29 June	1863	deserted
Mills, James H.	19	11 Aug	1862	H	Pte	31 May	1865	wounded at Gettysburg
Mitchell, Joseph H.	24	7 Aug	1862	D	Pte	5 July	1863	deserted
Moelter, Anthony	39	14 Aug	1862	K	Pte	19 Oct	1864	killed at Middletown
Monk, Frederick	18	6 Aug	1862	C	Pte	5 Dec	1863	transferred to First Independent Battery
Monroe, Albert	18	4 Aug	1862	C	Pte	16 Feb	1865	wounded 13 Sept 1864—discharged for disability

Name	Age on Enlistment	Enlisted	Company	Rank	Discharged/ Died	Remarks
Monroe, Francis F.	23	11 Aug 1862	C	Pte	23 June 1865	
Montague, John	22	28 March 1864	D	Pte	10 April 1864	deserted
Montgomery, Thomas	35	6 Aug 1862	K	Pte	3 Sept 1862	deserted
Moore, Charles W.	18	5 Aug 1862	K	Pte	1 July 1863	wounded at Fredericksburg— transferred to V.R.C.
Moore, Uriah D.	21	26 July 1862	F	Pte	absent at muster out	captured at Wilderness—paroled
Morgan, Henry B.	23	6 Aug 1862	F	Pte	23 June 1865	
Morris, William H.	21	13 Aug 1862	D	Pte	15 Dec 1863	transferred to First Independent Battery
Moser, Alanson	18	11 Aug 1862	C	Pte	12 July 1864	killed at Fort Stevens
Moses, Lucius	24	28 Aug 1862	F	Capt	24 Feb 1863	
Moses, Robert H.	18	26 July 1862	F, E	Capt	23 June 1865	
Mosher, Charles M.	18	31 July 1862	A	Corp	8 May 1863	died in hospital Washington, D.C.
Mosher, Charles W.	22	11 Aug 1862	G	Pte	1 July 1863	deserted
Mosier, William H.	24	11 Aug 1862	C	Pte	20 Oct 1862	deserted
Moss, Adelphin	18	1 Aug 1862	C	Pte	10 July 1865	transferred to V.R.C.
Moss, Willard H.	26	5 Aug 1862	D	Pte	29 June 1865	transferred to V.R.C.
Moss, William	32	6 Aug 1862	F	Pte	23 June 1865	
Moyer, Stephen	25	11 Aug 1862	H	Sgt	23 June 1865	
Mulray, Michael	26	15 Aug 1862	K	Pte	23 June 1865	
Munran, Patrick	43	5 Aug 1862	C	Pte	22 Dec 1863	
Munro, David A.	18	2 Aug 1862	H	Capt	23 June 1865	
Murphy, Dennis	19	25 July 1862	A	1/Lt	23 June 1865	
Murphy, James	21	13 Aug 1862	G	Pte	19 Sept 1862	deserted
Murphy, Michael	30	20 Aug 1862	D	Pte	23 June 1865	
Murray, Cassius W.	18	13 Feb 1864	E	Corp	23 June 1865	wounded at Fisher's Hill
Myers, John W.	25	7 Aug 1862	I	Pte	22 Sept 1862	deserted
Nash, James	39	4 Aug 1862	A	Pte	13 Oct 1862	deserted
Nellis, Theodore	18	13 Aug 1862	H	Pte	3 July 1863	deserted
Nelson, Leander	34	9 Aug 1862	I	Pte	23 June 1865	
Neupert, Lorenz	44	2 Aug 1862	E	Pte	23 June 1862	deserted
Nichols, Nelson	21	31 July 1862	E	Corp	12 Sept 1865	wounded at Wilderness
Nichols, Oliver	24	12 Aug 1862	D	Sgt	23 June 1865	

Name	Age on Enlistment	Enlisted		Company	Rank	Discharged/ Died		Remarks
Nicholson, David D.	21	15 Aug	1862	I	Pte	23 June	1865	
Nickerson, Linus M.	—	28 Aug	1862	—	Chaplain	23 June	1865	
Nims, Alfred	—	28 Aug	1862	C	Capt	23 Dec	1862	
Noble, James H.	18	9 Aug	1862	D	Pte	23 June	1865	wounded at Wilderness
Nolan, James	29	4 Aug	1862	E	Pte	22 Sept	1862	deserted
North, Augustus	23	19 July	1862	I	Pte	23 June	1865	
North, Belus F.	20	26 July	1861	F	Pte	23 June	1865	
North, Bradley S.	39	4 Aug	1862	G	Pte	28 Feb	1863	
North, Henry W.	29	13 Aug	1862	E	Pte	20 May	1865	
Northrup, Ebenezer W.	29	7 Aug	1862	C	Pte	absent at muster out		wounded at Wilderness
Northrup, Jerome	38	10 Sept	1864	E	Pte	23 June	1865	
Northway, Smith S.	18	1 Aug	1862	I	Sgt	6 May	1864	killed at Wilderness
Northway, Thomas	22	7 Aug	1862	K	Corp	6 May	1864	missing believed captured at Wilderness
Norton, Loren N.	25	9 Aug	1862	D	Pte	23 June	1865	
Norton, Willard	18	14 Aug	1862	F	Corp	23 June	1865	
Nye, Charles G.	32	28 Aug	1862	B	1/Lt	9 Feb	1863	
Oartel, John	20	13 Aug	1862	E	Corp	23 June	1865	wounded at Cold Harbor
O'Brien, Michael	22	24 Feb	1864	C	Pte	28 March	1865	wounded at Wilderness—discharged for disability
O'Donnell, John	21	11 Aug	1862	H	Pte	21 Jan	1863	deserted
O'Hara, Patrick	21	8 Aug	1862	K	Pte	1 June	1864	killed at Cold Harbor
Olmstead, Philo	34	11 Aug	1862	G	Corp	25 July	1864	wounded at Cold Harbor—died of wounds
Orr, James	32	14 Aug	1862	E	Pte	25 Dec	1862	deserted
Orr, John	25	19 Aug	1862	E	Pte	23 June	1865	
Osborn, Samuel	39	24 July	1862	E	Musician	23 June	1865	
Ostrander, Charles W.	28	25 July	1862	E, C	2/Lt	10 March	1865	wounded and captured at Wilderness—discharged for disability
Ostrander, John H.	34	9 Aug	1862	F	Corp	19 Sept	1864	killed at Winchester
Ostrander, Liberty	23	11 Feb	1864	C	Pte	15 June	1865	
Paige, Eliot	18	4 Aug	1862	C, F	Pte	15 Nov	1865	transferred to V.R.C.

Name	Age on Enlistment	Enlisted		Company	Rank	Discharged/ Died		Remarks
Palmer, Erastus B.	29	20 Aug	1862	D	Pte	25 Sept	1862	deserted
Palmer, Myron A.	22	6 Aug	1862	G	Pte	19 Sept	1862	deserted
Parish, Gates D.	33	4 Aug	1862	D	2/Lt	23 June	1865	
Parker, George S.	18	13 Aug	1862	H	Corp	8 July	1863	wounded at Gettysburg—died of wounds
Parmenter, Chauncey	35	13 Aug	1862	I	Pte	19 March	1865	wounded at Cedar Creek—discharged for disability
Parrisen, Otto W.	42	22 Feb	1864	F	1/Lt	23 June	1865	
Pattan, Henry J.	24	11 Aug	1862	H	Pte	23 June	1865	
Patten, George A.	20	9 Aug	1862	D	Pte	23 June	1865	wounded at Wilderness
Patterson, Albert H.	21	12 Aug	1862	E	Pte	18 Aug	1862	deserted
Patterson, Francis	21	4 Aug	1862	D	Corp	3 May	1865	wounded at Wilderness
Paul, William H.	30	5 Aug	1862	B	Corp	10 Jan	1864	died after railroad accident
Paulk, Noah W.	32	25 July	1862	I	Pte	6 July	1865	transferred to V.R.C.
Pease, David	22	6 Aug	1862	G	Pte	7 July	1863	deserted
Pease, Edmond	18	8 Aug	1862	G	Pte	23 June	1865	wounded at Gettysburg—captured at Wilderness
Peavy, Lorin M.	34	25 July	1862	A	Pte	1 Sept	1863	transferred to V.R.C.
Peck, Homer	24	13 Aug	1862	H	Corp	23 June	1865	
Peirce, Edwin L.	18	13 Aug	1862	I	Pte	6 Jan	1863	died of typhoid
Penfield, George H.	19	5 Aug	1862	A	Pte	6 May	1864	believed killed at Wilderness
Penn, John	22	14 Aug	1862	I	Corp	23 June	1865	wounded at Cold Harbor
Penoyer, Oscar	21	11 Aug	1862	E	Pte	13 May	1864	wounded at Gettysburg—discharged for disability
Perdue, Caesar	44	20 Aug	1862	D	Pte	28 Dec	1862	died near Fredericksburg
Perine, Charles W.	24	5 Aug	1862	A	Corp	23 June	1865	wounded at Wilderness
Perry, Albert B.	37	14 Aug	1862	E	Corp	23 June	1865	
Perry, Eli	44	8 Aug	1862	D	Pte	26 June	1865	transferred to V.R.C.
Perry, Eugene A.	18	14 Aug	1862	E	Pte	9 Jan	1866	discharged by court-martial
Perry, George H.	21	24 July	1862	E	Pte	13 July	1863	deserted
Petrie, Henry A.	32	14 Aug	1862	E	Pte	5 June	1865	wounded at Cedar Creek—discharged for disability

Name	Age on Enlistment	Enlisted	Company	Rank	Discharged/ Died	Remarks
Pettis, Austin	25	11 Aug 1862	G	Pte	31 Aug 1862	deserted
Pfeifer, John	22	18 July 1862	E	Pte	7 July 1865	wounded at Cold Harbor
Phelps, Jonathan H.	44	2 Aug 1862	H	Pte	24 April 1863	died in hospital
Phetiplace, George N.	24	23 July 1862	E	Sgt	25 Sept 1862	deserted
Phillips, Franklin	21	9 Aug 1862	E	Pte	1 June 1864	killed at Cold Harbor
Phillips, Samuel	25	11 Aug 1862	B	Pte	14 April 1863	discharged for disability
Picket, Frank E.	19	13 Aug 1862	D	Pte	10 July 1863	discharged for disability
Pilger, Peter	27	4 Aug 1862	I	Pte	15 May 1865	captured at Wilderness—discharged for disability
Pine, Daniel W.	37	12 Aug 1862	E	Pte	23 June 1865	
Pitcher, Abijah	23	4 Aug 1862	A	Pte	13 July 1864	wounded at Wilderness—died in hospital
Pitcher, William C.	36	21 July 1862	I	Pte	10 Sept 1863	deserted
Platt, George W.	24	15 Aug 1862	F	Capt	25 Oct 1864	wounded at Wilderness—discharged for disability
Poole, Herman	18	30 July 1862	C	Pte	28 Oct 1862	deserted
Poole, Theodore L.	22	29 July 1862	I, K	Capt	15 May 1865	wounded at Cold Harbor—discharged for disability
Porter, Samuel D.	28	6 Aug 1862	E	Pte	14 Aug 1862	deserted
Potter, Francis M.	26	13 Aug 1862	H	1/Lt	5 July 1865	wounded at Spotsylvania
Potter, John J.	18	23 July 1862	B	Corp	absent at muster out	wounded at Wilderness
Powell, James H.	21	25 July 1862	E	Pte	15 May 1865	wounded at Cold Harbor—discharged for disability
Prentice, Russell E.	23	1 Aug 1862	F	Pte	27 Oct 1862	deserted
Preston, John	18	15 Aug 1862	I	Pte	18 Aug 1864	wounded at Fort Stevens—died of wounds
Price, James	35	30 July 1862	C	Pte	29 July 1865	transferred to V.R.C.
Price, Nathan R.	44	7 Aug 1862	H	Pte	21 March 1865	discharged for disability
Prindle, Jesse H.	21	11 Aug 1862	B	Pte	30 June 1865	wounded at Gettysburg—transferred to V.R.C.
Pritchard, Phineas D.	28	5 Aug 1862	A	Pte	28 June 1863	deserted

Name	Age on Enlistment	Enlisted		Company	Rank	Discharged/ Died		Remarks
Pritchard, William H.	24	5 Aug	1862	A	Pte	2 July	1863	deserted
Putnam, Edward	25	17 July	1862	I	Pte	23 June	1865	
Quick, Charles M.	25	12 Aug	1862	D	Pte	26 Feb	1863	
Quinlan, John	24	2 Aug	1862	H	Pte	23 July	1865	
Rabee, William	24	8 Aug	1862	I	Pte	23 June	1865	
Ralph, John	35	30 July	1862	C	Pte	23 June	1865	
Randall, Albert	18	11 Aug	1862	B	Pte	8 Sept	1862	died of typhoid fever
Randall, Dempster	16	2 Aug	1862	E	Musician	23 June	1865	
Ranger, Gabriel	40	25 July	1862	I	Pte	absent at muster out		wounded at Petersburg
Raymond, Anthony	44	26 July	1862	F	Pte	29 Sept	1864	discharged for disability
Raymond, William	28	11 Aug	1862	F	Wagoner	23 June	1865	
Raymond, William K.	21	6 Aug	1862	C	Pte	21 Dec	1862	died of fever
Read, William	—	4 Aug	1863	E	Pte	25 March	1865	deserted
Reals, William	22	4 Aug	1862	C	Pte	28 Oct	1862	deserted
Reden, John A.	45	15 Aug	1862	I	Pte	16 Jan	1863	deserted
Reed, Hiram H.	18	8 Aug	1862	G	Corp	absent at muster out		wounded at Spotsylvania
Reed, Jack	30	1 Aug	1862	D	Pte	9 Aug	1863	discharged for disability
Reilay, Thomas	18	12 Aug	1862	C	Pte	23 June	1865	
Relyea, Daniel	20	26 July	1862	I	Musician	23 June	1865	
Remington, Henry	18	7 Aug	1862	C	Corp	18 Oct	1862	deserted
Renols, James	21	14 Aug	1862	I	Pte	2 March 1863		discharged for disability
Reynolds, Charles	29	24 July	1862	E	Wagoner	2 March 1863		transferred to 65th Infantry
Reynolds, John	34	5 Aug	1862	K	Pte	absent at muster out		under arrest for desertion
Reynolds, Myron L.	18	28 July	1862	B	Corp	23 June	1865	
Rice, Isaac B.	43	6 Aug	1862	H	Pte	6 Feb	1863	died at Falmouth, Va.
Rice, Judson	18	25 July	1862	A	Pte	17 March 1864		discharged for disability
Rich, Asa A.	21	12 Aug	1862	G	Corp	11 April	1865	wounded at Petersburg—died of wounds
Rich, Curtis L.	23	12 Aug	1862	F	1/Lt	23 June	1865	

Name	Age on Enlistment	Enlisted	Company	Rank	Discharged/ Died	Remarks
Richards, Isaac	23	29 July 1862	F	Corp	23 June 1865	captured at Wilderness—paroled
Richardson, George	21	22 Feb 1864	C	Pte	14 July 1864	wounded at Fort Stevens—died of wounds
Richardson, Joseph	32	7 Aug 1862	E	Pte	absent at muster out	wounded and missing at Wilderness
Richardson, Lyman	44	19 March 1864	C	Pte	25 March 1865	killed at Fort Fisher
Riechardt, William	34	24 July 1862	E	Pte	23 June 1865	
Riley, Frank	21	15 Aug 1862	I	Pte	23 June 1865	
Riley, John	19	14 Jan 1865	B	Pte	23 June 1865	
Riley, Patrick	22	25 July 1862	H	Pte	10 July 1865	transferred to V.R.C.
Riley, Patrick	21	14 Aug 1862	G	Pte	23 June 1865	
Riley, Thomas	18	6 Aug 1862	A	Pte	23 June 1865	wounded at Cedar Creek
Ripley, George W.	21	14 Aug 1862	F	Pte	23 June 1865	transferred to V.R.C.
Ritch, Ashley W.	23	25 April 1864	K	Pte	absent at muster out	
Robbins, Joseph S.	37	31 July 1862	K	Pte	2 April 1864	died at Sandusky, Ohio
Roberson, William	30	25 July 1862	I	Corp	18 Oct 1862	deserted
Roberts, John H.	31	14 March 1864	D	Pte	absent at muster out	captured at Wilderness
Robertson, Clarence H.	18	23 July 1862	B	Pte	20 Oct 1864	captured at Wilderness—died at Andersonville
Robertson, Lucien H.	26	11 Aug 1862	B	Sgt	19 May 1865	
Robinson, James	34	15 Aug 1862	H	Pte	23 June 1865	
Robinson, James B.	18	25 July 1862	A	Pte	22 Feb 1865	wounded at Cold Harbor—discharged for disability
Robinson, John	37	15 Aug 1862	K	Pte	29 June 1865	
Robinson, Rufus	28	11 Aug 1862	I	Pte	6 Nov 1862	died of typhoid fever
Rockwell, John W.	40	23 March 1864	D	Pte	23 June 1865	
Roe, Elisha	45	6 Aug 1862	I	Pte	23 June 1865	
Roell, Louis	22	14 Aug 1862	G	Pte	7 Jan 1863	
Roell, William	18	15 Aug 1862	G	Pte	2 July 1863	deserted
Rogers, Edgar	33	28 July 1862	E	Pte	7 July 1863	deserted

Name	Age on Enlistment	Enlisted		Company	Rank	Discharged/ Died		Remarks
Rogers, Niles	34	12 Aug	1862	G	Pte	16 June	1865	died in hospital
Rogers, Stephen W.	19	5 Aug	1862	A	Pte	26 June	1865	wounded at Winchester
Rooney, James J.	44	1 Aug	1862	K	Pte	23 June	1865	
Root, George H.	21	15 Aug	1862	G	Pte	20 Oct	1862	deserted
Roraback, Tarbell	20	28 July	1862	I	Pte	23 June	1865	
Rose, George C. W.	23	12 Aug	1862	G	Pte	26 Feb	1863	died at Harper's Ferry
Rose, William H.	18	1 Aug	1862	A	Pte	23 June	1863	wounded at Rappahannock Station
Roseboom, John R.	25	25 Aug	1863	D	Pte	6 May	1865	discharged for disability
Ross, James E.	26	12 Aug	1862	D	Corp	1 June	1864	killed at Cold Harbor
Rowe, Baltzer	33	26 July	1862	D	Pte	25 Aug	1863	discharged for disability
Rowland, Horace	30	20 Aug	1862	K	Corp	1 July	1863	deserted
Ruggles, Philo E.	19	21 July	1862	B	Sgt	7 Nov	1863	killed at Rappahannock Station
Ruggles, William	18 (16)	21 July	1862	B	Pte	23 June	1865	court-martialed for desertion
Russ, Henry J.	32	7 Aug	1862	C	Pte	23 June	1865	
Russel, William	24	17 Jan	1865	B	Pte	23 June	1865	
Russell, Horace	21	12 Aug	1862	D	Sgt	23 June	1865	wounded at Wilderness
Rust, John M.	38	13 Aug	1862	F	Pte	26 Oct	1862	died of disease
Ryan, Martin	25	11 Aug	1862	B, G	Capt	23 June	1865	
Ryan, Patrick	19	1 Aug	1862	F	Pte	23 June	1865	
Sage, Henry	19	9 Aug	1862	D	Pte	29 Aug	1865	transferred to V.R.C.
Salsbury, Edgar A.	22	25 July	1862	I	Sgt	22 Sept	1862	deserted
Salvage, John	21	14 Aug	1862	F	Corp	23 June	1865	wounded at Cold Harbor
Sanders, Benjamin	30	2 Aug	1862	H	Pte	25 Sept	1864	wounded near Winchester—died of wounds
Sanders, Carlton	24	2 Aug	1862	H	Pte	6 July	1863	wounded at Gettysburg—died of wounds
Sanders, James	38	15 Oct	1864	—	Asst/Surg	23 June	1865	
Sanders, John	27	15 Aug	1862	H	Pte	19 Oct	1864	transferred to First Independent Battery —killed in action
Sanderson, Henry H.	44	1 Aug	1862	C	Pte	26 June	1865	transferred to V.R.C.
Sanderson, John	18	1 Aug	1862	C	Pte	23 June	1865	
Sanford, Stephen H.	23	8 Aug	1862	I	Pte	28 April	1864	transferred to U.S. Navy

Name	Age on Enlistment	Enlisted		Company	Rank	Discharged/ Died		Remarks
Sax, Jacob	23	7 Aug	1862	I	Pte	6 May	1864	missing at Wilderness—believed killed
Schafer, Francis V.	25	5 Aug	1862	E	Corp	23 June	1865	
Scobey, George V.	34	14 Aug	1862	E	Pte	2 Jan	1863	deserted
Scott, James	35	21 July	1862	I	Pte	2 March	1863	died of consumption
Scott, Lorenzo	18	25 July	1862	B	Pte	13 Oct	1864	wounded at Fisher's Hill—died of wounds
Scott, Thomas H.	26	28 July	1862	B	2/Lt	30 June	1865	wounded at Gettysburg and Fort Stevens
Scott, Thomas L.	18	4 Aug	1862	B	Pte	30 Dec	1862	discharged for disability
Seager, Schuyler	21	11 Aug	1862	E	Corp	6 May	1864	missing at Wilderness
Secor, Oren W.	28	6 Aug	1862	D	Pte	17 Nov	1862	died at Cedar Spring
Segar, Peter	22	27 July	1862	D	Pte	23 June	1865	captured at Wilderness
Seibert, Peter	25	9 Aug	1862	K	Pte	22 July	1864	wounded at Wilderness—died of wounds
Senet, Henry C.	22	26 July	1862	F	Sgt	8 April	1865	wounded at Petersburg—died of wounds
Sharp, Benjamin	18	13 Aug	1862	H	Pte	29 June	1865	transferred to V.R.C.
Sharp, Bradley	37	4 Aug	1862	A	Pte	2 Feb	1864	died of smallpox
Sharp, John A.	24	24 July	1862	A	Pte	2 July	1863	deserted
Sharp, Peter	32	4 Aug	1862	A	Corp	3 July	1865	
Sheeley, George	19	14 Aug	1862	D	Pte	absent at muster out		wounded near Winchester
Sheffield, James M.	45	27 July	1862	A	Pte	23 Feb	1863	
Shelden, William	18	30 July	1862	C	Pte	23 June	1865	wounded at Wilderness
Shelp, Charles	25	7 Aug	1862	G	Pte	23 June	1865	
Shepherd, Charles	27	16 Aug	1862	D	Pte	28 Feb	1863	
Shepherd, John A.	24	16 Aug	1862	D	Corp	16 June	1865	wounded at Wilderness
Sherman, Alfred	21	6 Aug	1862	K	Pte	20 July	1865	transferred to V.R.C.
Shirley, Dudley G.	29	3 Aug	1862	D	Capt	20 Nov	1864	wounded near Winchester—discharged for disability
Shock, Peter	21	19 Aug	1862	K	Pte	19 April	1864	deserted
Shoens, Thomas H.	18	23 July	1862	B	Corp	19 Jan	1863	discharged for disability

Name	Age on Enlistment	Enlisted		Company	Rank	Discharged/ Died		Remarks
Sidman, Charles H.	18	15 Feb	1864	H	Pte	23 June	1865	wounded at Winchester
Sidnam, John	19	20 Aug	1862	H	Pte	3 July	1863	killed at Gettysburg
Simmons, John	22	6 Aug	1862	B	Pte	3 July	1865	transferred to V.R.C.
Sims, John V.	22	11 Aug	1862	H	1/Lt	19 Sept	1864	killed near Winchester
Sloat, Elias L.	24	9 Aug	1862	B	Sgt	23 June	1865	wounded at Wilderness
Slocum, John O.	42	14 Aug	1862	—	Asst/Surg	1 July	1863	transferred to 121st Infantry
Smith, Albert R.	21	12 Aug	1862	K	Corp	23 June	1865	wounded at Winchester
Smith, Alonzo A.	23	8 Aug	1862	G	Corp	1 July	1863	deserted
Smith, Andrew J.	25	26 July	1862	G	Capt	6 June	1865	
Smith, Calvin	21	11 Aug	1862	C	Pte	23 June	1865	
Smith, Chester	21	8 Aug	1862	A	Pte	13 Dec	1863	transferred to First Independent Battery
Smith, Daniel H.	42	11 Aug	1862	B	Pte	18 May	1865	wounded at Winchester
Smith, David	28	15 Aug	1862	K	Pte	23 June	1865	
Smith, Edwin	23	4 Aug	1862	C	Pte	28 June	1865	transferred to V.R.C.
Smith, Elisha A.	30	12 Aug	1862	B	Pte	31 Dec	1862	discharged for disability
Smith, Francis M.	26	15 Aug	1862	H	Musician	20 Feb	1863	deserted
Smith, George	23	14 Aug	1862	H	Pte	11 Dec	1863	transferred to First Independent Battery
Smith, Henry	35	5 Aug	1862	A	Pte	23 Feb	1863	discharged for disability
Smith, James W.	21	31 July	1862	B	Pte	18 Jan	1866	
Smith, John H. C.	21	5 Aug	1862	D	Pte	14 July	1865	transferred to V.R.C.
Smith, Joseph H.	19	30 July	1862	A, C	Capt	23 June	1865	
Smith, Lewis M.	21	9 Aug	1862	D	Pte	23 June	1865	wounded at Cold Harbor
Smith, Lyman	44	12 Aug	1862	K	Pte	2 Feb	1863	died of inflammation of lungs
Smith, Marshall	21	29 July	1862	B	Corp	13 June	1865	wounded at Cedar Creek
Smith, Merrick	23	14 Aug	1862	K	2/Lt	23 June	1865	wounded at Fort Stevens
Smith, Oren J.	22	9 Aug	1862	F	Pte	6 May	1864	killed at Wilderness
Smith, R. Fulton	26	14 Aug	1862	H	Pte	20 June	1863	deserted
Smith, Sidney	39	13 Aug	1862	K	Wagoner	23 June	1865	
Smith, Surreno S.	32	5 Aug	1862	F	Corp	23 June	1865	wounded at Wilderness
Smith, Timothy	28	15 Aug	1862	K	Pte	8 Sept	1862	deserted
Smith, Zebulon	21	6 Aug	1862	A	Pte	1 Oct	1864	deserted
Snedeker, Charles	18	26 July	1862	F	Pte	17 March 1865		wounded at Fort Stevens

Name	Age on Enlistment	Enlisted		Company	Rank	Discharged/ Died		Remarks
Soul, Alfred	36	11 Aug	1862	B	Musician	23 June	1865	
Spaulding, Eugene D.	20	10 Aug	1862	F	Corp	18 June	1864	wounded at Wilderness—died of wounds
Spear, Charles F.	20	12 Aug	1862	F	Corp	18 June	1864	wounded and captured at Wilderness, died of wounds
Spinks, Isaiah V.	23	14 Aug	1862	F	Pte	20 March	1863	discharged for disability
Spitzer, Gottfried	28	25 July	1862	E	Pte	2 July	1863	deserted
Springstad, Austin	20	3 Aug	1862	F	Pte	13 Nov	1862	died of disease
Sprulock, James F.	35	22 July	1862	B	Sgt	7 Nov	1863	killed at Rappahannock Station
Star, William	26	6 Aug	1862	G	Pte	30 June	1863	deserted
Steadman, Christopher P.	23	18 Aug	1862	E	Pte	absent at muster out		wounded at Wilderness
Stebbins, Daniel W.	18	2 Aug	1862	H	Pte	23 June	1865	
Stebbins, Menzies	25	6 Aug	1862	K	Pte	23 June	1865	wounded at Winchester
Stebbins, Peter	42	13 Feb	1864	H	Pte	21 July	1865	wounded at Fort Stevens—transferred to V.R.C.
Stebbins, Phineas S.	21	11 Aug	1862	K	Pte	1 June	1865	wounded near Strasburg—discharged for disability
Steele, Charles W.	23	24 July	1862	B	Corp	n.d.		
Stenson, John	22	9 Aug	1862	K	Pte	30 June	1865	transferred to V.R.C.
Sterner, Gottlieb	30	15 Aug	1862	E	Pte	absent at muster out		wounded at Cold Harbor
Steuben, Allen M.	24	28 July	1862	B	Pte	23 June	1865	
Stevens, Charles M.	30	8 Aug	1862	G	Pte	30 June	1864	discharged for disability
Stevens, Develois W.	19	6 Aug	1862	G	Corp	13 June	1865	wounded at Wilderness—discharged for disability
Stevens, George	18	6 Aug	1862	K	Musician	23 June	1865	
Stevens, Samuel	22	4 Aug	1862	A	Pte	28 March	1863	died of typhoid fever
Stevens, Theodore	19	11 Aug	1862	G	Pte	29 June	1865	wounded at Gettysburg—transferred to V.R.C.
Steves, Isaac R.	21	8 Aug	1862	B	Corp	29 June	1863	deserted
Stewart, Charles	31	15 Aug	1862	I	Pte	23 June	1865	

Name	Age on Enlistment	Enlisted		Company	Rank	Discharged/ Died		Remarks
Stone, Julius	19	12 Aug	1862	H	Pte	3 April	1863	died of typhoid fever
Stricknitz, Henry	21	29 July	1862	E	Pte	23 June	1865	
Stuart, John	35	2 Aug	1862	I	Pte	31 Aug	1862	deserted
Sullivan, Jerry	21	11 Aug	1862	H	Pte	1 April	1863	
Sullivan, Michael	32	11 Aug	1862	E	Pte	21 May	1863	deserted
Swartz, William Q.	35	21 July	1862	I	Sgt	3 Jan	1865	wounded at Fort Stevens—discharged for disability
Sweeney, Timothy	28	30 March	1864	E	Corp	23 June	1865	
Sweet, Russell	26	14 Aug	1862	F	Pte	23 June	1865	
Sweeting, Charles D.	19	14 Aug	1862	H	Pte	23 June	1865	
Swift, Oscar F.	40	14 Aug	1862	H	2/Lt	3 Dec	1862	
Swim, Lyman N.	18	15 Aug	1862	G	Corp	23 June	1865	
Talmadge, John	30	8 Aug	1862	A	Pte	6 July	1865	
Tappan, Burke M.	23	11 Aug	1862	H	Pte	23 June	1865	
Taylor, John W.	31	3 Aug	1862	D	2/Lt	1 March	1863	
Tefft, Nathan R.	54	24 July	1862	—	Surgeon	8 April	1864	
Teller, William S.	22	28 July	1862	E	Pte	absent at muster out		captured at Wilderness
Templeton, Thomas	36	22 July	1862	E	Corp	17 July	1865	wounded at Cedar Creek
Tenbroeck, Ezriah	31	5 Aug	1862	A	Pte	23 June	1865	
Terwilliger, James	26	15 Aug	1862	K	Pte	26 May	1864	deserted
Terwilliger, Joseph	37	6 Aug	1862	G	Pte	24 Sept	1862	deserted
Terwilliger, Richard	18	12 Aug	1862	K	Pte	10 Dec	1862	died of inflammation of lungs
Terwilliger, William	19	11 Aug	1862	K	Pte	17 Jan	1863	discharged for disability
Thayer, Stephen R.	35	14 Aug	1862	H	Pte	23 June	1865	
Thomas, Abram	45	30 July	1862	C	Pte	25 June	1865	
Thompson, Abner	18	11 Aug	1862	H	Corp	14 Oct	1864	wounded at Cold Harbor—discharged for disability
Thompson, David	29	7 Aug	1862	B	Pte	1 July	1863	deserted
Thompson, Miles	25	8 Aug	1862	K	Corp	23 June	1865	
Thompson, Patrick	35	1 Aug	1862	C	Pte	7 Dec	1863	discharged for disability
Thompson, Richard	21	1 Aug	1862	I	Pte	23 June	1865	

Name	Age on Enlistment	Enlisted	Company	Rank	Discharged/ Died	Remarks
Thompson, Stephen C.	28	30 July 1862	C	Pte	23 June 1865	
Thompson, William	37	11 Aug 1862	H	Pte	12 Nov 1862	deserted
Thompson, William	27	14 Aug 1862	K	Pte	20 July 1865	wounded at Fort Stevens—transferred to V.R.C.
Thornton, Thomas	24	21 March 1864	D	Pte	27 July 1864	deserted
Thorpe, Stephen B.	23	28 July 1864	F	Corp	16 Mar 1864	transferred to V.R.C.
Titus, Silas	—	28 Aug 1862	—	Col	23 Jan 1865	discharged for disability
Toms, Alexander	41	12 Aug 1862	G	1/Lt	23 June 1865	
Toms, Clinton D.	19	11 Aug 1862	G	Pte	14 April 1863	discharged for disability
Totten, Joseph	45	30 July 1862	C	Corp	11 April 1864	died of consumption
Town, George	32	12 Aug 1862	K	Corp	24 Jan 1864	
Tracy, Osgood V.	22	9 Aug 1862	I, G	Capt	23 June 1865	
Tracy, William G.	20	3 Nov 1862	I	2/Lt	29 July 1863	
Traganza, James D.	21	11 Aug 1862	E	Sgt	6 May 1864	killed at Wilderness
Trapp, Uriah	27	28 July 1862	A	Pte	3 July 1865	wounded at Cold Harbor
Traverse, John	31	15 July 1862	I	Pte	21 Sept 1862	deserted
Travis, John L.	29	12 Aug 1862	G	Corp	3 July 1863	killed at Gettysburg
Trenham, John J.	20	4 Aug 1862	A	Pte	11 Oct 1864	wounded at Winchester—died of wounds
Tripp, Humphrey L.	20	6 Aug 1862	I	Pte	29 June 1865	captured at Wilderness
Trowbridge, James	45	12 Aug 1862	B	Pte	25 May 1863	discharged for disability
Trowbridge, Samuel C.	20	8 Aug 1862	K, B	1/Lt	23 June 1865	wounded at Cold Harbor
Truesdell, Sanford N.	25	29 July 1862	K	Sgt	6 May 1864	killed at Wilderness
Tucker, Matthew T.	18	4 Aug 1862	H	Pte	21 Jan 1863	deserted
Tully, John	29	14 Aug 1862	H	Pte	23 June 1865	
Turner, George	22	26 July 1862	F	Pte	2 March 1864	died of disease
Turner, Uriah	23	5 Aug 1862	A	Pte	absent at muster out	wounded at Fisher's Hill
Tuttle, Edson	30	8 Aug 1862	I	Pte	19 Oct 1862	deserted
Tuttle, Philemon	22	2 Aug 1862	C	Corp	26 June 1865	
Twinum, Holland	25	5 Aug 1862	A	Pte	absent at muster out	wounded and captured at Wilderness

Name	Age on Enlistment	Enlisted	Company	Rank	Discharged/ Died	Remarks
Unckless, John	44	19 Aug 1862	D	Pte	2 June 1865	transferred to V.R.C.
Unckless, John A.	21	8 Aug 1862	I	Corp	23 June 1865	wounded at Cold Harbor
Underwood, Thomas	23	4 Aug 1862	C	Pte	23 June 1865	captured near Fairfax Court House
Vail, John	25	19 Aug 1862	K	Sgt	23 June 1865	
Van Alstine, Barney	39	13 Jan 1864	H	Pte	23 June 1865	wounded at Cold Harbor
Vanattas, William	35	14 Aug 1862	B	Corp	23 June 1865	wounded at Gettysburg
Van Dyke, Sanford	21	15 Aug 1862	G	Corp	23 June 1865	
Van Hoesen, Daniel	28	9 Aug 1862	B	Pte	24 April 1863	discharged for disability
Van Wormer, Daniel B.	23	25 July 1862	I	Sgt	22 Sept 1862	deserted
Vinton, Jefferson	33	12 Aug 1862	D	Pte	5 July 1863	deserted
Vosburgh, Hiram	21	28 July 1862	A	Pte	23 June 1865	
Vosseller, Henry H.	18	9 Aug 1862	H	Corp	23 June 1865	
Vosseller, Webster	21	12 Aug 1862	H	Corp	22 Oct 1864	wounded at Winchester—died of wounds
Vroman, Philip	26	28 July 1862	E	Corp	23 June 1865	wounded at Winchester
Wagner, Nathaniel J.	36	15 Aug 1862	H	Pte	25 Oct 1862	deserted
Wait, G. Addison	21	11 Aug 1862	K	2/Lt	24 May 1864	transferred to Tenth Infantry
Waldron, John A.	35	11 Aug 1862	G	Pte	27 Dec 1862	died of typhoid fever
Walker, Benjamin	18	1 Aug 1862	C	Pte	23 June 1865	wounded at Wilderness
Walker, Melvin B.	18	8 Aug 1862	F	Pte	2 Nov 1862	deserted
Walker, William A.	18	1 Aug 1862	C	Pte	absent at muster out	captured at Wilderness
Walpole, Horace H.	25	15 Aug 1862	E	Lt/Col	23 June 1865	captured at Spotsylvania—escaped
Walrath, Hezekiah	33	28 July 1862	E	Pte	5 March 1863	died of disease
Ward, Jeremiah	36	12 Aug 1862	B	Pte	19 Feb 1863	deserted
Warren, Griffin	21	18 July 1862	I	Wagoner	23 June 1865	
Waters, Mitchell D.	30	7 Aug 1862	C	Pte	12 Sept 1862	deserted
Wayne, John	22	7 Aug 1862	K	Pte	31 Jan 1863	died of typhoid fever
Weaver, Caius A.	18	11 Aug 1862	B	Pte	19 June 1865	wounded at Fort Stevens—discharged for disability
Webb, William J.	20	14 Aug 1862	B	1/Lt	28 Feb 1863	died of typhoid fever

Name	Age on Enlistment	Enlisted		Company	Rank	Discharged/ Died		Remarks
Weeks, Emanuel	40	18 Jan	1864	E	Pte	n.d.		wounded at Wilderness—discharged for disability
Welch, Gilbert	22	8 Aug	1862	B	Pte	16 Jan	1863	died of typhoid fever
Wells, Elas	33	11 Aug	1862	B	Pte	23 June	1865	
Wells, Herbert S.	24	6 Aug	1862	A, B	Capt	23 June	1865	wounded at Cold Harbor
West, Andrew F.	21	6 Aug	1862	D	Pte	23 June	1865	
Whaley, Francis E.	21	5 Aug	1862	D	Sgt	29 April	1865	wounded and captured at Wilderness
Wheaton, Victory B.	35	2 Aug	1862	H	Corp	19 Feb	1863	discharged for disability
Whertman, William	—	28 July	1863	E	Pte	23 Dec	1864	wounded at Cold Harbor—discharged for disability
Whipple, Hiram H.	18	9 Aug	1862	K	Pte	23 June	1865	
White, James	33	4 Aug	1862	E	Pte	31 Aug	1862	deserted
Whitworth, William	40	19 Aug	1862	K	Corp	3 July	1863	killed at Gettysburg
Wickham, James W.	37	9 Aug	1862	E	Pte	3 July	1863	killed at Gettysburg
Wicks, Hiram	28	14 Aug	1862	G	Corp	23 June	1864	wounded at Wilderness—died of wounds
Wiesmore, Charles H.	18	6 Aug	1862	E	Pte	26 July	1864	wounded at Gettysburg—deserted
Wiggens, Eugene	28	11 Aug	1862	B	Pte	23 June	1865	
Wilcox, Edward	31	30 July	1862	A	Pte	23 June	1865	
Wilcox, George S.	23	8 Aug	1862	G	Musician	20 July	1863	discharged for disability
Wilkin, Andrew W.	20	13 Aug	1862	H, I	Capt	23 June	1865	
Wilkins, John	24	22 March	1864	D	Pte	27 March	1864	deserted
Wilkinson, George	43	12 Aug	1862	D	Pte	12 March	1864	discharged for disability
Wilkinson, Lewis	19	5 Aug	1862	A	Pte	23 June	1865	
Will, William F.	20	30 July	1862	C	Sgt	1 April	1864	transferred to 39th Regiment, U.S. Colored Troops
Williams, Albert B.	18	15 Aug	1862	I	Pte	23 June	1865	
Williams, Augustus	40	15 Aug	1862	I	Corp	15 Nov	1863	transferred to V.R.C.
Williams, Charles M.	31	6 Aug	1862	C	Corp	19 Oct	1864	wounded at Gettysburg—killed at Cedar Creek
Williams, Edward	40	29 July	1862	A	Pte	23 June	1865	

Name	Age on Enlistment	Enlisted		Company	Rank	Discharged/ Died		Remarks
Williams, Ellis M.	32	8 Aug	1862	E	Sgt	31 Dec	1864	wounded at Spotsylvania—discharged for disability
Williams, John	34	20 Jan	1865	G	Pte	23 June	1865	
Williams, Justus N.	15	26 July	1862	F	Musician	23 June	1865	
Williams, Samuel	19	5 Aug	1862	D	Wagoner	30 June	1865	captured at Spotsylvania
Wilman, Adolph	21	26 July	1862	F	1/Lt	7 Jan	1865	wounded at Wilderness and Cedar Creek—discharged for disability
Wilson, George	23	18 July	1862	E	Corp	23 June	1865	
Wilson, James	43	11 Aug	1862	B	Pte	12 March	1864	died of typhoid fever
Wilson, Martin Luther	26	2 Aug	1862	A	1/Lt	19 June	1864	wounded at Rappahannock and Wilderness—died of wounds
Wilson, William H.	27	13 Aug	1862	E	Pte	12 July	1865	
Winney, Charles	23	21 March	1864	E	Pte	15 May	1865	discharged for disability
Winslow, William S.	35	3 June	1862	I	Corp	18 Oct	1862	deserted
Wood, Benjamin	27	12 Aug	1862	D	Pte	absent at muster out		
Woodcock, George A.	18	4 Aug	1862	H	Pte	28 Aug	1862	
Woodworth, Perry F.	18	6 Aug	1862	F	Musician	23 June	1865	
Woolsey, Hiram B.	21	11 Aug	1862	G	Corp	23 June	1865	wounded at Gettysburg
Wooster, Frank M.	25	16 Aug	1862	K, G	1/Lt	1 June	1864	killed at Cold Harbor
Wooster, William G.	23	11 Aug	1862	K	Sgt	23 June	1865	
Worden, Alfred	38	7 Aug	1862	C	Corp	23 June	1865	wounded at Cold Harbor
Worden, Charles H.	18	25 July	1862	B	Pte	23 June	1865	wounded at Cedar Creek
Worden, Isaac	22	11 Aug	1862	C	Pte	23 Jan	1864	transferred to V.R.C.
Worden, Palmer	19	6 Aug	1862	C	Drummer	23 June	1865	
Worker, Charles	31	15 Aug	1862	D	Q/M/S	23 June	1865	
Worlock, William W.	19	17 July	1862	F	Pte	30 Aug	1862	deserted
Wormwood, Eugene H.	37	7 Aug	1862	F	Sgt	14 May	1865	wounded at Cold Harbor—discharged for disability
Wright, Byron A.	21	11 Aug	1862	C	Pte	23 June	1865	
Wright, Charles	26	9 Aug	1862	C	Pte	18 Oct	1862	deserted
Wright, Charles V.	18	1 Aug	1862	C	Pte	10 Aug	1863	

Name	Age on Enlistment	Enlisted		Company	Rank	Discharged/ Died		Remarks
Wright, Edwin L.	18	1 Aug	1862	C	Pte	23 June	1865	wounded at Cold Harbor
Wright, James	24	9 Aug	1862	H	Pte	21 Jan	1863	deserted
Wright, Morris E.	29	8 Aug	1862	L	2/Lt	2 Oct	1863	
Wyatt, Henry	18	5 Aug	1862	G	Pte	23 June	1865	
Wyatt, James	21	31 July	1862	G	Sgt	23 June	1865	
Yates, Abram E.	26	21 Mar	1864	A	Pte	23 June	1865	
Yerdan, Ephraim	21	27 July	1862	E	Pte	23 June	1865	
Yoset, Francis	24	28 July	1862	A	Pte	31 Aug	1863	discharged for disability
Young, Joseph	34	30 July	1862	F	Pte	9 May	1863	deserted
Youngs, Chester C.	24	8 Aug	1862	G	Corp	23 June	1865	
Zellers, Nathan	26	9 Aug	1862	G	Pte	18 Jan.	1863	deserted
Zellers, William H.	30	7 Aug	1862	G	Pte	23 June	1865	
Zoellner, Mitchell	30	25 July	1862	A	Pte	21 July	1865	transferred to V.R.C.

SOURCE: *Annual Report of the Adjutant General of the State of New York for the Year 1903* (New York, 1904), no. 36.

| Place | Date | Killed | | Wounded | | | | Missing | | Aggregate |
| | | | | Died | | Recovered | | | | |
		Officers	Enlisted Men	Officers	Enlisted Men	Officers	Enlisted Men	Officers	Enlisted Men	
	1862									
Antietam, Md.	Sept 18									
Williamsport, Md.	Sept 19–20									
Manassas Gap, Va.	Nov 6									
Fredericksburg, Va.	Dec 11–15						5			5
	1863									
Marye's Heights and Salem Church, Va.	May 3–4				1	1	5			7
Deep Run Crossing, Va.	June 10					1				1
Gettysburg, Pa.	July 2–3		10		5	2	25		2	44
Boonsboro, Md.	July 10									
Funkstown, Md.	July 11–13									
Rappahannock Station, Va.	Nov 7		3		2	1	7			13
Mine Run Campaign, Va.	Nov 26–Dec 2									
	1864									
Wilderness, Va.	May 5–7		15	1	6	5	58	3	31	119
Spotsylvania Court House, Va.	May 8–21						20	1	3	24
North Anna, Va.	May 22–26									
Totopotomoy, Va.	May 27–30									
Cold Harbor, Va.	May 31–June 12		1			1	50			67
First Assault	June 1	1	8		6					

Place	Date	Killed		Wounded				Missing		Aggregate
				Died		Recovered				
		Officers	Enlisted Men	Officers	Enlisted Men	Officers	Enlisted Men	Officers	Enlisted Men	
Before Petersburg, Va.	June 17–July 9									
	Dec 12–April 2, 1865		1		1		10			12
	1865									
Assault of Petersburg, Va.	June 17–19						2			3
Weldon Railroad, Va.	June 21–23									
Washington, D.C. [Fort Stevens]	July 12–13	1	5		2		20			27
Charlestown, W. Va.	Aug 21		1				4			5
Opequon, Va. [Winchester]	Sept 19	1	5		4	4	20			34
Fisher's Hill, Va.	Sept 22		1		2		9			12
Cedar Creek, Va.	Oct 19	1	4			2	25			32
Petersburg Works, Va.	March 25	1	2		1		12			16
Appomattox Campaign, Va.	March 28–April 9									
Fall of Petersburg	April 2					1	7			8
Sailors' Creek	April 6									
Appomattox Courthouse	April 9									
Total loss		5	56	1	30	18	279	4	36	429

SOURCE: F. Phisterer, *New York in the War of the Rebellion,* 6 vols. (Albany, 1890), vol. 4, p. 3440.

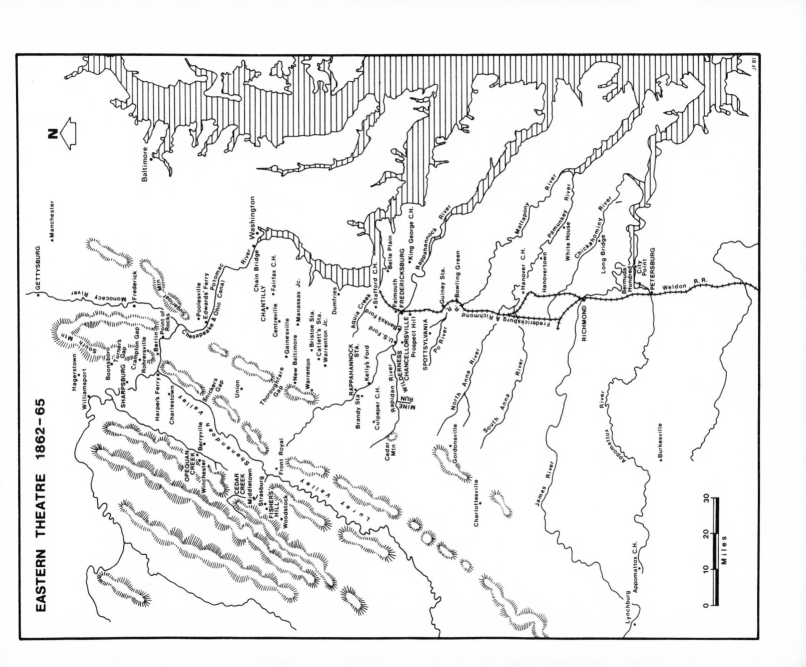

EASTERN THEATRE 1862–65

N

Baltimore

Manchester

GETTYSBURG

Washington

Frederick

Monocacy River

Poolesville

Chain Bridge

Fairfax C.H.

CHANTILLY

Centreville

Gainesville

New Baltimore

Warrenton

Catlett's Sta.

Bristoe Sta.

Manassas Jc.

Warrenton Jc.

Dumfries

Aquia Creek

Belle Plain

Stafford C.H.

King George C.H.

Rappahannock River

FREDERICKSBURG

Falmouth

Banks' Ford

U.S. Ford

Prospect Hill

SPOTSYLVANIA

WILDERNESS

CHANCELLORSVILLE

MINE RUN

Guiney Sta.

Bowling Green

Mattapony River

Pamunkey River

White House

Hanover C.H.

Hanovertown

Chickahominy River

Long Bridge

Bermuda Hundred

City Point

PETERSBURG

Weldon R.R.

RICHMOND

Fredericksburg & Richmond R.R.

Po River

North Anna River

South Anna River

Gordonsville

Charlottesville

James River

Appomattox River

Burkesville

Lynchburg

Appomattox C.H.

Hagerstown

Williamsport

Boonsboro

Turner's Gap

Crampton Gap

SHARPSBURG

Rohrersville

Berlin

Harper's Ferry

Charlestown

Berryville

Snicker's Gap

Union

Thoroughfare Gap

RAPPAHANNOCK STA.

Brandy Sta.

Kelly's Ford

Culpeper C.H.

Cedar Mtn

Rapidan River

South Mtn

Point of Rocks

Edwards Ferry

Chesapeake & Ohio Canal

Potomac River

Shenandoah Valley

OPEQUAN CREEK

Winchester

CEDAR CREEK

Middletown

Strasburg

FISHER'S HILL

Woodstock

Front Royal

Luray Valley

JF 81

0 10 20 30
Miles

NOTES

I The Road to War

1. *Syracuse Daily Courier*, 27 Aug. 1862.
2. Ibid. For a fuller discussion of Mrs. Gage's speech, see chap. 6.
3. W. W. Clayton, *History of Onondaga County, New York* (Syracuse, 1878), p. 103.
4. Ibid.
5. Ibid.
6. *Syracuse Daily Journal*, 2 Sept. 1862.
7. *Syracuse Daily Journal*, 1 Sept. 1862.
8. Ibid., 2 Sept. 1862.
9. A. B. Williams to Editor, *Syracuse Daily Journal*, 6 Sept. 1862.
10. Clayton, *Onondaga County*, pp. 105–6.
11. H to Editor, 19 Sept. 1862, *Syracuse Daily Journal*, 27 Sept. 1862.
12. Clayton, *Onondaga County*, p. 106.
13. H to Editor, 19 Sept. 1862, *Syracuse Daily Journal*, 27 Sept. 1862.
14. Clayton, *Onondaga County*, p. 106.
15. Our Regular Correspondent to Editor, 25 Oct. 1862, *Syracuse Daily Standard*, 7 Nov. 1862.
16. Ibid.
17. Ibid.
18. Ibid.
19. Letter from 122nd to Editor, 26 Oct. 1862, *Syracuse Daily Standard*, 3 Nov. 1862.
20. Our Regular Correspondent to Editor, 25 Oct. 1862, *Syracuse Daily Standard*, 7 Nov. 1862.
21. D to Editor, 23 Oct. 1862, *Syracuse Daily Journal*, 29 Oct. 1862.
22. Letter from 122nd to Editor, 28 Oct. 1862, *Syracuse Daily Standard*, 3 Nov. 1862.
23. H to Editor, 1 Nov. 1862, *Syracuse Daily Journal*, 7 Nov. 1862.
24. Ibid.
25. D to Editor, 1 Nov. 1862, *Syracuse Daily Journal*, 6 Nov. 1862.
26. D to Editor, 5 Nov. 1862, *Syracuse Daily Journal*, 13 Nov. 1862.
27. Letter from Capt. James M. Gere, 11 Nov. 1862, *Syracuse Daily Journal*, 18 Nov. 1862.

II From Fredericksburg to Gettysburg

1. P. J. Parish, *The American Civil War* (New York: Holmes and Meier, 1975), p. 192.
2. D to Editor, 11 Nov. 1862, *Syracuse Daily Journal*, 15 Nov. 1862.
3. Ibid.
4. D to Editor, 23 Nov. 1862, *Syracuse Daily Journal*, 28 Nov. 1862.
5. D. G. S. to Editor, 30 Nov. 1862, *Syracuse Daily Journal*, 9 Dec. 1862.
6. D to Editor, 9 Dec. 1862, *Syracuse Daily Journal*, 15 Dec. 1862.
7. *The Letters of Herbert Wells* (hereafter Wells), Onondaga Historical Association, near Bell Plains, Va., 10 Dec. 1862.
8. Clayton, *Onondaga County*, p. 107.
9. Ibid.
10. *The Times*, 13 Jan. 1863.
11. D to Editor, 23 Dec. 1862, *Syracuse Daily Journal*, 30 Dec. 1862.
12. Wells, near Fredericksburg, Va., 25 Dec. 1862.
13. D to Editor, 23 Dec. 1862, *Syracuse Daily Journal*, 30 Dec. 1862.
14. Ibid.
15. S. R. Watkins, *Co. Aytch: A Side Show of the Big Show* (N.Y., 1962), pp. 85–88.
16. D to Editor, 27 Jan. 1863, *Syracuse Daily Journal*, 31 Jan. 1863.
17. Ibid.
18. *Musket* to Editor, 24 Jan. 1863, *Syracuse Daily Journal*, 29 Jan. 1863.
19. Wells, near Falmouth, Va., 18 May 1863.
20. Clayton, *Onondaga County*, p. 109.
21. Ibid.
22. Ibid.
23. D to Editor, 9 June 1863, *Syracuse Daily Journal*, 13 June 1863.
24. D to Editor, 25 June 1863, *Syracuse Daily Journal*, 29 June 1863.
25. *Syracuse Daily Journal*, 2 July 1863.
26. Adj. O. V. Tracy to Mrs. Tracy, 4 July 1863, *Syracuse Daily Standard*, 8 July 1863.
27. Quoted in *Syracuse Daily Standard*, 8 July 1863.

III Into the Wilderness—And Out Again

1. Clayton, *Onondaga County*, pp. 109–10.
2. Wells, near Warrenton, Va., 5 Aug. 1863.

3. D to Editor, 6 Aug. 1863, *Syracuse Daily Journal*, 10 Aug. 1863.
4. Wells, near Warrenton, Va., 11 Sept. 1863.
5. Clayton, *Onondaga County*, p. 110.
6. Ibid.
7. D to Editor, 17 Nov. 1863, *Syracuse Daily Journal*, 21 Nov. 1863.
8. F. Phisterer, *New York in the War of the Rebellion* 6 vols. (Albany, 1890), p. 3440.
9. *Syracuse Daily Journal*, 13 Nov. 1863.
10. Clayton, *Onondaga County*, p. 110.
11. D to Editor, 6 Dec. 1863, *Syracuse Daily Journal*, 10 Dec. 1863.
12. Ibid.
13. Ibid.
14. Clayton, *Onondaga County*, p. 111.
15. Phisterer, *War of Rebellion*, p. 3440.
16. Quoted in Clayton, *Onondaga County*, pp. 112–13.
17. Quoted in Clayton, *Onondaga County*, p. 112.
18. Parish, *American Civil War*, p. 462.
19. Quoted in Clayton, *Onondaga County*, pp. 113–14.
20. Wells, Spotsylvania, 13 May 1864.
21. *Syracuse Weekly Recorder*.
22. Clayton, *Onondaga County*, p. 114.
23. Wells, Spotsylvania, 20 May 1864.
24. Clayton, *Onondaga County*, pp. 114–15.
25. Quoted in Clayton, *Onondaga County*, p. 115.
26. Wells, near Cold Harbor, Va., 5 June 1864.
27. Thomas B. Scott to Editor, 8 June 1864, *Syracuse Daily Journal*, 21 June 1864.
28. D to Editor, 12 June 1864, *Syracuse Daily Journal*, 18 June 1864.

IV The Road to Victory

1. Lt. Col. A. W. Dwight to Editor, 14 June 1864, *Syracuse Daily Journal*, 20 June 1864.
2. D to Editor, 18 June 1864, *Syracuse Daily Journal*, 23 June 1864.
3. D to Editor, 21 June 1864, *Syracuse Daily Journal*, 27 June 1864.

4. Wells, near Petersburg, Va., 27 June 1864.
5. D to Editor, 1 July 1864, *Syracuse Daily Journal*, 6 July 1864.
6. Parish, *American Civil War*, pp. 466–67.
7. D to Editor, 17 July 1864, *Syracuse Daily Journal*, 29 July 1864.
8. D to Editor, 15 July 1864, *Syracuse Daily Journal*, 21 July 1864.
9. Private letter from G, in *Syracuse Daily Journal*, 22 July 1864.
10. D to Editor, 15 July 1864, *Syracuse Daily Journal*, 21 July 1864.
11. Clayton, *Onondaga County*, p. 115.
12. D to Editor, 31 Aug. 1864, *Syracuse Daily Journal*, 5 Sept. 1864.
13. Jubal Early, *Memoir*, pp. 90–91, quoted in Angle, P. M. and Miers, E. S., *Tragic Years 1860–1865*, vol. 2, p. 893.
14. D to Editor, 19 Sept. 1864, *Syracuse Daily Journal*, 21 Sept. 1864.
15. Phisterer, *War of Rebellion*, p. 3440.
16. George C. Bates (122nd) to S. N. Holmes, 27 Sept. 1864, *Syracuse Daily Journal*, 14 Oct. 1864.
17. D to Editor, 28 Sept. 1864, *Syracuse Daily Journal*, 15 Nov. 1864.
18. Lt. A. W. Wilkin (Co. L) to Editor, 20 Oct. 1864, *Syracuse Daily Journal*, 26 Oct. 1864.
19. Act. Adj. R. H. Moses to Editor, *Syracuse Daily Journal*, 26 Oct. 1864.
20. Rev. I. O. Fillmore to Editor, 24 Oct. 1864, *Syracuse Daily Journal*, 28 Nov. 1864.
21. Wells, Camp Russell—near Winchester, Va., 20 Nov. 1864.
22. C to Editor, 14 Dec. 1864, *Syracuse Daily Journal*, 10 Dec. 1864.
23. Wells, near Petersburg, Va., 6 Jan. 1865.
24. Abraham Lincoln, *Collected Works*, ed. Roy P. Basler (New Brunswick, N.J.: Rutgers University Press, 1953), vol. 8, p. 330.
25. Horace H. Walpole to Carroll E. Smith, 26 March 1865, in *Syracuse Daily Journal*, 31 March 1865.

26. Private letter from Lt. Col. H. H. Walpole, in *Syracuse Daily Journal*, 22 April 1865.
27. Wells, near Burkesville, Va., 16 April 1865.
28. A. B. P. to Editor, 19 April 1865, *Syracuse Daily Standard*, 25 April 1865.
29. Clayton, *Onondaga County*, p. 116.
30. *Syracuse Daily Journal*, 27 June 1865.

V Life and Death in the Third Onondaga

1. Parish, *American Civil War*, p. 132.
2. Ibid., p. 133.
3. Ibid., pp. 134–37.
4. Clayton, *Onondaga County*, p. 103.
5. *Syracuse Daily Journal*, 28 June 1862, 18 July 1862, 6 May 1864.
6. *Syracuse Daily Journal*, 28 Nov. 1864, 31 March 1865.
7. *Syracuse Daily Journal*, 2 Sept. 1862.
8. Wells, near Falmouth, Va., 15 March 1863.
9. *Syracuse Daily Journal*, 2 Sept. 1862.
10. Ibid.
11. Ibid.
12. Ibid.
13. Wells, near Warrenton, Va., 5 Aug. 1863.
14. Hesseltine, W. B., *Lincoln and the War Governors* (New York: Knopf, 1948), p. 273ff.
15. Phisterer, *War of Rebellion*, p. 3440.
16. D to Editor, 23 Oct. 1862, *Syracuse Daily Journal*, 29 Oct. 1862.
17. Ibid., 28 Oct. 1862.
18. H to Editor, 1 Nov. 1862, *Syracuse Daily Journal*, 7 Nov. 1862.
19. D. G. S. to Editor, 30 Nov. 1862, *Syracuse Daily Journal*, 9 Dec. 1862.
20. D to Editor, 9 Dec. 1862, *Syracuse Daily Journal*, 15 Dec. 1862.
21. *Syracuse Daily Journal*, 22 June 1863.
22. Phisterer, *War of Rebellion*, p. 3440.
23. The figures quoted here have been derived from the return of regimental membership, etc., contained in the *Report of the Adjutant General for the State of New York for the Year 1903*

(New York, 1904), no. 36. This report provides the basis also of Appendix A.

24. D to Editor, 16 June 1864, *Syracuse Daily Journal*, 21 June 1864. When D writes of starting out with "over four hundred men," he is probably referring to the state of the regiment at the beginning of the Wilderness campaign. The original strength of the regiment was, of course, over twice that figure.

25. I. O. Fillmore to Editor, 24 Oct. 1864, *Syracuse Daily Journal*, 28 Nov. 1864.

26. *Syracuse Daily Standard*, 3 Nov. 1862.

27. D to Editor, 9 Dec. 1862, *Syracuse Daily Journal*, 15 Dec. 1862.

28. John D. Billings, *Hard Tack and Coffee* (Boston: George M. Small, 1888), pp. 47–50.

29. Wells, Bell Plains, Va., 10 Dec. 1862.

30. Wells, Warrenton, Va., 11 Sept. 1863.

31. D to Editor, 23 Oct. 1862, *Syracuse Daily Journal*, 29 Oct. 1862.

32. Parish, *American Civil War*, p. 131.

33. See chap. 7.

34. *Syracuse Daily Journal*, 2 Sept. 1862.

35. Ibid., 6 Sept. 1862.

36. *Syracuse Daily Standard*, 3 Nov. 1862.

37. Ibid., 25 April 1865.

38. Wells, near Bell Plains, Va., 10 Dec. 1862.

39. Wells, Camp Russell, 20 Nov. 1864.

40. D. G. S. to Editor, 30 Nov. 1862, *Syracuse Daily Journal*, 9 Dec. 1862.

41. Ibid.

42. War Department Adjutant General's Office, *General Orders*, 1861, no. 54 and 1864, no. 216.

43. Parish, *American Civil War*, pp. 377–78.

44. D to Editor, 26 June 1864, *Syracuse Daily Journal*, 2 July 1864.

45. D to Editor, 23 Oct. 1862, *Syracuse Daily Journal*, 29 Oct. 1862.

46. A. W. Dwight to Editor, 20 Oct. 1864, *Syracuse Daily Journal*, 26 Oct. 1864.

47. Wells, near Bell Plains, Va., 10 Dec. 1862.

48. D to Editor, 23 Nov. 1862, *Syracuse Daily Journal*, 28 Nov. 1862.

49. Wells, Warrenton, Va., 11 Sept. 1863.

50. D to Editor, 27 Nov. 1862, *Syracuse Daily Journal*, 12 Dec. 1862.

51. D to Editor, 23 Oct. 1862, *Syracuse Daily Journal*, 29 Oct. 1862.

52. *Syracuse Daily Standard*, 3 Nov. 1862.

53. Musket to Editor, 24 Jan. 1863, *Syracuse Daily Journal*, 29 Jan. 1863.

54. *Syracuse Daily Journal*, 11 July 1863.

55. Musket to Editor, 24 Jan. 1863, *Syracuse Daily Journal*, 29 Jan. 1863.

56. H to Editor, 19 Sept. 1862, *Syracuse Daily Journal*, 27 Sept. 1862.

57. Wells, near Petersburg, Va., 27 June 1864.

58. Wells, near Petersburg, Va., 6 Jan. 1865.

VI The Cause, Copperheads, and Butternuts

1. *Syracuse Daily Courier*, 27 Aug. 1862.

2. Bell I. Wiley, *Life of Billy Yank* (Indianapolis: Bobbs-Merrill, 1952), pp. 28–30.

3. Ibid., pp. 109–23.

4. Union to Editor, 27 June 1864, *Syracuse Daily Journal*, 29 June 1864.

5. D to Editor, 19 Sept. 1864; Ibid., 21 Sept. 1864.

6. Wells, Camp Russell, 20 Nov. 1864.

7. *Syracuse Daily Journal*, 21 Oct. 1864.

8. George H. Devoe, near Cedar Creek, Va., 15 Oct. 1864, *Syracuse Daily Journal*, 3 Nov. 1864.

9. Parish, *American Civil War*, p. 544.

10. Wells, near Burkesville, Va., 16 April 1865.

11. D. G. S. to Editor, 30 Nov. 1862, *Syracuse Daily Journal*, 9 Dec. 1862.

12. D to Editor, 6 Aug. 1863, *Syracuse Daily Journal*, 10 Aug. 1863.

13. D to Editor, 23 Dec. 1862, *Syracuse Daily Journal*, 30 Dec. 1862.

14. Wells, near Falmouth, Va., 15 March 1863.

15. D to Editor, 9 June 1863, *Syracuse Daily Journal*, 13 June 1863.

16. The "Berdans" were a regular army regiment of sharpshooters, commanded by Col. Hiram Berdan. Used mainly as skirmishers or for picking off rebel artillerymen, they figured prominently in the Gettysburg, Mine Run, and Wilderness campaigns; Wiley, *Life of Billy Yank*, p. 341.

17. D to Editor, 9 June 1863, *Syracuse Daily Journal*, 13 June 1863.

18. D to Editor, 23 Nov. 1862, *Syracuse Daily Journal*, 28 Nov. 1862.

19. D to Editor, 25 June 1863, *Syracuse Daily Journal*, 29 June 1863.

20. D to Editor, 6 Aug. 1863, *Syracuse Daily Journal*, 10 Aug. 1863.

21. D to Editor, 19 Sept. 1864, *Syracuse Daily Journal*, 21 Sept. 1864.

22. D to Editor, 6 Aug. 1863, *Syracuse Daily Journal*, 10 Aug. 1863.

23. Charles T. Wyman, Cartersville, Ga., 12 June 1864, *Syracuse Daily Journal*, 25 June 1864.

24. Andrew W. Wilkin to Editor, 20 Oct. 1864, *Syracuse Daily Journal*, 26 Oct. 1864.

VII Epilogue: The Ruggles Bequest

1. Last will and testament of Miss Reba Ruggles *Scottish Record Office*, ref. 14530, University of St. Andrews Minutes of Queen's College Council, 5 Jan. 1959. The real property had originally belonged to Dr. Agnes Rogers, a psychologist who spent most of her working life in the United States, before returning home to Craichie House. It was in America that she met Reba Ruggles who became her companion and beneficiary under her will.

2. Declaration for Pension, 21 Feb. 1907, National Archives, Washington, D.C.

3. In 1851 Noble Ruggles was nominated for constable of the Fourth Ward by the Liberty Party. *Syracuse Daily Standard*, 7 Feb. 1851.

4. *City Directories*, Syracuse, N.Y., 1851–91.

5. Certificate of Volunteer Enlistment, W. E. Ruggles, 21 July 1862, National Archives. William gave his age as eighteen, but this figure does not agree with the evidence of his age in other documents.

6. Certificate of Volunteer Enlistment, P. M. Ostrander, 27 Aug. 1862, National Archives.

7. Certificate of Volunteer Enlistment, W. E. Ruggles, 21 July 1862, National Archives.

8. Declaration for an Original Invalid Pension, 22 Oct. 1881, National Archives.

9. Company Descriptive Book, Co. B 122 N.Y.V., National Archives.

10. Company Muster Rolls, Co. B 122 N.Y.V., National Archives.

11. Descriptive list of deserters arrested, 15 March 1864, O. V. Tracy, 122 N.Y.V., to Capt. F. Actach, provost marshal, Sandusky, eighteenth dist. of Ohio, 12 March 1864, National Archives.

12. Company Muster Roll, Co. B 122 N.Y.V., National Archives.

13. Billings, *Hard Tack,* p. 157.

14. *Syracuse Daily Journal,* 18 and 30 May 1864.

15. *Syracuse Daily Journal,* 20 May 1864.

16. Company Muster Rolls, Co. B 122 N.Y.V., April 1865, National Archives.

17. Sentence of General Court-Martial, Special Orders no. 348, 3 July 1865, National Archives.

18. Ibid.

19. Billings, *Hard Tack* p. 162.

20. Asst. Adj. General, War Department, to Commissioner of Pensions, 27 Feb. 1883, National Archives.

21. Records of Onondaga Historical Society, Syracuse, N.Y.

22. *City Directories,* Syracuse, N.Y.

23. Ibid.

24. General Affidavit, Dwight Landon, 20 June 1890, National Archives.

25. *City Directories,* Syracuse, N.Y.

26. Declaration for an Original Invalid Pension, 22 Oct. 1881; Pension Drop Order and Report, 20 June 1907. National Archives.

27. *Syracuse Daily Standard,* 30 Aug. 1876, 29 Aug. 1878; *Syracuse Daily Journal,* 29 Aug. 1877, 29 Aug. 1881, 30 Aug. 1882, 29 Aug. 1884, 29 Aug. 1887, 1 Sept. 1888.

28. *Syracuse Weekly Recorder,* n.d.

29. General Affidavit, Nelson Greer, 12 June 1890, National Archives.

30. Declaration for Widow's Pension, Alida Ruggles, 1 June 1907, National Archives.

31. General Affidavit, Alida Ruggles, 3 July 1907, National Archives.

32. General Affidavit, John R. Collins, 3 July 1907, National Archives.

33. General Affidavit, Alida Ruggles, 3 July 1907, National Archives.

34. Widow's Pension Drop Report, Alida Ruggles, 21 Sept. 1927, National Archives.

35. Application for Reimbursement of Funeral Expenses, Sept. 1927, National Archives.

36. *City Directories,* Syracuse, N.Y.

37. According to the records of the Onondaga Historical Society, Ostrander was born on April 14, 1812 or 1813. Working back from the details in his death certificate, we arrive at April 13, 1812.

38. Death Certificate, Philip M. Ostrander, National Archives.

39. W. W. Beauchamp, *Past and Present of Syracuse and Onondaga County* (New York: S. J. Clarke, 1908), vol. 2, pp. 67–68.

40. Records of Onondaga Historical Society, Syracuse, N.Y.

41. *Syracuse Post-Standard,* 24 March 1918.

42. *Syracuse Post-Standard,* 24 March 1918.

43. Company Descriptive Book, Co. G, 81 N.Y.V., National Archives.

44. Company Muster-in Roll, Co. G, 81 N.Y.V., National Archives.

45. Company Muster Roll, 31 March 1862; Company Descriptive Book, 28 May 1862; Hospital Muster Roll, March–April 1862; Certificate of Disability for Discharge, 26 May 1862, National Archives.

46. Certificate of Volunteer Enlistment, Philip M. Ostrander, 27 Aug. 1862, National Archives.

47. Ibid.

48. Company Muster Roll, Co. A 149 N.Y.V., Jan.–Feb. 1863; Regimental Returns, n.d., Company Muster Roll July–Aug. 1863, National Archives.

49. Hospital Muster Roll, Sept.–Oct. 1864, National Archives.

50. Company Muster-out Roll, 12 June 1865, National Archives.

51. Declaration for Widow's Pension, Eliza Ostrander, 22 July 1890.

52. *City Directories,* Syracuse, N.Y.

53. General Affidavit, Milo Rosenthal, 1 Feb. 1883; General Affidavit, Sarah Stanley, 8 May 1888, National Archives.

54. Death Certificate, Philip M. Ostrander, 18 May 1888, National Archives.

55. *City Directories,* Syracuse, N.Y.

56. Ibid., 1883–85.

INDEX

LIBRARY OF CONGRESS CATALOGING IN PUBLICATION DATA

Swinfen, D. B.
  Ruggles' regiment.

  Includes index.
    1. United States. Army. New York Volunteers, 122nd—History. 2. United
States—History—Civil War, 1861–1865—Campaigns and battles. 3. United
States—History—Civil War, 1861–1865—Regimental histories—United States—
New York Volunteers—122nd. I. Title.
E523.5 122nd.s96   973.7′447   81–69940
ISBN 0–87451–230–1   AACR2